THE
WORST STREET
in
LONDON

Foreword by Peter Ackroyd

D1313031

Ian Allan

PUBLISHING

ACKNOWLEDGEMENTS

It would not have been possible to write this book without the excellent staff and resources at the Public Record Office, the British Library, the Metropolitan Archive, the Newspaper Library, the Bancroft Library, Westminster Reference Library and the Old Bailey Archives. My thanks is also extended to all those who generously shared their personal remembrances of Spitalfields with me. Finally, I would especially like to thank Sharon Hicks for her help, support and enthusiasm while researching this book and my long-suffering husband Robert for listening to my incessant ramblings.

First published 2008
Reprinted 2009, 2010

This impression 2010

ISBN 978 0 7110 3363 4

© Fiona Rule 2008

Published by Ian Allan Publishing

An imprint of Ian Allan Publishing Ltd, Hersham, Surrey, KT12 4RG
Printed and bound in the UK by CPI Mackays, Chatham ME5 8TD

Visit the Ian Allan Publishing website at www.ianallanpublishing.com

Distributed in the United States of America and Canada by Bookmasters Distribution Services.

Front cover and endpapers: reproduction from 1894 Ordnance Survey Map, with kind permission of Ordnance Survey

To the memory of Desmond Rule, otherwise known as Dad.

CONTENTS

Foreword by Peter Ackroyd   7

Introduction   9

Part One: The Rise and Fall of Spitalfields   15
1: The Birth of Spitalfields   16
2: The Creation of Dorset Street and Surrounds   22
3: Spitalfields Market   25
4: The Huguenots   27
5: A Seedier Side/Jack Sheppard   30
6: A New Parish and a Gradual Descent   46
7: The Rise of the Common Lodging House   51
8: Serious Overcrowding   54
9: The Third Wave of Immigrants (The Irish Famine)   58
10: The McCarthy Family   67
11: The Common Lodging Houses Act   70

Part Two: The Vices of Dorset Street   77
12: The Birth of Organised Crime in Spitalfields   78
13: The Cross Act   82
14: Prostitution and Press Scrutiny   87
15: The Fourth Wave of Immigrants   93
16: The Controllers of Spitalfields   96

Part Three: International Infamy   **105**
17: Jack the Ripper   106

Part Four: A Final Descent   **141**
18: The Situation Worsens   142
19: A Lighter Side of Life   147
20: The Landlords Enlarge their Property Portfolios   161
21: The Worst Street in London   164
22: The Murder of Mary Ann Austin   168
23: The Beginning of the End   181
24: Kitty Ronan   184
25: World War 1   190
26: The Redevelopment of Spitalfields Market   200

Part Five: A Walk Around Spitalfields   **218**

Bibliography   226
Index   229

Foreword
by
Peter Ackroyd

There are some parts of London that live in perpetual shadow, their air and atmosphere tainted by centuries of poverty and sorrow. They are the streets of darkness, running like a thread through the labyrinth of London. One such street has been traced here by Fiona Rule, in a book that is part history and part reverie, part celebration and part lament.

Dorset Street, laid down in 1674, some four hundred feet in length, was once unremarkable enough, but the weight of London soon fell upon it. It was part of the haunted ground of Spitalfields, a place of small and narrow houses that soon became a byword for misery. A report, written in the middle of the seventeenth century, describes the overcrowding caused by "poor indigent and idle and loose persons". They became the inhabitants of Dorset Street. Fiona Rule charts the evolution of misery. By the eighteenth century the houses had become ramshackle. In the early nineteenth century they were knocked together and became what were known as common lodging houses. The relatively spacious back-gardens were converted into cobbled courts so that more and more people could be accommodated. Crime and disease were rampant.

This book helps to elucidate what might be called the spiritual topography of London, whereby a certain neighbourhood actively influences the lives and characters of the people who live within it. So it is that the inhabitants of Dorset Street were described in the nineteenth century as evincing "the same want of hope – the same doggedness and half-indifference as to their fate". The houses themselves suffered the same weariness; there were cases when they simply collapsed. It is a street in which people disappeared, and where their suffering became invisible to the larger world. The various tides of immigrants – Huguenots, Jews and Irish – ebbed and flowed.

But this book is not simply a London history. Fiona Rule knows the names and addresses; she gives poverty and squalor a human face. She chronicles the simple or not so simple lives of the dispossessed. That is why, for example, she throws such an unusual and intriguing light upon the crimes of Jack the Ripper. Three of his victims lived or worked in Dorset Street and one of them, Mary Kelly, was butchered there. The cry of "murder" rang out that night, but no one paid the slightest notice.

Despite the attentions of journalists and philanthropists the condition of Dorset Street became worse in the last part of the nineteenth century. It was described by Charles Booth as "the worst street in London", and the police would venture through it only in pairs. It was known as "Dossett Street" because of the number of doss houses. It was filled with gamblers and prostitutes; dog fights and bare knuckle fights were common. It kept up these traditions well into the twentieth century, and the last man to be murdered here was found bleeding on its stones in February 1960.

Dorset Street has now gone, part of it turned into an unlovely car park. But in twilight and night, when the shadows grow longer, it may be wise not to come too close. The old darkness may engulf you. You may hear the cry of "murder", and the hands of the dead may reach out to claim you. This is a book for all lovers of London to read.

INTRODUCTION

On a cold February night in 1960, 32-year old nightclub manager Selwyn Cooney staggered down the stairs of a Spitalfields drinking den and collapsed on the cobbled road outside, blood streaming from a bullet wound to his temple. Cooney's friend and associate William Ambrose, otherwise known as 'Billy the Boxer', followed seconds later, clutching a wound to his stomach. By the time he reached the street, Cooney was dead.

The true facts surrounding Cooney's violent death are shrouded in mystery – investigations following his murder revealed gangland connections with notorious inhabitants of the criminal underworld such as Billy Hill and Jack Spot. Newspapers suggested his death was linked to a much further reaching battle for supremacy between rival London gangs. However, the mystery surrounding Cooney's murder is just one of the many strange, brutal and perplexing tales connected with the street in which he met his fate.

Halfway up Commercial Street, one block away from Spitalfields Market, lies an anonymous service road. The average pedestrian wouldn't even notice it existed. But unlikely though it may seem, this characterless, 400ft strip of tarmac was once Dorset Street, the most notorious thoroughfare in the capital: the worst street in London. The resort of Protestant fire-brands, thieves, con-men, pimps, prostitutes and murderers, most notably Jack the Ripper…

I first discovered Dorset Street by accident. Like many others who share a passion for this great city, its streets have always provided me with far more than simply a route from one location to another. They are also pathways into the past that reveal glimpses of a London that has long since vanished. A stroll down any of the older thoroughfares will reveal defunct remnants of a world we have lost. Boot scrapers sit unused outside front doors, hinting that before today's ubiquitous tarmac and concrete paving, the streets were often covered with mud. Ornate cast iron discs set into the pavements conceal the holes into which coal was once dispensed to fuel the boilers and ovens of thousands of households. On the walls of some homes, small embossed metal plaques remain screwed to the brickwork confirming long-expired fire insurance taken out at a time when fire was a much bigger threat to the city than it is in today's centrally-heated and electronically-powered world. For the history enthusiast, London's streets provide a wealth of treasure and their exploration can take a lifetime.

I had made many investigative sorties onto the streets of London before I ventured into Spitalfields, but what I found in this small, ancient district was unique and alluring in equal measure. At its centre lay the market. A far cry from the over-developed gathering place for the über-fashionable it is today, at the time of my visit it was a deserted hangar filled with a jumble of empty market stalls. Across from the abandoned market, Hawksmoor's masterpiece, Christ Church, loomed over shabby Commercial Street, looking decidedly incongruous next to a parade of burger bars, kebab houses and old fabric wholesalers whose window displays looked as though they hadn't been changed for at least twenty years. In the churchyard, tramps lounged around on benches searching for temporary oblivion in their bottles of strong cider.

On the other side of the church lay the Ten Bells pub. Paint peeled off its exterior walls and the interior was almost devoid of furniture save for a couple of well-worn sofas and some ancient circular tables near the window. However, despite its rather unwelcoming façade, there was something about the place that made it seem utterly right for the area. Moreover, it looked as though it hadn't altered a great deal since it was built, so I decided to go in. Once inside the Ten Bells, the feature that became immediately apparent was a wall of exquisite Victorian tiling at the far end of the bar, part of which was an illustration of 18th century silk weavers. Next to the frieze hung a dark wood board that reminded me of the rolls of honour that hung in my old secondary school listing alumni who had achieved the distinction of being selected Head Boy or Girl. However, the names on this board had an altogether more horrible significance. They were six alleged victims of 'Jack the Ripper'. A discussion with the barman about this macabre exhibit revealed that all six women on the list had lived within walking distance of where we were standing and may even have been patrons of the Ten Bells. They had earned their living on the streets, hawking, cleaning and when times were really tough, selling themselves to any man that would have them, often taking their conquest into a deserted yard or dark alley for a few moments of sordid passion against a brick wall. Unluckily for them, their final customer had in all probability been their murderer.

Of course, I had known a little about the career of Jack the Ripper before my visit to the Ten Bells. However, I had never previously stopped to consider the reality behind the story. The magnificence of Christ Church suggested that at one time, the area had been a prosperous and optimistic district. How had Spitalfields degenerated into a place of such deprivation and depravity that several of its inhabitants could be murdered in the open air, in such a densely populated area of London without anyone hearing or seeing anything untoward? My interest piqued, I returned home and began my research.

What intrigued me most about the Jack the Ripper story was not the identity of the perpetrator but the social environment that allowed the murders to happen. As I delved deeper into the history of the Spitalfields, I began to uncover a district of London that seemed almost lawless in character. By the time of the murders, the authorities seemed to have almost entirely washed their hands of the narrow roads and dingy courts that ran off either side of Commercial Street, leaving the landlords of the dilapidated lodgings to deal with the inhabitants in whatever manner they saw fit. The area that surrounded the market became known as the 'wicked quarter mile' due to its proliferation of prostitutes, thieves and other miscreants who used 'pay by the night' lodging houses, where no questions were asked, as their headquarters. These seedy resorts flourished throughout the district during the second half of the 1800s and were places to which death was no stranger. Even one of the landlords, William Crossingham, described them as places to which people came to die.

The sheer dreadfulness of the common lodging houses prompted me to investigate them further. During a particularly fruitful trip to the Metropolitan Archive, I uncovered the 19th century registers for these dens of iniquity, which gave details of their addresses and the men and women that ran them. As I turned the pages of these ancient old volumes, one street name cropped up time and time again: Dorset Street. By the close of the 19th century, this small road was comprised almost entirely of common lodging houses, providing shelter for literally hundreds of London's poor every night of the year. Most intriguingly, I remembered that the street's name also loomed large in the newspaper reports I had read about the Ripper murders; in fact the only murder to have occurred indoors had been perpetrated in one of the mean courts that ran off it. Dorset Street now became the focus of my research and as I uncovered more of its history, what emerged was a fascinating tale of a place that was built at a time of great optimism and had enjoyed over one hundred years of industry and prosperity.

However, with the arrival of the Victorian age came an era of neglect that ran unchecked until Dorset Street had become an iniquitous warren of ancient buildings, housing an underclass avoided and ignored by much of Victorian society. Left to fend for themselves, the unfortunate residents formed a community in which chronic want and violence were part of daily life – a society into which the arrival of Jack the Ripper was unsurprising and perhaps even inevitable.

The Worst Street in London chronicles the rise and fall of Dorset Street, from its promising beginnings at the centre of the 17th century silk weaving industry, through its gradual descent into debauchery, vice and violence to its final demise at the hands of the demolition men. Its remarkable history gives a fascinating insight into an area of London that has, from its initial development, been a cultural melting pot – the place where many thousands of immigrants became Londoners. It also tells the story of a part of London that, until quite recently, was largely left to fend for itself, with very little State intervention, with truly horrifying results. Dorset Street is now gone, but its legacy can be seen today in the desolate and forbidding sink estates of London and beyond.

Part One

THE RISE AND FALL OF SPITALFIELDS

Chapter 1

The Birth of Spitalfields

By the time of Selwyn Cooney's murder, Dorset Street's final demise was imminent. Within less than a decade, all evidence of its prior notoriety would be swept away, replaced by loading bays and a multi-storey car park. What remained of the 18th and 19th century housing stock was dilapidated and neglected. The general impression gained from a visit to the area – especially after dark – was of a seedy, rather threatening place with few, if any, redeeming features. However, Dorset Street, and indeed the whole district of Spitalfields, was not always a den of iniquity.

A closer inspection of the crumbling, filthy houses that lined its streets in the early 1960s would have revealed elaborately carved doorways, intricate cornices and granite hearths – clues from a distant past when the area had been prosperous with a thriving and optimistic community. Its location was excellent for business as it was close to the City of London, Britain's commercial capital, and the Docks, the country's main point of distribution. Ironically, Spitalfields' main asset, its location, was to prove the major factor in its decline.

Back in the 12th century, the area that would become Spitalfields was undeveloped farmland, situated a relatively short distance from

London. It was known locally as Lollesworth, a name that probably referred to a one-time owner. Amid the rolling fields that stretched out towards South Hertfordshire and Essex, farmers grew produce, grazed cattle and lived a quiet, rural existence. Unsurprisingly, the area was a popular retreat for city residents seeking the calm of the countryside and many rode out there at weekends to enjoy the unpolluted air and wide open spaces.

Two regular visitors were William (sometimes referred to as Walter) Brune and his wife Rosia, the couple responsible for putting Spitalfields on the map. The Brunes appreciated the tranquillity of the area so much that they chose it as the location for a new priory and hospital for city residents in need of medicines, care and recuperation. In the mid-1190s, building work began by the side of a lane that led to the city, and by 1197 the area's first major building was completed. The priory was constructed from timber and sported a tall turret in one corner. It must have been an imposing site in a district that was otherwise open farmland. The Brunes dedicated their creation to Saint Mary and the building was known as the Priory of St Mary Spital (or hospital). Sadly, nothing of Spitalfields' first major building remains today, but it was known to stand on the site of what is now Spital Square. Until the early 1900s, a stone jamb built into one of the houses on the square marked the original position of the priory gate. The Brunes' efforts were recognised 800 years later in the creation of Brune Street, which occupies an area that would have once been part of the priory grounds.

To the rear of the priory hospital was the Spital Field, which was used by inmates as a source of pleasant views and fresh air. Our modern definition of a hospital is a place that tends the sick. However, in the 12th century, a hospital would have taken in anyone who was needy and could benefit from what the establishment had to offer. Consequently, the poor were attracted to the hospital and the Spital Field began a centuries-long reputation for being a place to which the underprivileged gravitated. By the 16th century, the hospital had become so popular that the chronicler John Stow noted 'there was found standing one hundred and eight beds well furnished for the poor, for it was a hospital of great relief'.

Over the next two hundred years, a small community gradually developed around the hospital. As the priory's congregation grew, it developed a reputation for delivering enlightening and thought provoking sermons that could be heard by all who cared to listen from an open-air pulpit. At the time, religion in Britain was an integral part of everyday life and the Spital Field sermons became a popular excursion for city residents. By 1398, the sermons preached at the priory during the Easter holiday period had acquired such a reputation that the lord mayor, aldermen and sheriffs heard them. By 1488, the lord mayor visited the priory so frequently that a two-storey house was built adjacent to the pulpit to accommodate him and other dignitaries that might attend.

Such was the popularity of the Easter Spital Sermons that they survived Henry VIII's Dissolution of the Monasteries in 1534. Twenty years later, Henry's daughter, Elizabeth I, travelled to the Spital Field to hear the sermons. The sermons continued to be preached outside the Spital Field until 1649 when the pulpit was demolished by Oliver Cromwell's army.

The remainder of the Priory of St Mary Spital was not spared during the dissolution and all property was surrendered to the Crown. In 1540, Henry granted a part of the priory land to the Fraternity of the Artillery. This land had previously been known as Tasel Close and had been used for growing teasels, which were then used as combs for cloth. The fraternity turned the land into an exercise ground, primarily used for crossbow practice. Agas's map of London in 1560 clearly shows the 'Spitel Fyeld' complete with charmingly illustrated archers and horses being exercised.

By 1570, the lane next to the erstwhile priory had become a major thoroughfare known as 'Bishoppes Gate Street' and the area around Spital Field was redeveloped. The first new houses to be built were large, smart affairs with extensive gardens and orchards. These properties were occupied by city residents who could afford country retreats that were accessible to their place of work. As the old priory site became an increasingly popular residential area, the Spital Field was broken up and the clay beneath the grass was used to make bricks for more houses.

In 1576, excavators working in the Spital Field made a fascinating discovery. Beneath the topsoil were urns, coins and the remains of coffins, indicating that the site was once a burial ground for city folk during Roman times. Luckily for them, the excavators were not working under the same constraints that exist today and their discovery did not halt the breaking up of the field. Subsequently, the bricks made from the Spital Field clay were used to construct the first major development of the area.

While building work around the Spital Field continued, the area welcomed its first extensive influx of immigrants. During the 1580s, Dutch weavers, fleeing religious troubles in their homeland, arrived in the capital. Looking for a suitable place to live and carry out their business, they were immediately attracted to the new developments around the Spital Field. The area provided ample space to live and work, and was sufficiently close to the city for them to trade there. Thus, the area received the first members of a profession that was to dominate the area for centuries to come: weaving.

In 1585, as the Dutch weavers were moving into their new homes, Britain faced a threat of invasion from Spain. Queen Elizabeth I hastily issued a new charter for the old Artillery Ground and merchants and citizens from the city travelled up Bishoppes Gate Street to be trained in the use of weaponry and how to command common soldiers. Their training was exemplary and produced commanders of such high calibre, that when troops mustered at Tilbury in 1588, many of their captains were chosen from the Artillery Ground recruits. They were known as the Captains of the Artillery Garden. The training centre at the Artillery Ground was so efficient that it continued to be used by soldiers from the Tower of London as well as local citizens long after the Spanish threat passed.

As fate would have it, the Spanish threat of invasion inadvertently introduced the area around the Artillery Garden to a new wave of city dweller with the means to purchase a country retreat. By 1594, the entire site that had previously been occupied by the priory and hospital was redeveloped and, as Stow noted, it contained 'many fair houses, builded for the receipt and lodging of worshipful and honourable men'. This influx of new residents, combined with the constant presence of builders, allowed inns and public houses to flourish. The Red Lion Inn stood on the corner of the Spital Field and proved to be a popular meeting place as it was considered the halfway house on the route from Stepney to Islington. In 1616, the celebrated herbalist and astrologer Nicholas Culpeper was born in this inn. While a young man growing up in rural surroundings, Culpeper developed a fascination with the healing properties of plants and flowers and, after studying at Cambridge and receiving training with an apothecary in Bishopsgate, he became an astrologer and physician. He also wrote and translated several books, the most famous being *The Complete Herbal*, published in 1649.

While Nicholas Culpeper was enjoying his youthful love affair with nature, businesses around the Spital Field were gradually evolving from small, individual enterprises into organised companies. One skill much in demand was the preparation of silk for the weavers, otherwise known as silk throwing. In 1629, the silk throwsters were incorporated and put together a strict programme of apprenticeship whereby no one was allowed to set up a business unless they had trained for seven years. This move raised standards of silk throwing immeasurably and weavers were assured that they would receive quality goods and services from their suppliers. The silk weavers became more organised and the quality of their work was recognised when the Weavers' Company admitted the first silk weavers into their ranks in 1639.

The year before the silk weavers were accepted into the Weavers' Company, King Charles I had granted a licence for flesh, fowl and roots to be sold on the Spital Field. This licence marked the beginning of a market that would exist, with only one brief interruption, on the same spot for over 300 years. The increase in traffic to and from the new market also played its part in introducing more people to the area and a thriving community was established. The Spital Field and the surrounding area became a prosperous hamlet on the outskirts of the city, populated by affluent workers, market gardeners, weavers and suppliers to the weaving industry. 'Bishoppes Gate Street' became a major trade route and the inns rarely had room to spare.

Chapter 2

The Creation of Dorset Street and Surrounds

In 1649, William Wheler of Datchet, a small town in Berkshire, put 'all that open field called Spittlefield' in trust for himself and his wife. On their death, the land was to be passed to his seven daughters. Wheler had acquired the freehold to the land in 1631 after marrying into the Hanbury family, who had purchased the freehold to the Spittle Field from the church in the late 1500s. At this point in time, the Spital Field was still very rural.

A small development of houses, shops and market stalls had sprung up along the east side of the field and two local residents named William and Jeffrey Browne had recently employed builders to develop the land they owned along the north side of the field. The resulting road was named Browne's Lane in their honour and exists today as Hanbury Street. The south and west sides of the Spital Field remained open pasture, used by the locals for grazing cattle when it was not too boggy. In addition to the grazing areas, a series of footpaths stretched across the field, providing routes to and from the shops and market stalls. It was also considered a good shortcut to Stepney church.

The owners of land around the Spital Field watched with great interest as the area gradually became increasingly built up. Despite the area being semi-rural, its proximity to the city ensured that new developments were highly sought after and let for decent rents. Therefore, many landowners decided to take the plunge and get the builders in. Two such men were Thomas and Lewis Fossan. The Fossan brothers lived in the city and had purchased land just south of the Spital Field as an investment some years previously. In the mid-1650s, they decided to utilise their investment and employed John Flower and Gowen Dean of Whitechapel to build two new residential streets on their land. Both streets ran east to west across the Fossan brothers' field. The southernmost road took on the names of the builders and became known as either Dean and Flower Street or Flower and Dean Street, depending on whom you asked. Today it is known as the latter. The other road was named after the landowners and became known as Fossan Street. However, this unusual name was replaced by the more memorable Fashion Street, the name it retains to this day.

By the 1670s, development of the Spital Field began in earnest. That year, a road along the west side of the field, named Crispin Street, was finished and in 1672, William Wheler's trustees, Edward Nicholas and George Cooke, asked permission from the Privy Council to develop the south edge of the field. Their petition was welcomed by the locals as this part of the field was apparently 'a noysome place and offensive to the Inhabitants through its Low Situation.' What exactly was so 'noysome' and 'offensive' about the southern end of the field becomes clear when looking at an Order in Council dated 1669, where the 'inhabitants of the pleasant locality of Spitalfields petitioned the Council to restrain certain persons from digging earth and burning bricks in those fields, which not only render them very noisome but prejudice the clothes (made by the weavers) which are usually dried in two large grounds adjoining and the rich stuffs of divers colours which are made in the same place by altering and changing their colours.' Nicholas and Cooke offered their assurances to the Council that 'a large Space of ground ... will be left unbuilt for ayre and sweetnes to the place'. Their proposal was accepted, the Lord Mayor noting that the 'Feild will remaine Square and open and the wettnesse of the lower parts (would) be remedied.'

Once permission had been granted, Nicholas and Cooke acted quickly. Over the next 18 months, they issued 80-year building leases for sites at the southern end of the field and three roads were quickly laid out: on the southernmost edge of the field, a road named New Fashion Street (later known as White's Row), was constructed. Closer into the centre of the field, running parallel with New Fashion Street, was Paternoster Row (later known as Brushfield Street). A third road was laid in between these two roads in 1674. It was originally named Datchet Street, after the Wheler family's place of residence, but for some reason, it corrupted into Dorset Street. The road that was to become the most notorious in London had been built.

Dorset Street started life as an unremarkable road, 400 feet long by 24 feet wide, lined with rather small houses, the average frontage of which was just 16 feet. The street itself was originally intended to provide an alternative way of getting from the west to the east side of the Spital Field when Nicholas and Cooke closed some of the old foot paths. However, traffic could also travel along White's Row and Paternoster Row when crossing the field, so it is unlikely that Dorset Street was particularly busy. It was probably just as well that the road did not experience heavy traffic, as it appears that some of the first houses were not well built. The demand for property in the Spital Field area meant that builders found it difficult to keep up with demand. Consequently, houses tended to be 'thrown up' and by 1675, the situation had become so serious that the Tylers' and Bricklayers' Company were called in to investigate. The investigators were appalled at what they found and a number of builders were fined for the use of 'badd and black mortar', 'work not jointed' and 'bad bricks'. It seems that the first major developments around the Spital Field were destined to have a short life.

Chapter 3

Spitalfields Market

As more and more people moved into the area around the Spital Field, it became clear that a more regular market would be a most profitable venture. Charles I had originally granted a licence for a market on the Spital Field back in 1638. However, it appears that this licence was revoked during the Commonwealth period (1649-1660) as between these dates only an occasional fair seems to have been held on the field. By the early 1680s, a plan for a market on the Old Artillery Ground was put forward by the Crown, but plans fell through and the market never materialised. However, in 1682, John Balch, a silk throwster who was married to William Wheler's daughter Katherine, was granted the right to hold two markets a week (on Thursdays and Saturdays) on or around the perimeter of the Spital Field. Thus the new Spitalfields Market was born.

Alas, Balch did not live to see his idea come to fruition as he died just one year after the market licence had been granted to him. However, in his will, Balch left his leasehold interest and market franchise to his great friend Edward Metcalf. Seeing the possibilities, Metcalf acted quickly and issued 61-year building leases to a number of developers and soon construction of a permanent market building was underway. Metcalf's design for the market included a cruciform market house situated in the middle of the Spital Field, around which were market stalls. In each corner of the field were L-shaped blocks of terraced houses. Four streets (known as North St, East St, South St and West St), radiated out from the market house, in between the L-shaped blocks. The market house itself was a grand building, built in the style of a Roman temple, possibly in reference to the Roman burial ground that had once occupied the field. Today, this building is long since demolished, but a miniature model of it can be seen on the silver staff belonging to the church wardens of Christ Church on Commercial Street.

Not long after the market was built, Metcalf died and the lease and franchise was taken over by George Bohun, a merchant from the City. Under Bohun, the market continued to increase in popularity as a place to trade meat and vegetables, and in 1708, was described by the commentator Hatton as 'a fine market for Flesh, Fowl and Roots.' By this time, the upper storey of the market house was being used as a chapel by the Spital Field's second wave of immigrants, French Protestants known as Huguenots.

Chapter 4

The Huguenots

In 1685, King Louis XIV of France revoked the Edict of Nantes, which had allowed non-Catholics freedom to use their own places of worship and co-exist with their neighbours without fear of persecution. As a result, some areas of France became downright dangerous for people who did not hold with the Catholic faith, and Huguenot Protestants began to arrive in the City of London in their hundreds. Many of the Huguenots were highly skilled silk weavers and so the Spital Field, with its established community of weavers and throwsters seemed the logical place for the Huguenot weavers to settle. The first Huguenots to arrive at the Spital Field set up for business in the Petticoat Lane area. The historian Strype, who was himself from an old Dutch weaving family, noted that Hog Lane (as Petticoat Lane was then known) soon became a 'contiguous row of buildings' all occupied by Huguenot silk weavers.

The Huguenots were welcomed by Spital Field locals with open arms. In 1686, a public collection raised a massive £40,000 for the 'relief of French Protestants' and the Dutch weavers and throwsters, no doubt remembering that they too had once been immigrants, helped the French weavers to set up business. Their generosity was no doubt influenced by the fact that the weaving industry in Spitalfields was enjoying a period of great prosperity and more weavers would present no threat to jobs.

The Huguenots soon developed a reputation for being extremely self- sufficient. In addition to producing absolutely beautiful silks, which were the envy of the world, they built houses, workshops, hospitals and even churches for themselves. In the period 1687-1742, ten French Protestant churches were built around the Spital Field. The last one seated up to 1,500 people, which gives an indication of how many Huguenots were living in the area by this time.

By 1700, the Spital Field had gone from being a sleepy, rural hamlet to the bustling centre of the silk weaving industry. Times were good and businesses were enjoying increasing prosperity. The Spitalfield weavers jealously guarded their craft and began to develop a reputation for insurrection, should their business be threatened in any way. In 1697, a group of weavers mobbed the House of Commons twice to show their support of a Bill to limit foreign silk imports by the East India Company. Their attempts to protect their industry certainly paid off, and 1720, it was a globally recognised fact that English silk was every bit as good as that made in France. Silk exports were at record levels and Spitalfields was acknowledged as the epicentre of this thriving industry. Flushed with success, the silk weavers began tearing down the old and often shoddily-built houses that lined the streets of Spitalfields and erected large, elegant homes that reflected their elevated status. These new properties were often used to both live and work in. The attics were built with large windows so that as much light as possible could flood in and illuminate the looms for as many hours as possible. Downstairs, sumptuous drawing rooms were used as showrooms for the weavers' work and buyers were entertained there.

The quality of these houses was such that many still stand today. Fournier Street contains some particularly good examples of 18th century weavers' homes, complete with restored attics and brightly coloured shutters at the windows. Number 14 was constructed in 1726 by a master weaver. It has three floors and a large attic with the customary lattice windows behind which once stood the loom. According to local legend, the silk for Queen Victoria's wedding dress was woven there.

Chapter 5

A Seedier Side/Jack Sheppard

Despite its newfound fortune and thriving industry, early 18th century Spitalfelds did have its seedier side. The wealth of many residents made the area very popular with thieves, pickpockets and housebreakers, many of whom set up shop in the locality so as to be close to their victims. In fact Jack Sheppard, one of London's most notorious criminals, was born in New Fashion Street (now White's Row) in 1702. Jack's father died when he was just six years old and the young lad was sent to Bishopsgate Workhouse as his impoverished mother could no longer afford to keep him.

At the time, Workhouses tried to place children in their care in apprenticeships, taking the view that once their training was completed, the child would become self-sufficient. However, Jack's initial placements were beset with bad luck. After two disastrous apprenticeships with cane-chair manufacturers he eventually found work with his mother's employer – the wonderfully titled Mr Kneebone – who ran a shop on The Strand. Kneebone took Jack under his wing, taught him to read and write and secured him an apprenticeship with a carpentry shop off Drury Lane.

Jack showed an aptitude for carpentry and for the first five years of his seven-year indenture, he progressed well. However, as he reached adulthood, he developed a taste for both beer and women and began to regularly frequent a local tavern named The Black Lion. The Black Lion was a decidedly unsavoury place, its main clientele being prostitutes and petty criminals, but Jack seemed to enjoy its edgy atmosphere and before long, became involved with a young prostitute called Elizabeth Lyon, known to her clients as 'Edgworth Bess'. Now with a girlfriend to impress, Jack decided it was time to supplement his paltry income by stealing.

At first, he concentrated on shoplifting, no doubt fencing the goods he stole at his local. However, as his confidence increased, Jack moved on to burgling private homes. At first the burglaries were very successful but in February 1724, the inevitable happened. Jack, Bess and Jack's brother, Tom, were in the throes of escaping from a house they had just burgled when Tom was discovered and caught. Fearful that he may be hanged for the crime, Tom turned informer and told the authorities his accomplices' whereabouts. Jack was duly arrested and sent to the Roundhouse Gaol in St Giles. It was from the top floor of this prison that Jack began to earn the dubious reputation as an expert escapologist; a reputation that would eventually bring him national notoriety. Employing his knowledge of joinery and making full use of his slender, 5' 4" frame, Jack managed to break through the Roundhouse's timber roof. He then lowered himself to the ground using knotted bed linen and silently disappeared into the crowd.

Although Jack had proved adept at escaping from gaol, he was less talented when it came to pulling off robberies undetected. By May 1724, he was in trouble again, this time for pickpocketing in Leicester Fields. He was sent to New Prison in Clerkenwell on remand and soon got a visit from Edgworth Bess. Bess allegedly claimed to be Jack's wife and begged the gaoler to allow them a little time in private. The sympathetic (and rather stupid) gaoler agreed and the couple immediately got to work filing through Jack's manacles, presumably using tools that Bess had concealed about her person. The couple worked quickly and soon managed to break a hole in the wall through which they clambered, only to find themselves in the yard of a neighbouring prison! Somehow, the pair managed to scale a 22-foot high gate and made off back to Westminster.

By now, Jack Sheppard's reputation was beginning to cause a stir and the subsequent publicity caught the attention of Jonathan Wild, an unpleasant character with strong links to the criminal underworld. Wild was a shrewd operator and consummate self-publicist, who had manufactured himself as London's 'Thief-taker General' by shopping his cohorts to the authorities whenever it suited him. Wild was keen to fence goods stolen by Jack, but Jack was not so enthusiastic about the proposed partnership and refused, thus prompting Wild's wrath. From that moment on, Jonathan Wild began plotting Sheppard's downfall.

One summer evening, Wild chanced upon Edgworth Bess in a local inn. Knowing Bess's fondness for liquor, Wild plied her with drink until she was so inebriated that she revealed Jack's whereabouts without realising what she had done. Jack was caught and once again imprisoned, this time at Newgate Gaol. At the ensuing trial, Jonathan Wild testified against him and Jack was sentenced to hang on 1 September 1724.

Although Newgate Gaol was more secure than the previous two, the threat of having his life cut short was enough to ensure that Jack effected a means of escape. During a visit from a very repentant Bess and her friend, Poll Maggot, Jack managed to remove a loose iron bar from his cell, and while Bess and Poll distracted the lustful guards, he slipped through the gap to freedom. As a final insult to prison security, he left the gaol via the visitor's gate, dressed as a woman in clothes provided by Poll and Bess.

By now, Jack's escapades had attracted nationwide attention. This was a disaster for Jack because it meant there were very few places he could go without fear of being recognised. Just nine days after his escape, he was found hiding in Finchley and taken straight back to Newgate.

This time, the authorities were taking no chances and placed him in a cell known as the 'castle', where he was literally chained to the floor. During his incarceration, Jack (who by now had become something of a folk hero), was visited by hundreds of Londoners curious to meet the notorious gaol-breaker. This, of course, gave him the opportunity to acquire various escape tools donated by well-wishers. Unfortunately, these tools were found by guards during a routine search of the cell. Many men would have accepted defeat at this stage, but Jack Sheppard was made of stronger stuff. In fact he was on the verge of accomplishing his greatest escape.

On the 15 October, the Old Bailey was thrown into chaos when a defendant named 'Blueskin' Blake attacked the duplicitous Jonathan Wild in the courtroom. The ensuing mayhem spilled over into the adjacent Newgate Prison and Jack saw his chance. Using a small nail he had found in his cell, he managed to unchain his handcuffs but failed to release his leg irons. Undaunted, he tried to climb the chimney but found his way blocked by an iron bar, which he promptly ripped out and used to knock a hole in the ceiling. Jack managed to get as far as the prison chapel when he realised that his only route of escape was down the side of the building – a 60-foot drop. Showing incredible nerve, he decided to retrace his steps back to his cell to retrieve a blanket with which he could lower himself down the wall, onto the roof of a neighbouring house. He did this and after breaking through the house's attic window, walked down the stairs and out into the street, once again a free man.

This time, Jack managed to evade capture for two weeks until his fondness for drink proved to be his downfall. He was arrested on 1 November and sent back to Newgate for a third time. This time, the authorities were determined not to let him out of their sight and so Jack was put on permanent watch, weighed down with 300lb-worth of ironmongery. During his brief stay at Newgate, he was once again visited by all manner of inquisitive Londoners and even had his portrait painted. A petition was raised appealing to the court to spare his life, but the judge was not prepared to comply unless he informed on his associates, which he was not prepared to do. Jack's execution date was set for 16 November at Tyburn.

On the day of the hanging, Jack made one final escape attempt, hiding a small pen-knife in his clothing but unfortunately it was found before he was put onto the condemned man's cart. 18th century hangings were macabre, curious and ultimately barbaric affairs. They were regarded as public spectacles and were attended by hundreds of spectators. The general atmosphere was similar to that of a modern-day carnival and well-wishers cheered Jack on his way down the Oxford Road while men, women and children jostled for the best seats on the gallows' viewing platforms.

As Jack made his final journey, he had one last plan up his sleeve. He knew that the gallows were built for men of a much heavier build than he, so it was unlikely that his neck would be broken by the drop. If he managed to survive the customary 15 minutes hanging from the rope without being asphyxiated, then his friends and associates could quickly cut down his body, whisk it away ostensibly for a quick burial and take him to a sympathetic surgery where he could be revived. Jack's final plan may have worked, had it not been for the heroic reputation he had acquired during his escape attempts. Sadly, once his body was cut down from the gallows, it was set upon by the baying mob of spectators, who by now had worked themselves into mass hysteria. Word got around that medical students were in the crowd, waiting to take Jack's body for medical experiments. Jack's new found fans crowded round his body to protect it from the student dissectors, making it impossible for his friends to reach him in time to revive him. By the time the crowd dispersed, Jack was dead.

With the exception of Jack the Ripper, Jack Sheppard has over the centuries become Spitalfields' most notorious son. His daring exploits have provided inspiration for numerous books, films, television programmes and plays, the most famous being *The Beggar's Opera*, which in turn formed the basis of *The Threepenny Opera* by Kurt Weill and Bertolt Brecht.

That said, the punishment he received for his crimes seems extreme to our modern sensibilities. The early 18th century was not a good time to be caught committing an offence in London. During Jack's last year of escapades, no less than 41 other criminals were sentenced to death at the Old Bailey, while over 300 more were condemned to endure humiliating corporal punishments or exile. A wide variety of crimes were reported in the Old Bailey Proceedings for 1724: Simple Grand Larceny (the theft of goods without any aggravating circumstances such as assault or housebreaking) was by far the most common offence; 39% of convicted prisoners were found guilty of this crime. This was followed by shoplifting and pickpocketing (just under 12% and just over 9% of all prisoners respectively) and burglary (5% of convicted prisoners). Violent crime was relatively rare: five defendants were found guilty of robbery with violence, four were found to have committed manslaughter and just three were found guilty of murder. Other crimes brought to trial that year included bigamy, coining (counterfeiting coins), animal theft and receiving stolen goods.

Punishments for defendants who were found guilty varied enormously. In cases of theft and fraud, the strength of the sentence was usually commensurate with the amount of money involved. On 26 February 1724, Frederick Schmidt of St Martins in the Fields was brought up before the judge accused of coining. As the trial unfolded, it became apparent that Schmidt had been caught changing the value of a £20 note to £100. His accuser, the Baron de Loden, deposed that Schmidt erased the true value from the bank note then 'drew the Note through a Plate of Gum-water, and afterwards having dried it between Papers, smooth'd it over between papers with a box iron, and afterwards wrote in the vacancy (where the twenty was taken out) One Hundred, and also wrote at the Bottom of the Note 100 pounds.' The Baron also added that Schmidt boasted to him that 'he could write 20 sorts of Hands and if he had but 3 or 400 pounds he could get 50,000 pounds.'

The Baron's accusation was supported by Eleanora Sophia, Countess of Bostram, who had also seen Schmidt altering the note. It appears that Schmidt's boastful ways caused his downfall. The jury found him guilty of coining and, as this was a capital offence, he was sentenced to death. In contrast, later that year, John and Mary Armstrong were prosecuted for the lesser but potentially very lucrative offence of passing off pieces of copper as sixpences. One witness deposed that 'the People of the Town of Twickenham (where the Armstrongs resided) had been much imposed upon by Copper Pieces like Six Pences' and when the defendants were apprehended, 'several Pieces of Copper Money, and a parcel of tools were found upon the man.' Fortunately for the Armstrongs, the jury did not consider their offence to be worthy of capital or even corporal punishment; both were fined three Marks for their misdemeanour.

Theft also carried a very wide range of punishments. On 17 January 1724, Edward Campion, Jonathan Pomfroy and Thomas Jarvis of Islington stood trial for feloniously stealing three geese. On 9 December the previous year, the prisoners were stopped by a night watchman who was understandably curious to find out why the men had geese under their arms. The men admitted to the watchman that they had taken the birds out of a pond. However, once they realised they were going to be prosecuted, they changed their story and said they found the geese wandering around in the road. The jury felt inclined to believe the night watchman's account and found the trio guilty as charged. The judge, no doubt hoping that a bit of public humiliation might make them see the error of their ways, sentenced them to be whipped.

While being publicly flogged was hardly a pleasurable way to spend an afternoon, it was infinitely preferable to the fate of another animal thief, who had appeared at the Old Bailey in January of the same year. The case was reported succinctly in the Court Proceedings, which in a way makes it all the more shocking to 21st century minds. The entry read, 'Thomas Bruff, of the Parish of St Leonard Shoreditch, was indicted for feloniously stealing a brown mare, value 5 pounds, the property of William Sneeth, the 25th of August last. The Fact being plainly proved, the jury found him guilty of the Indictment. Death.'

Throughout the 18th century, the death penalty was meted out for all manner of offences, from murder to pickpocketing. Hanging was by far the most common method of carrying out the sentence and mercifully most convicts did not have to wait more than a few weeks for their appointment at Tyburn. By the 18th century many of the more horrific, medieval methods of execution had long since been banned. However, for a few unfortunate individuals found guilty of Treason, two truly appalling relics from the Middle Ages remained. Women found guilty of either Treason or Petty Treason could be sentenced to be burned alive at the stake. Amazingly, coin clipping (filing or cutting down the edges of coins so more could be forged) was included in the offences for which being burned was punishment; three women were burned alive in the 1780s for this very crime. However, many other women who suffered this most dreadful of ends had been found guilty of murdering their husbands (which was considered Petty Treason).

Just 18 months after the execution of Jack Sheppard, a woman named Catherine Hayes was sentenced to death by burning after persuading her two lovers to kill her husband with an axe and then dispose of his body. Any appeals for clemency went unheeded after the trial and the date of Catherine's execution was set for 9 May at Tyburn. No doubt horrified at the fate that awaited her, Catherine managed to procure some poison while incarcerated at Newgate. However, her plan was discovered by her cellmate and the poison taken away. The details of her execution were recorded by the Newgate Calendar, which reported, 'On the day of her death she received the Sacrament, and was drawn on a sledge to the place of execution. When the wretched woman had finished her devotions, in pursuance of her sentence an iron chain was put round her body, with which she was fixed to a stake near the gallows.

'On these occasions, when women were burned for Petty Treason, it was customary to strangle them, by means of a rope passed round the neck and pulled by the executioner, so that they were dead before the flames reached the body. But this woman was literally burned alive; for the executioner letting go the rope sooner than usual, in consequence of the flames reaching his hands, the fire burned fiercely round her, and the spectators beheld her pushing away the faggots, while she rent the air with her cries and lamentations. Other faggots were instantly thrown on her; but she survived amidst the flames for a considerable time, and her body was not perfectly reduced to ashes until three hours later.'

Men convicted of Treason could be sentenced to a different but just as terrible method of execution: that of being hanged, drawn and quartered. Most men who suffered this fate had been accused of conspiring against the monarch and therefore they became martyrs to those who shared their ideals. Perhaps sensitive to this, the Newgate Calendar's reports of executions of this nature are generally composed with much more taste than the accounts of female murderers such as Catherine Hayes. This does not however negate the fact that this form of execution was ghastly. Before undertaking his final journey, the condemned man would be tied to a hurdle which was in turn attached to a horse. The prisoner was then drawn through the streets in full view of the thousands of onlookers who had turned out to see the macabre spectacle. On reaching the gallows, the man would be placed on the back of a horse-drawn cart and a noose put around his neck. The horses would then be scared into bolting forwards, thus dragging the body from the back of the cart and leaving it to swing in the air. At this point, those who had been sentenced only to hang would be left on the gallows until it was presumed that life was extinct.

A much worse fate met those convicted of Treason. The executioner watched carefully to decide when the prisoner was about to lose consciousness and at that point, the body was cut down and quickly disemboweled and castrated; the executioner making a point of showing the dying convict his own innards and amputated genitalia before he passed out. Once the prisoner had been disemboweled, the corpse was beheaded and the torso cut into quarters. Heads of traitors were often displayed publicly at the entrances to bridges or major thoroughfares as a warning to others, although many were 'rescued' by members of the deceased's family so they could be buried with the rest of the corpse.

Given the sickening nature of all three forms of 18th century capital punishment, being sentenced to death must have devastated all but the most resilient of convicts. However, for those receiving this most awful of sentences, all was not lost. After sentence was passed, the prisoner's family, friends and associates could petition for mercy via the Recorder of London who in turn, produced a report on each capital sentence and sent it to the reigning monarch for consideration. If the king felt that the prisoner had a good enough case, he could issue one of two types of pardon: a Free Pardon was issued when the monarch and his cabinet felt there was some doubt as to the prisoner's guilt. Once issued, the accused was free to leave his or her place of incarceration without further ado. More common was the Conditional Pardon. This was issued when it was felt that the sentence delivered was too severe. Receivers of Conditional Pardons generally had their sentences commuted to a lesser punishment. During the 18th century, around half of all those sentenced to death were pardoned.

The death penalty could also be avoided altogether by using two methods, the first of which one involved a mechanism known as 'Benefit of Clergy'. This ancient system was originally introduced in the Middle Ages to allow the Church to punish its members without going through a civil court. If a prisoner could prove he was a God-fearing Christian, the judge might be persuaded to hand sentencing over to the clergy, whose punishments were far less severe. In order to test the convict's faith, judges generally asked them to read a passage from the Bible, and Psalm 51 was usually selected due to its theme of confession and repentance. As a result, the Psalm became commonly known as 'neck verse' because of the number of necks it had saved from the gallows.

The second method of avoiding the death penalty was to secure a 'partial verdict' from the jury. As the accounts above show, the death penalty could be issued for all manner of relatively minor crimes. In fact, theft of goods to the value of just ten shillings or more could carry the penalty of death if the judge was so inclined. However, many jurors felt that this punishment was far too severe and so allowed the defendant to escape the risk of a death sentence by valuing the goods stolen at under ten shillings, which carried a much more lenient sentence. A good example of the partial verdict in action occurred at the trial of Ann Brown, who went on trial at the Old Bailey on 17 January 1724 accused of shoplifting. Ann had been caught red handed stealing stockings from two shops a month previously. At the trial, she had very little to say in her defence bar the fact that she had been cajoled into committing the crimes by another (anonymous) woman. However, despite having no reasonable excuse for her actions, the jury decided to spare her the prospect of a death sentence by valuing the items at four shillings and ten pence. Ann was spared the noose, but did not escape another, almost equally feared punishment: transportation.

By the beginning of the 18th century, the number of defendants using the 'Benefit of Clergy' device to escape the death penalty was at an all time high. This meant that numerous miscreants were released into the community after trial, where they were soon up to their old tricks again.

The authorities addressed this problem by legislating that men and women convicted of 'Clergyable' offences could be transported to serve their sentence working in Britain's colonies. Those found guilty of capital offences could also be transported if the monarch upheld their appeal. In 1718, the Transportation Act was passed through Parliament and proved to be an immediate hit with British judges, who saw it as a way of offering clemency to convicted prisoners while at the same time removing them from British society. A pamphlet from 1731 neatly described the process as 'Draining the nation of its offensive rubbish, without taking away their lives'. Between 1718 and 1775, two thirds of all convicted criminals at the Old Bailey were sentenced to transportation.

Once committed, convicts were held in the cells of a local gaol before being handed over to a 'convict merchant' who would transport his human cargo to the colonies in return for a fee paid by the Government. When the ship docked at its destination, the convicts were sold on contract as servants to local colonists, who in turn sold produce from their tobacco plantations and arable farms to the convict merchant who would then sail back to Britain with a ship full of a very different sort of cargo.

During the early years of criminal transportation the majority of convicts were sent to either the West Indies or the east coast of America (usually Maryland or Virginia). The journey to these far-flung destinations was both arduous and treacherous. Many of the convicts were not in the best of health when they embarked and consequently, outbreaks of disease were rife. Others found the prospect of servitude in a foreign land too much to bear and, sadly, suicides were not uncommon. According to contemporary landing certificates, mortality rates for convicts during the early years of transportation ran at between 11% and 16%. However, conditions gradually improved and by the 1770s, transporting agents were reporting just 2-3% fatalities per voyage.

The length of sentence received by transported convicts largely depended on the seriousness of the crime. Prisoners convicted of Clergyable offences were sent away for seven years while felons who had secured conditional pardons for capital crimes were transported for a period of anything from 14 years to life.

The vast majority of transported convicts were male. Women were generally considered to be less of a threat to the public and therefore were often given corporal punishment for non-capital offences rather than being sentenced to transportation. Historian A. Roger Ekirch studied the Maryland census return for 1755 and found that 79.5% of all transported convicts living there were either men or boys, most of whom were between the ages of 15 and 29 years. Their social status and professional backgrounds were surprisingly diverse. Ekirch noted that the prisoners ranged 'from soldiers to silversmiths to coopers and chimney sweeps, including a former cook for the Duke of Northumberland. One Irish convict styled himself a metal refiner, chemist and doctor while another jack-of-all-trades was reputedly "handy at any business" '. Other felons found by Ekirch include a former barrister who supplemented his income by smuggling rare books out of university libraries to be sold on the black market and a gentleman who despite being independently wealthy got his kicks from stealing silver cutlery.

Although the majority of transported convicts were not dangerous and many provided useful, cheap labour for the local plantation owners and farmers, many colonists found the concept of transportation insulting in the extreme. This is unsurprising considering it was patently obvious that the courts on the British mainland viewed their North American and West Indian colonies as perfect dumping grounds for the members of society they had rejected. Some colonies attempted to halt the process of transportation by levying taxes on the convict ships but the British Government soon stopped this practice. It was only at the outbreak of the War of Independence in 1775 that transportation to America finally ground to a halt. In total, around 30,000 prisoners were transported to America between 1718 and 1775 representing up to a quarter of all British immigrants to America during the 18th century.

When America declared independence from Britain in 1776, the courts were left with the dilemma of what to do with felons sentenced to transportation. Although the practice had proved unpopular in the colonies receiving the prisoners, transportation had proved to be hugely successful as a means of disposing of criminals on the British mainland and the courts were reluctant to dispense with the punishment. Various proposals were discussed and ultimately dismissed until the authorities finally realised that the answer to their problem lay many thousands of miles away in a land that had only been visited by a handful of Englishmen.

Earlier in the decade, Royal Navy Lieutenant James Cook had returned to Britain after a long expedition to the South Pacific announcing that he had claimed a new territory for the Crown named New South Wales. Cook and his crew reported that despite its remote location, the land and climate were very favourable for settlement. The courts reviewed Cook's reports of the land, came to the conclusion that New South Wales would be a perfect destination for transported criminals and on 26 January 1788, the 'First Fleet' of ships docked at Port Jackson, Sydney, with a human cargo of around 700 convicts. British colonisation of Australia had begun.

Life was exceptionally hard for Australia's first colonists. Due to the sheer number of convicts on board the first fleet, the ships could only be loaded with a relatively small amount of provisions, meaning that on arrival at Sydney, the convicts and accompanying marines had to become self-sufficient very quickly. The voyage itself was far longer than any previous convict transportations and by the time the ships reached port, many of the passengers were in very poor physical health and unable to work. The absence of any established farms or plantations exacerbated the problem and many people, convicts and free settlers alike, starved to death. The arrival of a second fleet in 1790 only made the situation worse as the starving colonists had to deal with an influx of yet more people who had to be fed.

At this point, the successful establishment of a penal colony in New South Wales seemed an almost impossible task and the venture may have failed completely were it not for the vision and enthusiasm of the colony's first Governor, Arthur Philip. On accepting the post, Philip envisaged the development of a colony that comprised a mix of convicts and free settlers. British citizens looking to begin a new life overseas were to be encouraged to come to New South Wales by the offer of a generous financial relocation package from the Government.

Once they had arrived, they would be given assistance in setting up their chosen business and would have a large workforce at their disposal in the form of convicts. In reality, the Government showed little interest in developing the fortunes of its new colony. Financial incentives for those wishing to emigrate were much lower than Philip had hoped and to cap it all, stories of the appalling conditions in New South Wales began to filter through to the homeland. Between 1788 and 1792, just 13 people decided to emigrate to Australia. In contrast, over 4,000 convicts arrived.

The almost total absence of new, free settlers combined with the arrival of a never-ending stream of convicts presented Philip with a problem that seemed almost insurmountable. He had to find a way to deal with an ever-expanding population of convicts, many of whom were either unable or unwilling to work. In addition to this, a sizeable proportion of the convicts were professional criminals who were constantly looking for ways to abscond or cause trouble. Some were dangerously violent; others suffered from mental illness. None of them wanted to be in Australia. Philip met the challenge with a mixture of prudence and authority. Provisions were constantly in short supply and so he took great care to ensure that they were shared amongst the population equally, regardless of status. The condition in which prisoners were received in New South Wales was significantly improved by the introduction of hygiene and care standards on the convict ships. Convicts that displayed exemplary behaviour were rewarded with better-paid, more responsible jobs and any crimes committed were dealt with in a fair but firm manner.

Gradually, the situation began to improve. New businesses were set up by convicts who had served their sentences but could not afford the passage home. Marriages were conducted and children born, thus strengthening community bonds. Convicts and settlers became less homesick as they slowly adjusted to their new surroundings. On arriving in New South Wales, Major Robert Ross had summed up the opinion of virtually everyone present by describing the place as the 'outcast of God's works'. By the time Philip finished his term as Governor in 1792, the colony was beginning to become a fully functioning community, though it would be nearly 60 years before the Gold Rush of the 1850s enticed any significant numbers of free settlers to build a new life in Australia. By then, most of the pioneers were dead but their refusal to quit in the face of adversity left an enduring legacy that helped shape the former penal colony into one of the 21st century's wealthiest nations.

Despite the undeniably harsh conditions faced by transported convicts, there is little evidence to suggest that the threat of exile deterred the populace from breaking the law. Just two years after the passing of the Transportation Act, the East India Company infuriated the Spitalfields weavers for a second time when it began importing cheap printed calico from India. When made up into a garment, printed calico took on the look of woven silk, but cost a fraction of the price. Therefore it became very popular throughout the City, much to the silk weavers' disgust. The weavers referred to women who wore dresses of this printed cloth as 'calico madams' and were known to attack them in the street. One poor unsuspecting woman was assaulted by a crowd of weavers who 'tore, cut, pulled off her gown and petticoat by violence, threatened her with vile language and left her naked in the fields'. The printed calico problem came to a head when a group of weavers tried to march to Lewisham to destroy some calico printing presses but were met by troops, who shot one of the weavers dead. As a result, the Government passed the Calico Act in 1721, which banned the use and wear of all printed calicos.

Chapter 6

A New Parish and a Gradual Descent

By the 1720s, Spitalfields had become so densely populated that the old chapels and churches could not accommodate enough people. The Huguenots were well-served by their own chapels, but many Spitalfields residents were not French Protestants and needed their own place of worship. There was an old chapel on Wheler Street and a Friends Meeting House in the aptly-named Quaker Street, but both these places were far too small to serve the burgeoning population. The decision was made in 1728 to create a new parish in the area. This parish was named Christ Church and its church was built by the great ecclesiastical architect Nicholas Hawksmoor on Red Lion Street (now Commercial Street), almost opposite the market. Christ Church was consecrated on 5th July 1729 and is distinguished by its exceptionally tall spire, which measures 225 feet.

By the 1740s, Spitalfields was at the height of its prosperity. The parish clerk, John Walker, noted that there were at the time 2,190 houses in Spitalfields, not counting those in Norton Folgate, the Old Artillery Ground or Spital Square. The properties along the major thoroughfares were occupied by master weavers and silk merchants, while the artisans and journeymen lived in the side turnings, such as Dorset Street and Fashion Street. In the Ten Bells pub on Commercial Street, a 19th century tiled frieze depicts a Spitalfields street scene in the mid-18th century. The picture shows a busy, cheerful community of craftsmen and merchants, doing business with one another and evidently taking great pride in their work. However, the good times were not destined to last for long and by the 1760s, cracks began to show in the hitherto closely-knit weaving community that by now formed the backbone of the area.

For some time, journeymen silk weavers had been unhappy about the level of wages they received. An article from the *Gentleman's Magazine* dated November 1763 illustrates how this dissatisfaction sometimes descended into violence: 'in a riotous manner (the journeymen weavers) broke into the house of one of their masters, destroyed his looms and cut a great quantity of silk to pieces, after which they placed his effigy in a cart, with a halter round its neck, an executioner on one side, and a coffin on the other; and after drawing it through the streets, they hanged it on a gibbet, then burnt it to ashes and afterwards dispersed.'

This particular act of aggression against an employer was by no means an isolated incident. By 1768, these outbreaks of violence had become so widespread that an act of Parliament was passed making it punishable by death to break into any house or shop with the intention of maliciously damaging or destroying silk goods in the process of manufacture. The fiery-tempered journeymen were undeterred by the act and continued to loot the homes and workplaces of employers who they felt had treated them unfairly.

As time went on, the attacks on the master weavers' homes became more organised and it soon became clear that the journeymen were becoming a cohesive unit, capable of severely damaging the local industry. As a result, troops were employed to break up meetings of journeymen whenever and wherever they took place. In 1769, a meeting at the Dolphin pub in Spitalfields was raided by troops, who opened fire on the journeymen, killing two and forcing the ringleaders to beat a hasty retreat from the area. Two of them were subsequently caught and hanged at the crossroads at Bethnal Green (also a weaving area) as a warning to others.

The Government realised that while force could be employed to calm the journeymen weavers' tempers, the silk weaving industry was facing problems of a much more far-reaching nature. As news of Spitalfields' burgeoning silk weaving industry spread throughout the 18th century, the area experienced a dramatic influx of poor from all over the British Isles looking for work. At first, the master weavers welcomed this state of affairs because it meant they could buy cheap labour, but by the middle of the century, there were simply too few jobs to go round.

In 1773, the Government passed the Spitalfields Acts and attempted to remedy the situation by restricting the number of people entering the industry and having independent local Justices set the journeymen's wages. However, this external control of wages and restricted employment meant that the master weavers found it difficult to operate their businesses day to day. This, coupled with the introduction of mechanised looms and the fact that woven silks were gradually slipping out of fashion, meant that the master weavers began to move out of the area to towns in Essex, where they had the freedom to run their businesses as they pleased, with lower overheads. The Spitalfields silk industry was in decline.

Despite the exodus of master weavers to the Essex countryside, the influx of poor coming to Spitalfields looking for work continued unabated. Soon the cheaper accommodation in the alleys and courts became overrun with people. Disease spread quickly in such a claustrophobic atmosphere and the more desperate residents resorted to petty crime in order to make ends meet.

However, all was not doom and gloom just yet. Many weaving businesses continued to employ journeymen weavers and throwsters from the area and other businesses, such as Truman's Brewery, which had stood in Black Lion Street since 1669, were also major employers. Dorset Street and Spitalfields in general was also considered an attractive location for manufacturers' London showrooms due to its proximity to the City. In the early 1820s,

Thomas Wedgwood opened a showroom for his family's world famous china at number 40 Dorset Street. The Wedgwood family had been potters for generations, however, it was the creative vision and sound business acumen of Thomas' great, great uncle, Josiah Wedgwood, that brought the pottery international success. Josiah was responsible for the creation of the pottery's signature Queen's Ware, a simple, classical design with a plain cream glaze, which is still available today.

Queen's Ware is named after Queen Charlotte, a regular Wedgwood customer who appointed the firm 'Queen's Potter' in 1762. Ironically, Josiah Wedgwood was an active campaigner for social reform and led the way for improved living conditions for the poor by building model dwellings for his workers in Stoke on Trent. It is a pity he was not alive to see the overrun and dilapidated courts and alleyways that surrounded his company's London showroom in the early 19th century. Despite its good location, Thomas Wedgwood left the Dorset Street property in the mid-1840s, no doubt realising the area was in slow but unstoppable decline. He retired soon after and lived out his days in rural Bengeo, Hertfordshire, where he died in 1864.

Another business that had grown to dominate the area was Spitalfields Market. The market had been gradually improved and enlarged throughout the latter part of the 18th century and by 1800 was a major supplier of fruit and vegetables (mainly potatoes) to the masses. The market offered a wide variety of job opportunities from administrative positions for those who could read and write, to portering and selling for workers who had not benefited from a formal education (or preferred more physical work). Freelance opportunities were also available for costermongers who took produce from the market on their barrows and wheeled it round the streets looking for buyers. Workers from all around the London area and beyond travelled to the market to do business.

Many men who travelled some distance to the market found it easier to stay in the area overnight rather than face a long journey home after a hard days work. Consequently cheap lodgings and an evening's entertainment became widely sought. Public houses sprang up on any available land within a short walk from the market. One of the earliest market pubs was the Blue Coat Boy at 32 Dorset Street. Situated a mere two minutes away from the market gates, this pub was certainly in existence by 1825 and had probably stood on the site for much longer. Although fairly small, it provided an opportunity to relax with colleagues before the next day's hard work began. Some pubs offered rooms to let above the bar but it soon became clear that a significantly larger amount of accommodation was required to satisfy the rapidly increasing demand from itinerant workers. Thus, one of the major forces in the downfall of Spitalfields arrived – the common lodging house.

Chapter 7

The Rise of the Common Lodging House

The Spitalfields common lodging houses evolved purely in response to demand. If the residents had known what they would do to the area, there is little doubt they would have banned them on the spot. However, as more itinerant workers arrived, locals realised that good money could be earned by letting out spare rooms on a nightly basis. When it transpired that the spare rooms could be let virtually all year round, empty properties were sought, which could be turned into yet more sleeping quarters, yielding more cash.

Until 1851, there were virtually no regulations regarding the running of common lodging houses. Anyone could run one, so long as they could pay the rent on the property. Consequently, conditions in common lodging houses could be horrendous. An inquest into the death of James Parkinson, aged 36, was printed in the *Morning Herald* newspaper in 1836. It gives a shocking depiction of day-to-day life in one of these establishments: Parkinson, a dealer in cats' meat, had apparently arrived at a 'low lodging house for travellers' in Saffron Hill (an area well known for this type of establishment), paid for his bed and promptly retired for the night. At some stage during the night, the poor man died in his sleep. Incredibly, the landlady did not realise that he was dead for several days, despite seeing his body in the bed on several occasions. Perhaps even more incomprehensible is the fact that none of the other lodgers reported anything odd about their room-mate and seemed oblivious to the terrible smell brought on by decomposition of the corpse. By the time Parkinson's death was recorded, his face had turned black. When questioned about the incredible lack of perception demonstrated by her and the other lodgers, the landlady shrugged 'they go in and out without seeming to care for each other.'

Although the above report is an extreme example of disregard for fellow human beings, inmates from the lowest type of common lodging house could ill afford to be too concerned about their fellow man. During the peak winter season, up to three people could be forced to share a bed. Possessions had to be kept about one's person for fear of theft while asleep and it truly was a situation of 'every man for himself.' It seems remarkable that houses offering such terrible conditions remained in business. However, it must be remembered that the lodgers were almost always poor and desperate for somewhere to sleep for the night. Unable to afford a more salubrious establishment, they were forced to resort to the common lodging houses.

Lousy surroundings and the prospect of another day's hard graft in front of them made the lodgers yearn for home comforts and in particular, female company. Consequently, the second scourge of Spitalfields arrived – prostitution. At first, the Spitalfields prostitutes were just another part of life for a busy market area with a highly transient population. However, by the middle of the 19th century, Spitalfields was undergoing a period of damaging social change that would transform the area for nearly 150 years.

In 1826, the remaining Spitalfields silk weavers were dealt a devastating setback when, in the spirit of free trade, the Government finally allowed French silk to be imported to the UK. Although a 30% tariff was levied on the imports, the market was flooded and in consequence, the weavers' wages were halved virtually overnight. Had this state of affairs occurred 50 years previously, the weavers may have had the energy and resources to protest and halt the trade, but by the 1820s, the departure of most of the master weavers from Spitalfields had left their erstwhile workers barely able to scratch a living. The fact that their already insufficient wages were now halved made their position impossible. The vast majority of the firms that had stayed in Spitalfields either packed up shop or moved out to the country, where at least their overheads would be lower.

The journeymen weavers and throwsters were left with the option of either deserting the area in search of work elsewhere or staying put and finding a way to supplement their wages. Crime increased as impoverished weavers were compelled to steal food for their families and some of their womenfolk were forced into the ultimate indignity of prostitution. Families were forced to move to cheaper lodgings and some even had to resort to the foul common lodging houses.

In 1846, the Spitalfields silk weaving industry received its final, fatal blow when the duty on French silk was halved. This time, the impoverished weavers resigned themselves to the fact that the good times were never coming back and didn't even bother to register much of a protest. The devastating blow suffered by Spitalfields as a result of the demise of the silk weaving industry is clearly shown in statistics from the period. In 1831, (when it must be remembered that many weaving firms had already left the area) there were up to 17,000 looms in Spitalfields and 50,000 residents were dependent on the silk weaving industry. By 1851, just 21,000 individuals were employed in the silk industry in the whole of London.

The Huguenot families who had made their fortunes in Spitalfields tried their best to help their impoverished ex-employees. For example, in 1834, George Fournier left a large bequest to the Spitalfields poor in his will. His generosity was remembered by renaming the road that ran along the side of Christ Church, Fournier Street. However, the silk industry was by this stage terminally sick and nothing could be done to prevent its ultimate demise.

Chapter 8

Serious Overcrowding

By the 1830s, the plight of the silk weavers had created a problem the parish couldn't ignore. As Spitalfields' fortunes faded, local properties, particularly those around Christ Church, became ridiculously overcrowded as residents attempted to reduce individual rent bills. In addition, the buildings into which the poor families were crammed were very old and had been neglected for so many years that they were beginning to fall apart at the seams. These rookeries posed two problems for the Parish Council and local members of Parliament.

Firstly, the old and dilapidated houses had not only become home to hundreds of Spitalfields poor, but their maze of ancient alleyways and courts also attracted felons who found them perfect hideouts and meeting places. In addition to this, Spitalfields market had become so successful that traders were finding it increasingly difficult to gain access to it via the ancient, narrow streets that led from Whitechapel and the City. In order to solve both problems in one fell swoop, a new road was proposed that would connect the market with Whitechapel. This road was to be aptly named Commercial Street and its construction would necessitate the demolition of the rookeries that so troubled the local Councillors.

Plans for the first phase of Commercial Street were duly approved and by 1845 all the rookeries had been swept away and replaced with the new trade route. Exactly what the Councillors expected to happen to the hundreds of rookery dwellers once they had been made homeless remains a mystery. Perhaps it was assumed that they would simply disappear once their homes were destroyed. Unsurprisingly, they did not disappear. They simply moved to either side of the new road, thus making already congested thoroughfares such as Dorset Street, Whites Row and Fashion Street more crowded than ever.

Canny property owners in the streets affected by the overcrowding problem recognised the extra money that could be made by converting all available space into extra housing. One such property-owner was John Miller. Miller was a butcher by trade, who worked out of his shop at 30 Dorset Street. He and his family had moved to the area in the 1830s, just as many older residents associated with the weaving industry were moving out. As a result, properties came up for sale at a regular rate and when funds could be found, John Miller acquired them. In addition to number 30, Miller also owned numbers 26 and 27 Dorset Street.

These two properties were joined together and had sizeable gardens to the rear, which were reached via a covered passage that ran between the ground floors of the houses. Attracted by the prospect of extra rental income, Miller decided to destroy the gardens and in their place threw up three 'one up, one down' cottages set around a flagged courtyard. By 1851, the houses were completed and the new development was given the name Miller's Rents, an apt description of what they were. Over the years, this poorly built little square of slum-dwellings acquired three more mean cottages and its name evolved from Miller's Rents into Miller's Court, a name that was to become notorious in 1888 when Jack the Ripper's final victim was horrifically mutilated in one of its squalid rooms. But more of that story later.

The dispersal of the rookery inhabitants offered more custom for the already busy common lodging houses. Enterprising proprietors eagerly searched for more old houses suitable for conversion. By that time, there were still virtually no regulations attached to running a common lodging house and setting one up was a reasonably easy exercise. The interiors of countless once-elegant weavers' homes were ripped out and all dividing walls demolished to create huge, open rooms on each floor. The only room to remain intact was the kitchen, although in some houses that too was ripped out and the tenants expected to share a kitchen with the house next door.

The upper floors were then filled to capacity with cheap beds, often only comprising a rude timber frame and straw-filled sacking that served as mattress. There were rarely any washing facilities, lighting was poor and heat non-existent apart from the fire in the kitchen. The proximity of the beds (and the fact that they were often shared) made disease spread fast. The conditions in the lodging houses were so appalling that by 1844 they had attracted the attention of Parliament and consequently came under the scrutiny of the Royal Commissioners.

Their inspectors were not surprisingly disgusted at what they found and concluded that something had to be done about them. The Commissioners' subsequent report on the 'Health of Towns and Other Populous Places' advised that some enforceable regulations should be placed on the running of common lodging houses, with a view to improving the situation. However, although their advice was acted upon, in the long run it was to have little effect on the terrible evolution of the Spitalfields lodging houses.

Although the common lodging houses were dreadful places for their inhabitants, the owners of these establishments were able to carve out very lucrative careers for themselves. Many of the lodging house keepers at this time were long-term residents of Spitalfields who were fortunate enough to have the resources to buy up suitable property and convert it quickly and cheaply. One such man was John Smith. Smith, who was a greengrocer by trade, was initially attracted to the area by the market, and by the early 1800s, had set up retail premises in Spitalfields with his wife Elinor. As the area declined, Smith noticed the demand for cheap lodgings and gradually acquired property, converting it to house the poor. The business proved to be extremely successful and Smith expanded his property portfolio whenever he could. He concentrated his efforts in and around Brick Lane, an old road that had originally led to fields in which the clay for bricks was dug.

By the 1860s, John Smith's main business had evolved from greengrocer to lodging house keeper. By this time he and Elinor had seven children, three of whom would go on to continue the business of keeping common lodging houses into the next century. Indeed, his eldest son James (known locally as Jimmy) and daughter Elizabeth would go on to become two of the most influential people on the streets of Spitalfields at the time of Jack the Ripper.

Chapter 9

The Third Wave of Immigrants
(The Irish Famine)

While the Royal Commissioners were busy inspecting the common lodging houses, the overcrowding problem in Spitalfields was about to get worse. Almost as soon as Dorset Street and its surrounds had adjusted to the resettlement of ex-rookery residents, it faced yet another influx of people to the area. This time, the cause was not road building, but a fungus named Phytophthora Infestans.

Early in 1845, an American ship docked in Ireland with a deadly cargo. Some of the produce on board carried the Phytophthora fungus, which was capable of causing devastation to potato crops. At the time, potatoes were big business in Ireland. Almost half the population relied on potatoes to keep from starvation and consumed them in large quantities. Irish potato crops were mainly comprised of two, high-yielding varieties, both of which were affected by the fungus with frightening speed. An unusually cool and wet summer allowed the fungus to thrive and that year's potato crop was almost a complete failure across the country.

At first, the Irish people did their best to remain optimistic about the future. On 2 September, the *Cork Examiner* reported that in at least one other year (1765), the potato crop had been ruined and noted that communities had recovered from that crisis: 'We have no apprehension that the potato is gone from us. There will be some to make another venture apon it next year and probably, in 1848 there will be such a crop as has not been witnessed within the time of the oldest man living.' That said, the underlying emotion was that of utter dread and two days later, the *Examiner* reported that, 'all is alarm and apprehension. The landlord trembles for the consequences; so does the middleman; so does the tenant farmer.'

Believing the situation to be temporary, many landlords did their best to improve conditions for their tenants. For example, in September 1846, a group of landlords from Fermanagh vowed to employ as many impoverished farm workers as they possibly could to work on their property. They also sought to establish a depot in Enniskillen that would distribute 'Indian Meal' (ground corn) to the starving. Similar plans were laid throughout the country. However, the populace found the Indian Meal unpalatable to the point of being inedible and driven by hunger, men resorted to insurrection in order to obtain food for their families.

Workers employed by a Mr Fitzgerald of Rocklodge, near Cloyne, refused to allow their master to send his corn to ships at Cork or to the market, stating that they would give him the price he demanded for it. There were serious riots in Dungarvan and in late September 1846, bakers' shops in Youghal were raided in an attempt by the starving mob to prevent the export of bread. The mob was eventually dispersed by the military.

By October 1846, vast tracts of land throughout Ireland were home to communities that had become utterly destitute. Father Daly of Kilworth reported in the *Cork Examiner* that many of his congregation were subsisting purely on cabbage leaves. Given this state of affairs, it is little wonder that the people were growing increasingly angry and frustrated with their remote Government on the British mainland. Sir Robert Peel's cabinet had provided a modicum of relief during the initial stages of the famine, but when Peel's party were succeeded by the Whigs (under Lord John Russell) in June 1846, much of the financial burden of providing for the starving Irish workers was passed to the landowners.

However, despite offering precious little assistance, the Government was wary of the increasing insurrection and dispatched army regiments to trouble spots with the intention of stamping out any trouble before it began. The army presence only increased the animosity towards the British Government. On 8 October, 'A Pauper' wrote to the *Cork Examiner*, 'On yesterday morning the 7th instant, on my way to the Union-house in company with my three destitute children, so as to receive some relief in getting some Indian meal porridge, to our great mortification the two sides of the road were lined with police and infantry – muskets with screwed bayonets and knapsacks filled with powder and ball, ready to slaughter us, hungry victims… If the Devil himself had the reins of Government from her Britannic Majesty he could not give worse food to her subjects, or more pernicious, than powder and ball.'

By the end of 1846, thousands of Irish had become so poor that they could no longer afford to keep their own homes. Although many landlords had done their best to waive as much rent as possible, they had to collect some money in order to pay their own staff. Consequently, the previously loathed Workhouses were becoming ridiculously overcrowded, especially as the fast-approaching winter made sleeping rough too awful to contemplate. On 23 October, the *Evening Post* reported that the Workhouses of Cork, Waterford and some other towns contained more inmates than they were calculated to accommodate.

Altogether, the increase as compared with the previous October was fifty per cent. The fact that even the Workhouses had reached capacity was, for some, the end of the line, as this sad article from the *Tipperary Vindicator* illustrates: 'A coroner's inquest was held on the lands of Redwood in the Parish of Lorha, on yesterday, the 24th (October) on the body of Daniel Hayes, who for several days subsisted on the refuse of vegetables and went out on Friday morning in a quest of something in the shape of food, but he had not gone far when he was obliged to lie down, and, melancholy to relate, was found dead some time afterward.'

In an attempt to provide the destitute with at least some form of income, the Government-run Board of Works set up 'task work'. This employment took the form of extremely menial, repetitive jobs such as ditch digging, drain clearing and road laying and workers were treated in a similar manner to that of common criminals. The task work was despised by the Irish and most chose to work for the landowners rather than join the task work gang. However, by the end of 1846, the landowners had problems of their own. Despite their best efforts to provide relief (by December 1846, many landowners had completely waived any yearly rents due), their funds were not limitless and the famine had proved to be a massive drain on their resources. The landowners were gradually running out of money.

By the end of 1846, Ireland was in an unprecedented and truly horrific state of destitution. The once hardy population had withered away to skeletons. Disease was rife, with dropsy, cholera and typhus raging through and destroying entire communities. Coffins were so scarce that most of the dead were buried in the clothes they had died in. Entire fields that had once contained the potato crop became makeshift graveyards. The crisis had become an utter catastrophe.

1847 brought with it yet more problems. Once again, the populace's worst fears were realised as the potato crop succumbed yet again to the devastating blight and the country was on its knees. The Government-run task work groups ground to a halt as workers became too ill and malnourished to perform any useful jobs and with the wage earner jobless, families literally starved to death. Despite this dreadful state of affairs, the Government still refused to subsidise alternative foodstuffs such as meat and bread. Starving Irish stood on the docks and watched as container-loads of the food they craved disappeared across the sea. The military was required less and less as communities became too apathetic and weak to organise any form of protest. The dead lay undiscovered in deserted villages for days on end.

The landlords who had done so much to help their tenants, were finally coming to the end of their resources and, fearing another blight the following year, searched for a solution. It came in the form of passenger ships bound for the New World and the British mainland.

In a bid to literally save the lives of their countrymen, many Irish landowners offered to pay their tenants' passage on ships bound for America, the British mainland and other English-speaking countries. Their offer was accepted by thousands, who felt that they simply had no other choice. The prospect of a new life in the New World appealed greatly, but the ships used to flee the island carried dangers of their own. Disease was often rife on board and once the ship arrived at its destination, passengers were forced to stay in infected, low boarding houses while waiting to be naturalised.

In the first six months of 1847, 567 people died on the passage from Great Britain to New York. Conditions on ships working the passage between Ireland and Canada were even worse. It was not uncommon for half of passengers to die before reaching the Canadian ports. Newspapers in Quebec carried eyewitness reports of the terminally sick being thrown from vessels onto the beach, where they were left to die. Emigration carried an immense degree of risk, but for many, it appealed more than remaining in the wasteland that had once been their home.

By the time the famine finally began to subside in 1849, up to 1.5 million Irish families had fled their homeland. During that period, it is estimated that 46,000 Irish arrived in London and by 1851, the census recorded that 109,000 Londoners had been born in Ireland. Due the circumstances surrounding their arrival in the capital, the vast majority of Irish immigrants had virtually no money at their disposal and so settled in areas where work could be found quickly and housing was cheap. According to the contemporary writer John Garwood, the most popular parts of London for the Irish immigrants to settle were St Giles, Field Lane, Westminster, parts of Marylebone, Drury Lane, Seven Dials, East Smithfield, Wapping, Ratcliff, The Mint in Southwark and the 'crowded lanes and courts between Houndsditch and the new street in Whitechapel'. However, virtually any area that possessed a rookery became home to impoverished Irish families.

London became home to many of the poorest families simply because they couldn't afford to escape anywhere further afield. The opportunities in the new world of North America made it the preferred destination for most displaced Irish. Even those who came to London initially hoped that they would eventually be able to afford the passage across the Atlantic. John Garwood noted 'they do not regard England with any fondness, excepting that they generally consider the English as honest, although heretics, who will keep their word and pay them what they agree for. They generally simply desire to come, in order to obtain money to get over to America.' In the cases of the poorest families, it was common for one or two of the fittest men to travel from Ireland to the British mainland or North America.

Once they had secured some reasonably-paid work, they began either sending money home or purchased sea passage on behalf of other family members. This method of gradually evacuating entire families from Ireland became extremely popular: in 1852, the Colonial Land and Emigration Commissioners noted, 'the misery which the Irish have for many years endured has destroyed the attachment to their native soil, the numbers who have already emigrated and prospered remove the apprehension of going to a strange and untried country, while the want of means is remedied by the liberal contributions of their relations and friends who have preceded them. The contributions so made, either in the form of prepaid passages, or of money sent home, and which are almost exclusively provided by the Irish, were returned to us, as in:

> 1848, upwards of £460,000
> 1849, upwards of £540,000
> 1850, upwards of £957,000
> 1851, upwards of £990,000.'

The majority of famine refugees who migrated to Spitalfields took up residence in the courts and dilapidated lodging houses in the southernmost part of the district, close to the Whitechapel and Commercial Roads. However, the overcrowded streets that lay closer to Christ Church also provided much-needed accommodation when space allowed. Since the silk-weaving industry had gone into decline, Dorset Street had received a steady stream of Irish settlers, many of whom set up boot and shoe-making workshops in the old weavers' garrets.

One such immigrant was James Rouse who had lived and worked on the street since at least 1840. Rouse possessed a talent for his trade combined with shrewd business sense. By 1861, he had accrued sufficient savings to relocate to more spacious premises in Lamb Street and described himself in the census of that year as a 'master boot maker'. Two of his sons are listed as apprentices. The profit made from the business in the following decade allowed him to retire in the 1870s and live a comfortable life in the middle-class suburb of Bromley.

In 1851, there were 50 people living in Dorset Street who had been born in Ireland. Some like James Rouse and his family had lived in London for some time while others almost certainly arrived on the street as a direct result of the famine in their homeland. At number 16, William Keefe and his family shared their home with four women who had almost certainly escaped deprivation in Ireland and were attempting to make new lives for themselves in the British mainland. Three of the women, Margaret Casey, 35, Margaret Lynch, 20, and Mary Ann Doughan, 35, hailed from Cork while their room-mate, Catherine Allen, 27, hailed from Galway. None of the women were married and so it was entirely up to them to ensure the rent was paid on time. The two Margarets and Catherine worked as seed potters (probably for one of the merchants in Spitalfields Market). This type of work was both home-based and seasonal. One can imagine the mess as flowerpots were filled with soil ready for seeds to be planted in the spring and the growing anxiety felt by the women as summer approached and work became increasingly scarce.

Irish refugees with families in tow found emigration to London particularly challenging, both emotionally and financially. Back in Ireland, even the largest cities such as Dublin were nowhere near as noisy, dirty and frenetic as mid-19th century London. In order to lessen the inevitable homesickness and to keep a rein on rental expenditure, many set up home with members of their extended kin. The Keating family arrived in Dorset Street in the late 1840s. Like so many other Irish immigrants to the East End the head of the family, John Keating, was a boot maker who brought not only his young wife and child with him but also his mother-in-law, brother-in-law, niece and an apprentice. Although the family comprised six adults and a seven-year-old, they all lived in one room at number 25 Dorset Street while John attempted to make a go of his business.

The arrival of famine refugees on the streets of Spitalfields was not well received by the locals, including other Irishmen. The migrants soon gained a reputation for attempting to fit far too many members of their family into one room in order to save money (see the Keatings above). The resulting noise and constant comings and goings irritated their neighbours who did not understand that the extreme overcrowding was due to poverty rather than choice. In 1853, John Garwood unkindly noted 'in the days of Queen Elizabeth, it was customary to divide the Irish in to three classes: the Irish, the wild Irish and the extreme wild Irish… The same divisions may be made in the days of Queen Victoria… And the class of Irish with which we are most familiar in the courts and alleys of London, are by no means the most favourable specimens of the nation.'

Many Londoners resented the fact that the majority of refugees used their city as a stepping-stone to their goal of reaching America. This even caused divisions between the immigrants and their own countrymen. Garwood explained, 'of the Irish immigrants who remain in London, few have any such intention at first. But they gradually become accustomed to the place and its habits, and at length settle down in it. Their descendants are called "Irish Cockneys," and the new-comers are called "Grecians.' By these names they are generally distinguished among themselves. And the two divisions of this class are most distinct. The animosity which subsists between them is very bitter, far beyond that which often unhappily exists between the Irish and the English. The Cockneys regard the Grecians as coming to take the bread out of their own mouths, and consider their extensive immigration as tending to lower their own wages. Having also succeeded in raising themselves, at least some steps, from that abject poverty and nakedness which distinguished them on their first arrival, they now look on the Grecians as bringing a discredit on their country by their appearance and necessities. There are constant quarrels between the two, and they are so estranged that they will not live even in the same parts of the town, after the first flow of generous hospitality has passed over.'

To the immense relief of all concerned, the 1850 Irish potato crop finally survived. However, it did not yield as much as it had done before the outbreak of the fungal virus and many communities continued to exist in great hardship. By this time, over one million people had died as a result of the worst famine to occur in Europe in the 19th century. As the statistics on page 63 show, the amount of contributions towards passages out of the country steadily increased into the 1850s and, although the worst of the famine was over, the Irish continued their exodus in the hope that a better life could be found elsewhere. Their migration was helped immeasurably by competition between the steam-boat companies who slashed their prices in order to attract more custom. Passage from Cork to London, which normally cost around 10 shillings, could be obtained for as little as one shilling. There were even reports of some companies bringing passengers over to the British mainland for no charge whatsoever.

Chapter 10

The McCarthy Family

One Irish family that took advantage of the new, rock-bottom prices were destined to become Dorset Street's most influential residents. In 1848, Daniel McCarthy and his pregnant wife Margaret, boarded a ship sailing from Cork harbour and left their homeland behind them. After a brief stay in Dieppe (where it is likely Daniel sought work in the Docks), the McCarthys, who by now had a baby son named John, arrived in England.

Daniel had previously been used to agricultural work so the family initially made for Hertfordshire, where it was hoped that permanent farm work could be secured. However, this was not to be and for the next five or so years, the family travelled across London and the home counties, picking up menial jobs wherever they could. However, like so many of their countrymen before them, they were eventually forced into the metropolis permanently, where work, however demeaning and badly paid, was in greater supply.

The McCarthys settled in Red Cross Court, in Southwark. This mean yard was a typical London address for impoverished Irishfolk fleeing the famine in their homeland. It had originally been the back yard of the Red Cross Inn – a hostelry on Borough High Street. However, as the population of The Borough exploded in the early 19th century, the yard was built over. Two-storey cottages lined its perimeter and a row of dilapidated stables ran down the centre. By the 1860s, the occupants of Red Cross Court were far too poor to keep horses so the stables served as stockrooms for oranges that were bought at Borough Market and sold cheaply on the streets by the Court's inhabitants.

By the time Daniel and Margaret McCarthy arrived in Red Cross Court, their family had increased significantly. Joining John were four brothers: Denis, Jeremiah, Timothy and Daniel. In 1865, a daughter named Annie was born. During the following years, Red Cross Court became something of a Mecca for members of the McCarthy clan. By 1881, there were McCarthys living at numbers 1, 4, 9, 10 and 12 plus two more McCarthy families living at number 2 and 24 May Pole Alley, which was situated next door. By this time Daniel and Margaret had moved across the river to Whitechapel where they lived out the rest of their lives in quiet obscurity. However, their eldest son John harboured grand ideas about his future and set about laying plans to escape the grinding poverty of London's slums – plans that were to be more successful than probably even he would have imagined.

Like the Borough across the river, Spitalfields – and roads such as Dorset Street in particular – became an attractive destination for impoverished Irish immigrants because it offered insalubrious but cheap accommodation and was close to the potential workplaces of the City, the Docks and, of course, the market. Many of the working-class Irish immigrants found work as costermongers, buying fruit and vegetables from the market and taking them round the streets on a barrow to sell to the residents. During his investigation into how London's poor lived and worked, Henry Mayhew studied the Irish costermongers in depth. At the time, it was officially estimated that there were 10,000 Irish street-sellers in London. However, Mayhew reckoned the figure to be higher. He noted, 'of this large body, three-fourths sell only fruit, and more specifically nuts and oranges; indeed the orange season is called the "Irishman's Harvest." The others deal in fish, fruit and vegetables… some of the most wretched of the street Irish deal in such trifles as Lucifer-matches, water-cresses, etc.'

In addition to street-selling, many Irish immigrants who had previously been employed on farms took to labouring in the building trade. Some took casual labouring work at the docks, while others took on the back-breaking work of excavating and wood chopping. When work was thin on the ground (as it often was), both men and women would take to the streets and beg.

This hand-to-mouth existence meant that accommodation was hard to find. Families barely had enough money to feed themselves, let alone enough to find rent money for a reasonably furnished room. Consequently the common lodging houses that lined Dorset Street (and many other streets in Spitalfields), experienced an unprecedented boom. However, their burgeoning business was soon to come under the scrutiny of social reformers, journalists and ultimately, the Government.

Chapter 11

The Common Lodging Houses Act

By the beginning of the 1850s, the already pitiful plight of the poor in Spitalfields had been exacerbated to an almost unbearable degree by the arrival of the Irish immigrants. The area was now among the poorest in the whole of London and was beginning to attract the attention of the press. In 1849, the journalist Henry Mayhew visited Spitalfields in search of acute poverty for an article he was writing for the *Morning Chronicle* newspaper. He was particularly touched by the plight of the old silk weavers, who he found living 'in a state of gloomy destitution, sitting in their wretched rooms dreaming of the neat houses and roast beef of long ago.' Mayhew went on to note that the remaining Spitalfields weavers seemed resigned to their reduced circumstances and no longer had the energy to do anything about it: 'In all there was the same want of hope – the same doggedness and half-indifference as to their fate.'

Spitalfields was not the only area of the metropolis that was experiencing poverty on an unprecedented scale. Across the river, the ancient area of Bermondsey was experiencing similar problems, as this heartbreaking excerpt from a coroner's report on the death of a poverty-stricken young woman shows: 'she lay dead beside her son upon a heap of feathers which were scattered over her almost naked body, there being no sheet or coverlet. The feathers stuck so fast over the whole body that the doctor could not examine the corpse until it was cleansed. He then found it starved and scarred from rat bites.'

Similar accounts of abject poverty began appearing regularly in the London press. Under particular scrutiny once again were the already notorious common lodging houses which, according to the journalists who visited them, had plumbed even greater depths. The scathing press reports, combined with the report from the Royal Commission forced Parliament to address the common lodging house problem and an act was passed in 1851 in a bid to improve the situation.

In their wisdom, the politicians responsible for drawing up the act came to the conclusion that the common lodging houses caused problems not because of the wanton lack of facilities and the type of person that frequented them, but because they lacked supervision and clear rules and regulations. The new act stipulated that every common lodging house should have clear signage outside stating what the building was used for. Inside, every sleeping room should be measured. From these measurements, the number of beds allowed in each room would be calculated and a placard hung on the wall stating the allocation. Beds were to have fresh linen once a week and all windows were to be thrown open at 10am each day for ventilation purposes. All lodgers had to leave the lodging house at 10am and would not be allowed back in until late afternoon. These regulations were to be enforced by the local police.

While the regulations imposed by the Common Lodging Houses Act were well meaning, they were at best badly thought out and at worst laughable. Measuring the rooms to allocate beds was all very well and good if only one person was going to sleep in each bed. However, it had been a long-standing practice for people to share beds in order to save money, thus doubling or even tripling the room capacity on particularly cold nights. The fact that each room had a sign stating the number of beds allowed was of virtually no use because few inmates could read and those that could were not about to report their only source of shelter to the authorities. Fresh bed linen once a week would have been a good idea if the act had also made the laundries obliged to take it in. In reality, few self-respecting laundries would touch lodging-house bed linen as it was often riddled with vermin, which infected the whole laundry.

In winter, the throwing open of all windows during the day made the unheated rooms bitterly cold. The fact that lodgers were thrown out on the street at 10 in the morning may have made for a quiet day for the lodging house management, but was cruel to the lodgers, many of whom were sick and malnourished. They had to take all their belongings and walk the streets for up to six hours in search of money for their bed for the next night. In the case of Spitalfields, the police knew only too well what type of characters inhabited the lodging houses and officers were unwilling to walk into the 'lion's den' for fear of being attacked. Consequently, few lodging houses were inspected regularly.

The Common Lodging Houses Act of 1851 had many failings, but probably its biggest fault was that it did not provide any regulation on the way the proprietors made their money. Consequently, prices for a bed were self-regulating. Anybody could go into business running common lodging houses, so long as they had a suitable property at their disposal. In Spitalfields, the downward slide of the local economy meant that by the mid-19th century, property prices were at an all-time low as no self-respecting house-hunter would even consider living there. The elegant master weavers' homes that had been so lovingly designed and furnished in the 1700s were now suffering from severe neglect. Roofs leaked, plaster fell off the walls, the kitchen ranges were clogged with grease and floorboards began to fall away. In 1857, *The Builder* magazine reported on the collapse of a house in Dorset Street, which resulted in the death of a child and warned that virtually every house in the street was in a similarly dangerous state of decay.

Consequently, these houses (which had once only been within the reach of the reasonably wealthy) could now be picked up for next to nothing. The combination of inexpensive property and a huge demand for cheap housing made Spitalfields one of the key areas for men and women keen to make their living from the misfortune of the poor. Most of the new landlords were previously itinerant entrepreneurs who acquired their property with money won by gambling on the horses or, as Henry Mayhew described, 'by direct robbery.' Furnishings were often obtained from hospitals or houses in which contagious disease had been rife. The furniture from this type of place was cheap as no one else wanted to risk buying it for fear of infection. Aspiring property magnates with little or no collateral soon hit on the idea of selling shares of their business in order to raise the start-up capital. Advertisements appeared in the newspapers offering a 4% return to investors in common lodging houses. Once a project had a sufficient number of investors, the property was converted and quickly let out. Most of the investors in this type of scheme lived far away and had little or no idea of how their 'customers' were being treated. If they had, it is doubtful they would have slept easily, as this description by Henry Mayhew clearly illustrates:

'Padding-kens (common lodging houses) in the country are certainly preferable abodes to those in St Giles, Westminster or Whitechapel; but in the country as in the town, their condition is extremely filthy and disgusting; many of them are scarcely ever washed, and to sweeping, once a week is miraculous. In most cases they swarm with vermin. Except where their position is very airy, the ventilation is very imperfect, and frequent sickness the necessary result. It is a matter of surprise that the nobility, clergy and gentry of the realm should permit the existence of such horrid dwellings.' Mayhew then goes on to describe the lodging houses in glorious detail: 'One of the dens of infamy may be taken as a specimen of the whole class. They generally have a spacious, though often ill-ventilated kitchen, the dirty dilapidated walls of which are hung with prints while a shelf or two are generally, though barely, furnished with crockery and kitchen utensils. In some places, knives and forks are not provided, unless a penny is left with the deputy or manager till they are returned. Average numbers of nightly lodgers is say 70 in winter, reducing to 40 in summer, when many visit the provinces... The general charge to sleep together is 3d per night or 4d for a single bed. There are family rooms that can be hired and crammed with children sleeping on the floor...

'The amiable and deservedly popular minister of a district church, built among the lodging houses, has stated that he has found 29 human beings in one apartment and that having with difficulty knelt down between two beds to pray with a dying woman, his legs became so jammed that he could hardly get up again. Some of the lodging houses are of the worst class of low brothels, and some may even be described as brothels for children... At some of the busiest periods, numbers sleep on the kitchen floor... a penny is saved to the lodger by this means. More than 200 have been accommodated in this way in a large house.'

The Spitalfields common lodging houses catered for three major types of customer: those too ill or old to work, those too lazy to work and the common criminal. Consequently, the day-to-day running of them was not a job for the faint-hearted. Generally, lodging house proprietors employed a 'deputy' whose job it was to make sure that all inmates had paid for their beds and a 'night watchman', who acted as a bouncer, keeping unwanted individuals away. Both the deputy and the night watchman had to possess the ability to throw out anyone who could not pay for their bed, regardless of their situation. As this often meant ejecting pregnant women and sick, elderly persons, knowing full well that they would have to sleep rough, it can be assumed that lodging house employees did not possess much of a conscience.

The lodging house proprietors possessed even less concern for their fellow man. In addition to allowing desperate people to sleep in disgusting conditions, they made more money from their pathetic customers by seizing the local monopoly on essentials such as bread, soap and candles, which they sold on to lodgers at hugely inflated prices. Detective Sergeant Leeson, who patrolled the Spitalfields area in the late-19th century, wrote of the common lodging houses, 'the landlords of these places…are to my mind, greater criminals than the unfortunate wretches who have to live in them.'

In addition to the wretched lodging houses, Dorset Street and much of Spitalfields became overrun with mean tenements that were let out on a weekly basis. These tenements were usually let out by the room, which came sparsely furnished with ancient and often dilapidated furniture. Thomas Archer wrote about such tenements in his report on 'The Terrible Sights of London', saying, '…each ruined room is occupied by a whole family, or even two or three families, houses which are never brought under the few and not very effective restrictions of the law, and where, from garret to basement, men, women and children swarm and stifle in the foul and reeking air. It is here that poverty meets crime, and weds it.'

These tenements were particularly popular with prostitutes as they provided the privacy required to service a client that was denied them in the huge dormitories of the common lodging houses. Landlords welcomed the prostitutes because they could charge higher rent to allow for the risk of them being found to be living off immoral earnings. As the number of prostitutes operating in Spitalfields dramatically increased in the second half of the 19th century, the landlords of the tenements realised that additional money could be made out of becoming more organised in the way they controlled their tenants.

Part Two

THE VICES OF DORSET STREET

Chapter 12

The Birth of Organised Crime in Spitalfields

The term 'organised crime' inevitably conjures up images of suit-wearing, cigar-chewing, gun-toting gangsters such as Al Capone. However, this type of highly efficient, sophisticated gang leader didn't emerge until the 20th century. The organised crime that evolved in Spitalfields (and many other parts of London) in the 1870s was on a much more primitive level. Far from being criminal geniuses, the leaders of the Spitalfields underworld were simply men who wanted to make money, but did not possess the education or background to go about it in a strictly legal manner.

By the 1870s, Spitalfields landlords were becoming highly organised in the way they made their money. Common lodging houses represented the legitimate, if morally dubious, side of their business, as did the chandlers' shops (which sold household essentials such as candles, soap and oil) and general stores that proliferated in the area. However, the occupations and tastes of their lodgers created a huge demand for three services that were on the wrong side of the law: prostitution, the fencing of stolen goods and illegal gambling.

A typical tenant of a common lodging house in Dorset Street and the surrounding roads was male and aged between 20 and 40. By day he would find casual work at one of the markets, on a building site or down at the docks. All these places of work provided a copious, never-ending supply of commodities well worth pilfering. Disposal of stolen goods was easy and quick; the chandlers' shops and general stores were more than happy to purchase foodstuffs and household essentials, which were then sold on at the usual, highly inflated prices. The lodging house proprietors were also not averse to fencing, as the journalist Henry Mayhew discovered while investigating London's poor: 'In some of these lodging houses, the proprietor(s)… are "fences", or receivers of stolen goods in a small way. Their "fencing"… does not extend to any plate, or jewellery, or articles of value, but is chiefly confined to provisions, and most of all to those which are of ready sale to the lodgers. Of very ready sale are "fish got from the gate" (stolen from Billingsgate); "sawney" (thieved bacon), and "flesh found in Leadenhall" (butchers' meat stolen from Leadenhall market).' If a more ambitious robbery was planned, the local shopkeepers' in-depth knowledge of the population usually meant that a buyer could be found for virtually anything within hours.

By night, lodging house residents, being young, free and mostly single, sought the company of women. Recognising a gap in the market, the canny landlords installed prostitutes in their properties thus creating a new, highly lucrative revenue stream for themselves. Although the lodging houses were supposed to be patrolled by the police, this rarely happened, allowing brothels and prostitution rings to be run without impediment. In October 1888, the *East London Observer* complained of the common lodging houses that 'No surveillance is exercised, and a woman is at perfect liberty to bring any companion she likes to share her accommodation.' The newspaper then went on to blame the prostitutes for the proliferation of criminals in the lodging houses, which was unjust: 'If loose women be prevented from frequenting common lodging houses, their companions the thieves, burglars and murderers of London would speedily give up resorting to them.' As the lodging houses provided the 'thieves and burglars' with 'no questions asked' accommodation at an affordable price, it is unlikely they would have deserted them due to the lack of prostitutes.

As vice in Spitalfields' lodging houses and furnished rooms increased, men known as 'bullies' were employed by the landlords. Their job was ostensibly to act as a doorman to the establishment, thus keeping undesirables away from the tenants. However, in reality, the bully's main job was to ensure that punters didn't leave without paying their dues. A typical bully was either ex-army or recently out of gaol. Some would work their way up the ranks until they had enough money to purchase a lodging house of their own. However, most were indolent ruffians who enjoyed lounging around during the day and exercising their muscle at night. Their only fear was of the police, which was unsurprising as many of them had a criminal record and would have easily landed themselves back in gaol after even the most minor altercation with the boys in blue. Consequently, the bullies avoided the police like the plague.

By the 1870s, Dorset Street was comprised almost entirely of common lodging houses, furnished rooms and general shops run by the landlords. Simply by catering for demand, the average Dorset Street landlord had, by the 1870s, quite a number of 'employees'. In addition to the prostitutes who worked out of his properties (from whom he would have received a cut from any money earned in addition to the rent); there were 'deputies' who acted as lodging house managers, doormen or bullies and assistants for the adjacent general stores or chandler's shops. Times were good and if a landlord was smart, a lot of money could be earned from these little empires.

The police found it easier to turn a blind eye to the goings on in the lodging houses and, without feedback from the police, the authorities were oblivious to the plight of the law-abiding residents. The only threat to the lodging house proprietors' empires came from competitors, keen to expand their operations. Consequently, common lodging houses became highly sought-after by anyone who could raise enough money to acquire them. Enterprising young men saw how well established lodging-house keepers such as the Smiths of Brick Lane were doing and began to hatch plans to obtain their own properties. The only stumbling block was how to scrape together enough start-up capital. However, soon an Act of Parliament was about to bring their dreams much closer to reality.

Chapter 13

The Cross Act

Throughout the 1870s, the Government had become increasingly troubled about the extreme poverty and lawlessness that was prevalent in areas such as Dorset Street. Of particular concern were the properties in which the poor were forced to live. The politicians listened to the social commentators and developed sympathy for the honest poor who had to share living accommodation with prostitutes, thieves and conmen. In an attempt to improve matters, the Artisans and Labourers' Dwellings Act (otherwise known as the Cross Act) was passed in 1875.

This act allowed the Government-run Metropolitan Board of Works (the predecessor of the London County Council,) to purchase and demolish large swathes of 'unfit' property, with a view to replacing the houses with more salubrious dwellings. The Board of Works responded to the act with enthusiasm and over the following two years purchased 16 slums comprising 42 acres, mainly located in the Boroughs of Stepney, Finsbury, Islington and Whitechapel (which included Spitalfields.) Many of London's most notorious slums were demolished, including a massive site in Flower and Dean Street.

Despite its good intentions, the Cross Act produced disastrous results. It had been the Metropolitan Board of Works' intention to sell the land on which the slums had once stood to housing charities. These charities would then build new, model dwellings in which the poor of the area could be re-housed. The new properties would be clean, bright and warm and with any luck, would have a miraculous effect on the inhabitants, who would eschew their life of crime in favour of a hard-working, God-fearing existence.

In reality, the only people to truly benefit from most of the slum clearances were the landlords of the properties earmarked for demolition. These canny property owners made sure their houses were packed to the rafters with tenants when the surveyors called in order to ensure maximum compensation for lost income. Once a property had been condemned, the landlord naturally lost all interest in repair and maintenance work thus subjecting his tenants to truly abominable conditions, while he used the money from the compulsory purchase to buy up more suitable housing close by that was not earmarked for demolition. When the condemned properties were ready to be demolished, the tenants were cast out into the street, while the landlord counted his compensation money – paid to him by the rate-payers of the Borough. The displaced slum dwellers, now desperate for somewhere to stay, crowded into the remaining lodging houses, thus lining the pockets of the landlords once again. The landlords responded to the surge in demand by raising their prices.

An estimated 22,868 people were evicted as a result of the Cross Act. Most were from the poorest sectors of the population whose irregular income or home-based work made them ineligible for the smart new model dwellings that replaced their previous homes. Consequently, many became permanently homeless.

The Cross Act also proved to be a disaster for the Metropolitan Board of Works. Between 1875 and 1877, the Board purchased property to the value of over £1.5 million. However, when the demolished sites were sold on to the housing charities, little more than £330,000 was raised. Realising that they were never going to recoup their losses through the charities, the Board of Works refused to sell some sites for affordable housing. In Spitalfields, many of the demolished slum sites were reserved for commercial development in a bid to gain a better price for the land. Few developers were interested and, despite some warehousing being built, the area did not benefit from the relocation of any major employers. Thus, Spitalfields acquired yet more destitute, homeless individuals on a permanent basis. The landlords, who had already received fat compensation payments for the demolition of their slum properties must have rubbed their hands with glee.

By this time, overcrowding in Dorset Street was worse than ever before. Rooms no larger than 10 square feet became home to two, three or even four families. Sleeping could only be achieved if done in shifts, the other tenants either spending their time at work or in the pub. Despite their poverty, the tenants of these awful places did their best to give their children a decent start in life. Schools sprang up in even the most dangerous and overcrowded tenements, as evidenced by the report of Mr Wrack, a housing inspector from the Metropolitan Board of Works who visited Miller's Court, Dorset Street in 1878.

On arriving in the court, Mr Wrack found that the ground floor of number 6 was being used as a school room during the day and a sleeping room at night. At the time of his visit there were 19 people in the 12 foot square room, namely 17 children, all under 7, the schoolmaster and his wife. This overcrowding, coupled with the fact that the room was directly adjacent to three privies and the communal dustbin, prompted Mr Wrack to deem the room an inappropriate place in which to educate children. He informed the schoolmaster of his findings and two days later the school was relocated.

By the closing years of the 1870s, Spitalfields resembled a bomb site. Large swathes of land in roads such as Goulston Street and Flower and Dean Street were a mess of bricks, mud and cement as developers built model dwellings for the housing charities. Other sites that had previously housed rookeries stood empty. Any private property-owners who could afford to sold up and moved out.

Property values hit an all-time low. It was at this point that the area acquired a new generation of landlords. Most of these men had come from poor, working-class backgrounds. Some had come to London from Ireland during the famine. Others had lived in Spitalfields all their lives but had never before been presented with the opportunity to acquire property. All of them wanted to make money from housing the poor and destitute.

Most of the new landlords did not go into the business of running a registered common lodging house immediately. A preferred route to this goal was to initially secure the lease on a property and let it out on a weekly basis as furnished rooms. Rooms let in this manner had not been included in the regulations set out in the Common Lodging Houses Acts (only those let on a nightly basis had to be registered with the Police). This loophole allowed aspiring landlords to rent rooms with little interference from the authorities, just as long as they were prepared to trust their tenants for a whole week before they paid their dues.

Investing this amount of trust in tenants who were desperately poor was a risky business and nearly every slum landlord in London had experienced 'bunters': men and women who made a profession out of taking lodgings in which they stayed for some time before absconding without paying the rent. Henry Mayhew met with a 'bunter' named 'Swindling Sal' from New Cut in Lambeth who told him about 'Chousing Bett', a particularly notorious bunter: 'Lord bless me, she was up to as many dodges as there was men in the moon. She changed places, she never stuck to one long; she never had no things to be sold up, and, as she was handy with her mauleys (fists), she got on pretty well. It took a considerable big man, she could tell me, to kick her out of a house, and then when he done it she always give him something for himself, by way of remembering her. Oh, they had a sweet recollection of her, some on' them.' Swindling Sal and her kind justified their actions through prejudice; making the sweeping generalisation that most lodging-house keepers subscribed to the Jewish faith (which was actually untrue), they reasoned that their victims 'was mostly Christ-killers, and chousing (defrauding) a Jew was no sin'.

In order to protect themselves against losses incurred through bunters, landlords charged highly inflated rents so that the money paid by their honest tenants more than covered losses due to fraudulence. This practise earned them little respect from the more educated classes. Henry Mayhew himself described keepers of low lodging houses as 'rapacious, mean, and often dishonest.' This opinion was shared by many other social commentators of the era, and their criticism was not unjust. However, it should be borne in mind that had it not been for the existence of low lodging houses, the very poor (of which there were many) would have had nowhere else to go. Making money from the starving was certainly not a career to be proud of, but the virtual absence of any form of welfare for the very poor inevitably resulted in housing being created for profit. It could reasonably be suggested that the Government was the real villain of the piece.

Once they had gained control over their properties, the new Spitalfields landlords quickly became aware of the type of clientele from whom they could make the most money as a seemingly endless stream of prostitutes enquired after rooms to let. This state of affairs was by no means unusual. Indeed, Henry Mayhew suggested that 'those who gain their living by keeping accommodation houses... are of course to be placed in the category of the people who are dependent on prostitutes, without whose patronage they would lose their only means of support.'

Chapter 14

Prostitution and Press Scrutiny

Despite its less than salubrious atmosphere, Dorset Street and the surrounding area was a good hunting ground for prostitutes as there was a large and mixed supply of punters. Spitalfields Market offered a regular supply of market workers and out-of-town traders. The Docks, with their never-ending supply of sex-starved sailors were well within walking distance and it even became fashionable for West End gentlemen to visit the area for an excursion known as 'slumming'. Consequently, any woman finding it hard to make ends meet and able to disregard her self-respect, could earn money by plying her trade on the streets.

The landlords of lodging houses (particularly those not subjected to Police scrutiny) used prostitution to feather their own nests. Many acted as quasi-pimps; although they would not find punters for the girls, they would provide them with protection from the numerous gangs that prowled the streets extorting money from the street-walkers. These gangs usually comprised between three and ten youths. Most lived just outside the area they stalked. The Old

Nichol estate, which lay just north of Spitalfields, spawned many of these gangs. The youths would walk down to Spitalfields in the evenings and generally make a nuisance of themselves, pestering elderly street-vendors and intimidating the local prostitutes from whom they would often extort money. However despite their frightening appearance, these gangs were comprised of cowards who only singled out those weaker than themselves for rough treatment. The appearance of one of the lodging-house doormen would usually send them packing. Consequently, the doormen became indispensable to the working girls.

Many of the local prostitutes were rather pathetic, gin-soaked women whose alcoholism had caused their families to abandon them many years earlier. Most were in their forties and possessed rapidly fading looks. They plied their trade on the streets, taking punters down the nearest alleyway for a quick knee-trembler. The lucky few managed to make enough money to hire their own room in one of the numerous courts. Miller's Court, off Dorset Street was a perfect location for prostitutes. The fact that the court only had one exit meant that punters going in and out could be observed and the girls' nightly intake could be easily assessed. Additionally, the proximity of the neighbouring rooms meant that the girls were afforded a much larger degree of mutual protection than they would have enjoyed had they resorted to doing their business out in the street.

The new landlords' acquisition of property in the Dorset Street area really paid off in 1883 when the now rather aged Spitalfields Market began a phase of massive redevelopment. Over the next 15 years, the main market area acquired a new iron and glass roof and the old 17th-century buildings surrounding it were demolished. In their place, new buildings were built around the market area, including four blocks containing shops at street level, basements below and three-storey residential accommodation above. These new buildings still survive today at the eastern side of the market. The huge amount of building work at the market meant that, in addition to the traders and porters, masses of men involved in the building trade arrived in the area seeking somewhere cheap to sleep.

Obviously, the streets closest to the market benefited the most from this sudden influx of workers and landlords of property in Dorset Street, Whites Row and Brushfield Street really reaped the benefits.

However, while the lodging-house keepers were busy cashing in on the development of Spitalfields Market, their properties and their dubious business activities were about to come under the spotlight of public scrutiny. Journalists decided it was time that the more educated classes got to know how the poor really lived. Soon a flurry of articles and pamphlets appeared, most of which dealt with the deplorable housing conditions suffered by the poor.

One of the first journalists to write about the issue was George Sims, who composed a series of articles for *Pictorial World* entitled 'How The Poor Live' early in 1883. Later the same year, he followed with a series called 'Horrible London' in the *Daily News*. In October 1883, William C. Preston, using the pseudonym Reverend Andrew Mearns, wrote 'The Bitter Cry of Outcast London', a 20-page penny pamphlet that highlighted the plight of the poor. The *Pall Mall Gazette* published a selection of passages from the pamphlet, including the following, rather prosaic tract that deals with conditions in lodging houses:

> 'One of the saddest results of (this) overcrowding is the inevitable association of honest people with criminals. Often is the family of an honest working man compelled to take refuge in a thieves' kitchen (referring to the shared facilities in the common lodging houses)... who can wonder that every evil flourishes in such hotbeds of vice and disease?... Ask if the men and women living together in these rookeries are married and your simplicity will cause a smile. Nobody knows. Nobody cares... Incest is common; and no form of vice or sensuality causes surprise or attracts attention... The low parts of London are the sink into which the filth and abominable from all parts of the country seem to flow.'

Preston's pamphlet started an avalanche of public comment but few of its readers actually took practical steps to improve matters. One man that did his utmost to make a difference was an East London vicar called the Reverend Barnett.

In the same year as Preston's pamphlet was published, Barnett and a group of public-spirited investors formed the East London Dwellings Company with a view to buy, rehabilitate or rebuild on slum properties. Unlike the Metropolitan Board of Works, Barnett and his colleagues wanted to bring relief to the very poorest inhabitants of London. In return, investors would be able to sleep the sleep of the just, and receive 4% in dividend. Barnett's idea proved to be more than just hot air and by 1886, the East London Dwellings Company had completed Brunswick Buildings in Goulston Street and Wentworth Buildings in Wentworth Street (previously one of the most run-down streets in Spitalfields). The success of these two schemes attracted other developers to the area including the banking family, Rothschild.

The Rothschilds had settled in the East End when they first arrived in Britain and had evidently not forgotten their roots. They purchased the land in Flower and Dean Street that had been demolished by the Metropolitan Board of Works and under the name of the 'Four Per Cent Dwellings Company' they built Rothschild Buildings. These developments housed over 200 Jewish families and although residents complained of bed bugs and overcrowding, the conditions were comparatively sanitary. The design of Rothschild Buildings was not unlike that of an army barracks and critics believed that these surroundings would make it impossible for a community to flourish.

However, research shows that this was far from the truth. Against the odds, a strong sense of community and mutual support developed in the blocks and the tenement rules (which looked very forbidding on paper,) were generally enforced by the tenants themselves in the interests of safe and orderly communal living. In his book *Rothschild Buildings*, Jerry White notes that 'after that first and crucial decision about who could have a flat and who could not, the people of

Rothschild Buildings were largely on their own. The myth of an all-powerful rooting system of "rebuke and repression" which kept the people orderly owed more to bourgeois prejudice than reality... the community life which centred on the landings of Rothschild Buildings was friendly and vibrant. "At Rothschild, we were like one family" is a frequently heard description of the relationship between neighbours'.

However, life was not this rosy at all tenement blocks. However good their intentions, most philanthropic housing developers sought tenants that were poor but hard working and honest. They were not in the business of providing housing for the indolent, criminal or chronically sick. Consequently, most people that frequented the common lodging houses in Spitalfields were ineligible as tenants and Spitalfields became unattractive to developers. The sites the housing companies wanted were in Finsbury and Westminster, where there were plenty of people willing and able to pay 6/- or 7/- a week, not in the East End, where flats remained empty and rents were often unpaid. Only 2% of the population of Tower Hamlets and 2.8% in Southwark, lived in charity tenements in 1891, compared to 8% in Westminster. Several slum clearance sites in Wapping, Shadwell, Limehouse and Deptford were rejected by housing charities in the 1870s and 1880s, and remained undeveloped until the LCC took them on.

Over 4% of London's population lived in philanthropic housing blocks in 1891, but as we have seen, the charities did not provide shelter for the very poor and the demolitions which they encouraged and depended upon intensified the plight of the destitute. For example, the 1884-5 Royal Commission was convinced that the really poor, including those evicted in the demolition schemes undertaken to satisfy philanthropic developer the Peabody Trust's need for land, did not find places in the Peabody Buildings, and that preference was given to respectable artisans and families with more than one income.

Poor families with nowhere to go moved into Spitalfields with alarming regularity and despite the efforts of men such as the

Reverend Barnett and the Rothschilds, the area continued to be overrun with honest poor rubbing shoulders with criminals. In 1885, an old woman spoke to the Royal Commission on Housing of the Working Classes: 'I came to London 25 years ago and I've never lived in any room for more than two years yet: they always say they want to pull down the house to build dwellings for poor people, but I've never got into one yet.' The Government could not fail to ignore the deplorable situation regarding the housing of the very poor in many areas in London. In a bid to improve the situation, the Housing of the Working Classes Act was passed in 1885. However, housing of the poor was not tackled with any real success until four years later, when the Metropolitan Board of Works was replaced with the London County Council. By then, the already sizeable problem with overcrowding in Dorset Street and its surrounds had worsened.

Chapter 15

The Fourth Wave of Immigrants

On 1 March 1881, Tsar Alexander II of Russia was assassinated by a gang of revolutionaries. This act, although seemingly unconnected to religion, proved to be a catalyst for an outbreak of extreme violence and animosity towards Jewish communities in Russia, Poland, Austro-Hungary and Romania and provoked an exodus on an unprecedented scale.

Following the assassination, rumours abounded throughout Russia that the Jews were responsible (in actual fact, only one of the gang was Jewish). Word spread that the new Tsar had issued a decree instructing all Russians to avenge the death of his father by attacking any Jew they might happen to come across. Although this decree never existed, it gave many Russians the opportunity to vent their frustrations at the sorry economic state their country was in by providing a scapegoat. In April 1881, an anti-Jewish riot (known as a pogrom) broke out in Elisavetgrad. In scenes that were to be repeated in Nazi Germany, Jewish businesses were attacked, shops ransacked and homes burned. Jews were beaten, insulted and spat on. Word spread fast about the attack and soon pogroms were breaking out all over Eastern Europe.

The Russian Government pandered to the anti-Jewish feeling and passed a hastily-written act that was designed to remove any of the power and status held by Jews that so upset the rest of the population. This act, known as the 'May Laws' required all Jews to live only in urban areas. Even the ownership or purchase of countryside land was forbidden. In addition, restrictions were applied to Jewish businesses, university quotas for Jews were halved and Jews were no longer allowed to practice professions such as medicine or law.

The May Laws, coupled with the constant fear of violence resulted in a mass exodus of Jews from Eastern Europe. Between 1880 and 1914, nearly three million Jews emigrated from Russia and her neighbouring countries. Most went to America but 150,000 came to Britain.

Once admitted to Britain, many of the Eastern European immigrants headed for the East End, mainly because there were established Jewish communities there where they could buy kosher food, speak languages they understood and perhaps even meet up with old friends. Spitalfields had a well-established Jewish community by the 1880s and so seemed to be a perfect destination for the newly arrived immigrants. However, not all Spitalfields Jews welcomed the new arrivals.

By the late-19th century, London's Jewish community had created a comfortable niche for itself. Wealthier Jews held office in parliament and were even part of the Royal family's inner circle. Working-class Jews had to work no harder than their non-Jewish counterparts in order to make a living. Most importantly, Jews could live in London without fear of anti-Semitism ruining their lives. The arrival of the Eastern European Jews, many of whom were peasant country folk, worried the British Jewry. Many felt their position in society was jeopardised. Others were simply embarrassed by their country cousins. Even the Chief Rabbi urged his counterparts in Eastern Europe to dissuade the population from travelling to Britain. However, their attempts at restricting the amount of Jews arriving at the ports failed miserably.

Although the British Jews were understandably wary of the sudden rush of Jewish immigrants, once the immigrants arrived, they did their very best to help them. In much the same way as the Huguenots had operated 200 years previously, the Jews set up schools, adult education centres and employment agencies to help the new arrivals integrate into English society as easily as possible. Much of this work was funded by established families such as the Rothschilds. However, the sheer numbers of Jewish immigrants flooding into areas such as Spitalfields caused problems with the existing population, mainly because there was already very little room to spare. The Jewish immigrants did their best to cram as many people as they could into the space available, causing one wit to note, 'give a Jew an inch and he'll put a bed in it; give him two and he'll take in a lodger.'

Chapter 16

The Controllers of Spitalfields

By the 1880s, living conditions in Dorset Street and many other roads in Spitalfields had reached an all-time low. The area was vastly overcrowded, extremely poor and largely ignored by the authorities. Unable to take on the labouring jobs available to men, poor, single women fared the worst and as we have seen, many resorted to selling themselves on the street in order to put food in their stomachs and a roof over their head.

The women roamed the badly-lit streets and alleyways of Spitalfields for hours on their nightly quest for bed money. They couldn't afford to be choosy when it came to punters and copious amounts of alcohol helped to dull their judgement. These sad, desperate women were sitting ducks for any man with a sadistic streak and assaults were common. However, the autumn of 1888 brought with it the spectre of something much more sinister, that would leave an indelible mark on Dorset Street, Spitalfields and its people for well over a century.

The women who were forced to prostitute themselves tended to live in the roads to the east of Commercial Street plus Dorset

Street, Whites Row and further north, the Great Pearl Street area. Due to the distinctly brutal and lawless nature of many of the inhabitants, these roads became known as the 'wicked quarter mile'. Amazingly, it was from this tiny area that virtually every character involved in the Jack the Ripper mystery came.

By 1888, the vast majority of the 'wicked quarter mile' was owned or let by just six families of lodging house proprietors. The area to the north of Spitalfields Market, bordered by Quaker Street, Commercial Street and Grey Eagle Street fell under the control of a man named Frederick Gehringer, who lived in Little Pearl Street. Gehringer, who was from German stock, also ran a very successful haulage business from his premises and no doubt had business connections at nearby Spitalfields Market. In addition to this, he also ran the City of Norwich public house in Wentworth Street.

The southern end of Brick Lane was largely run by longstanding resident and erstwhile greengrocer Jimmy Smith and his son (also Jimmy), who resided for much of the 1880s in their common lodging house at 187 Brick Lane. Jimmy Smith Junior was to become one of the most influential figures on the streets of Spitalfields. As a young lad, he had shown the enterprising side to his nature by setting up a small coal dealership, selling mainly to the residents of nearby Flower and Dean Street (where he rented a coal shed). Realising that many residents were too weak to carry the coals back to their rooms, he offered a delivery service, thus enabling him to sell the coal at quite an inflated price.

By the time he reached adulthood, Jimmy Smith had also gained a reputation for being the man who 'straightened up the police', especially when it came to illegal street gambling. Local resident Arthur Harding remembered Jimmy's antics thus: 'The street bookies gave him money to share out among the different sergeants and inspectors and they relied on him to keep out strangers. He had a good team against anybody who caused trouble. He was the paymaster – the police trusted him and the bookies trusted him. He was a generous man, always good for a pound when anybody was hard up. He was the governor about Brick Lane.'

After the Cross Act-induced slum clearance at the western end of Flower and Dean Street, the remaining slums and lodging houses were run by Jimmy Smith's sister Elizabeth and her husband Johnny Cooney, who lived at number 54. These lodgings were among the most notorious in Spitalfields and it was common knowledge that many operated as brothels. Like Fred Gehringer, Cooney also had interests in the beer trade and ran the Sugar Loaf in Hanbury Street. The pub was a popular meeting place for music hall artistes not least because it was frequented by Cooney's cousin, the most famous music hall star of them all – Marie Lloyd.

The lodgings in nearby Thrawl Street and George Yard were controlled by Irishman Daniel Lewis and his sons. Little is known of the Lewis family. They had close links with the Smith and Cooney clans and may even have been related but this cannot be confirmed.

Dorset Street, by this time the worst street of the lot, was presided over by another Irishman – the ex-Borough resident Jack McCarthy and his close friend and colleague, William Crossingham, an ex-baker from Romford in Essex. Jack McCarthy had endured an impoverished childhood on the streets of The Borough but his entrepreneurial spirit had enabled him to climb out of the gutter at a relatively early age. While working in the building trade as a bricklayer, he supplemented his income by dealing in old clothes and then used the money to set himself up as a letting agent of furnished rooms along Dorset Street and in Miller's Court. As more money was earned, McCarthy progressed from agent to proprietor and by the time he was 50, owned a considerable amount of slum property throughout the East End.

Probably through his fellow landlord Johnny Cooney of Flower and Dean Street, Jack McCarthy became involved in the Music Halls. His involvement in the theatre inspired his offspring and he became the founder of quite a theatrical dynasty, which included music hall celebrities, variety performers and even a Hollywood star (of which more will be written later.)

Jack McCarthy also developed an interest in boxing and, together with the Smith family of Brick Lane, was involved in the organisation of prize fights in the London area. These fights proved to be extremely popular and attracted hundreds of spectators eager to gamble their hard-earned cash in the hope of backing the winner. However, the fights did not pay particular attention to the Queensberry Rules and the gambling that was inherent to the event was illegal. As we have seen, Jimmy Smith was adept at bribing the local Spitalfields police to turn a blind eye to his exploits; however, officers from further afield were more difficult to handle. Consequently, fights held outside the Spitalfields area often received unwanted attention from the local constabulary.

In 1882, Jack McCarthy and Jimmy Smith's brother Richard were involved in an ugly confrontation with the police during an illegal prize fight they had organised at St Andrew's Hall in Tavistock Place. Both men were arrested and eventually found themselves in front of the judge at the Middlesex Sessions House in Clerkenwell. Although neither man could deny they were present at the fight, Jimmy Smith managed to persuade Sergeant Thicke of the Whitechapel Division to give both men glowing character references, thus saving them from incarceration. Instead, McCarthy was fined and Smith (who had assaulted a policeman during the fracas) was bound over to keep the peace and made to pay £5.

The final man who exerted control over the mean streets of Spitalfields was Jack McCarthy's neighbour and business associate, William Crossingham. Like most of his fellow landlords, Crossingham was not native to Spitalfields and had been brought up in semi-rural Essex before coming to London in his early twenties to work as a baker. After a stint of living in Southwark (possibly where he first met McCarthy), Crossingham married and changed his career to lodging-house keeper. He enjoyed a close relationship with the McCarthy family for many years – his daughter married McCarthy's brother, Daniel – but always maintained a link with his birthplace; he moved back to Romford in the early 1900s but retained an interest in Dorset Street until his death.

Being a landlord of some of the most notorious properties in London required a fearless temperament combined with shrewd business sense. In this, the Spitalfields landlords did not disappoint. They were hard men who had no qualms about forcing their tenants to live in often filthy, degrading and hopeless conditions. They thought nothing of forcing the sick, elderly and infirm out onto the street if they had insufficient money for a bed. They remained unmoved as desperate women were forced to prostitute themselves in order to pay their rent. However, as the State offered absolutely no assistance to those on the bottom rung of society, the landlords also provided an invaluable service. Were it not for the common lodging houses, many Spitalfields residents would be forced to sleep rough every night. The neighbourhood recognised this and consequently the landlords enjoyed grudging respect from their tenants and more importantly, the freedom to run their businesses as they pleased with little or no interference from the authorities.

A feature of the Spitalfields landlords was the additional services they provided for their tenants. Both the McCarthy and the Smith families ran general shops close to their lodging houses that sold all manner of essentials, from soap to string, at highly inflated prices. These shops operated long hours and were in many ways the forerunners of today's corner shops. They were generally open every day (except Sundays) and many only closed for a couple of hours (at around 2am) before opening again to catch the market porters on their way to work. These long hours meant that members of the family would take it in turns to work in the shop and, while McCarthy and Smith's children were small, local people were employed to help out.

As we have seen, another service provided by the lodging house keepers was that of the public house. There were an incredibly large number of pubs in Spitalfields during the latter part of the

19th century. Dorset Street alone had the massive Britannia at the Commercial Street end, the particularly rough Horn of Plenty at the Crispin Street end and the Blue Coat Boy slap bang in the middle. The Blue Coat Boy was a relatively small concern when compared to the gin-palace grandeur of some East End pubs but it held the honourable distinction of being the only building along Dorset Street that never changed usage.

Built during the halcyon days of the silk weaving boom, the pub was run by a variety of owners and landlords throughout the 19th century. In 1896, it was sold to the City of London Brewery for the princely sum of £2,000. By this stage, the pub was beginning to show irreparable signs of decay and in 1909 was torn down and completely rebuilt. It survived another 20 years before falling victim to the London County Council's redevelopment plans for Spitalfields Market. The Britannia pub was run for a large part of the 19th century by the Ringer family, who let the upper floors as furnished rooms and eventually took over the building next door. These properties became collectively known as 'Ringer's Buildings' and over the years played host to some particularly suspicious tenants including a couple of spinsters who appear to have run a brothel comprised of under-age girls.

While the general shops and public houses provided an additional (and legal) revenue stream for the Spitalfields landlords, other opportunities presented themselves that were not so above board. As we have already seen, the very nature of the landlords' clientele meant that opportunities to fence stolen property, run protection rackets and pimp for the local prostitutes existed in abundance.

As each Spitalfields landlord bought up more property and expanded his miniature empire, divisions began to appear on the landscape. This was primarily due to the latest influx of Jewish immigrants. All of a sudden, the Irish (including McCarthy, Lewis and Cooney) were no longer the new kids on the block. While some Irishmen joined forces with their old enemies the English in order to make the newly arrived Jews feel as unwelcome as possible, many agreed it was less trouble to try to get along with their new neighbours. However, cultural differences meant that by the end of the 1880s, Spitalfields was far from an integrated society.

The Jews, believing there was safety in numbers, began to heavily populate the streets to the south of Dorset Street such as Butler, Freeman, Palmer and Tilley Street. Rothschild Buildings was only let to Jews. Thus, all the non-Jews that had previously lived on these streets got pushed north towards the market and the common lodging houses became unbearably overcrowded. Displaced youths became furious at the Jews for taking over what had been their homes and roads such as Dorset Street became so full of anti-Semitic feeling that some Jews couldn't walk past the end of the road without being called 'Christ killers', let alone venture down it.

As these new divisions embedded themselves within Spitalfields' society, youths began to form gangs, partly out of mutual distrust, partly for their own safety. Admission rules to the gangs were strict: the Jews only accepted Jews; the Irish cockneys only accepted non-Jews. Gang members were fiercely protective of their own kind and socialising between the two factions was strictly prohibited. Heaven help any Irish girl who became friendly with a Jewish boy as both would be ostracised by their respective peers. However, these gangs often tired of racial warfare and began to look for other forms of entertainment, one of which was hassling, robbing and sometimes violently assaulting the local prostitutes.

Whether English Protestant, Irish Catholic or Eastern European Jew, all the gang members held a pretty dim view of the local prostitutes. This was not without cause. Far from being exotic ladies of the night such as were found further west, the vast majority of Spitalfields prostitutes were middle-aged, rough women. For many, a love affair with alcohol had driven them away from their families to a life living hand-to-mouth in the common lodging houses. Needless to say, these were not women who commanded respect from any quarter. They plied their trade in and around the pubs and most 'tricks' comprised taking their client up the nearest alley for a 'fourpenny touch', thus earning themselves enough money for a lodging house bed or another hour in the pub.

Many chose the latter option. Some women took up with thieves and lured unsuspecting clients down dark passages to be promptly robbed by their accomplice. Others worked for brothels that specialised in charging hugely inflated prices for services rendered. Any punter that protested was robbed, threatened with violence and thrown out, sometimes without his clothes.

Part Three

INTERNATIONAL INFAMY

Chapter 17

Jack the Ripper

Due to their unsavoury profession and dishonest ways, the Spitalfields prostitutes seemed fair game for the gangs of young men. However, sometimes their taunting of the women went much further. On 8 December 1887, Margaret Hames, a prostitute from Daniel Lewis's lodging house at 18 Thrawl Street was plying for trade when she was set upon by a gang of men who beat her so badly on the face and chest that she was admitted to Whitechapel Infirmary and wasn't released until after Christmas. Four months later, her neighbour Emma Smith suffered a worse fate...

Emma Smith was a 45-year-old alcoholic who, like so many other Spitalfields women, had resorted to prostitution in order to fund her habit. At the time of the attack, she had been living at Lewis's lodging house for about 18 months. On the evening of 2 April 1888, Emma left her lodgings on her usual quest for money and alcohol. By the early hours of the next morning she had made her way to the Whitechapel Road and as she ambled down the thoroughfare, she noticed a group of men outside Whitechapel Church. Naturally wary of male gangs, Emma crossed the road to keep her distance but the men turned and followed her. By the time she had reached the corner of Osborn Street, the men had caught up with her. *En masse*, they violently assaulted her, beating her around the face and ripping her ear (possibly in an attempt to steal her earrings). The assailants then took away her money and as a parting gesture, rammed an unidentified blunt instrument into her vagina with such force that it ruptured the peritoneum and other organs. Satisfied with their work, they turned and left, leaving Emma bleeding and trembling on the pavement.

Although in utter agony, Emma had the presence of mind to try to get back to her lodgings where she could be assured of help and unbelievably, she managed somehow to stagger the short distance to 18 George Street where she was met by the deputy, Mary Russell. Mrs Russell was so horrified by Emma's injuries that she decided to take her to hospital immediately and enlisted the assistance of another lodger named Annie Lee. Once at the hospital, Emma was seen by the house surgeon, Dr Hellier and immediately admitted. Sadly however, peritonitis had set in and she died of her injuries the following day.

Considering the rough and constantly dangerous atmosphere that pervaded Spitalfields, it is interesting to note that the press thought the murder of Emma Smith, who was, after all only a common prostitute, notable enough to report on. In fact, the murder made the front page of *Lloyds Weekly News* on the Sunday following her death, suggesting that, despite its dreadful reputation, Spitalfields was not host to as many incidents of extreme violence as one might have expected.

Emma's murder no doubt had a profound effect of her fellow prostitutes, not least because the attack seemed to be completely random. But as the women still had to eat and find shelter each night, they had little choice but to risk taking to the streets unless they could afford their own room in one of the many ramshackle houses, which, of course, cost more than a bed in a lodging house. One way of affording a private room was by getting a boyfriend who could not only pay half the rent, but could also offer some degree of protection should the need arise. Recognising the benefits of such a set up, many prostitutes paired up with any man that would have them.

Some time in January 1888, one such prostitute arrived in Dorset Street and made her way to Jack McCarthy's shop. Claiming her name was Mary Kelly, she introduced her male companion as her husband and asked if McCarthy had any suitable rooms to let.

Mary Kelly was unlike the majority of her colleagues inasmuch as she was a good twenty years younger than most of them and was reasonably attractive. Brought up in Wales, she had married very young (about 16) to a man named Davis who worked at the local coal mine. However, soon after their marriage, Davis was killed in a pit explosion and Mary was left to fend for herself. She went to Cardiff and, with her cousin as a companion, got sucked into prostitution.

After a stint on the streets of Cardiff, the bright lights and wealthy punters of London's West End beckoned and Mary moved to the capital, taking up residency in one of the many brothels that existed close to the theatres and night life. Whilst working there, she met a man who made her an offer she couldn't refuse.

During the mid-to-latter part of the 19th century, there was a huge demand for English girls to work in brothels across the channel. The ports of Boulogne, Havre, Dieppe and Ostend had large English communities and were also, of course, a stop-off point for sailors. Consequently, an equally large number of brothels or 'maisons de passé' existed in these towns and English girls were much in demand to work in them. The only problem was that very few girls wanted to go and work across the Channel, in a land where they didn't understand the language and were far away from their friends and family. In a bid to satisfy the burgeoning demand (and to line their own pockets) the brothel owners resorted to nefarious methods of procuring English prostitutes.

Men and women representing the brothels were sent to London with the instruction to use any means necessary to entice new girls over to France. Some procurers posed as wealthy gentlefolk looking for below-stairs staff to join them on a trip to the Continent. Others were more direct, explaining that although the establishment they represented was a brothel, the girl could expect to earn so much money that, once they had their fill of Continental life, they could return to England and set up their own business (such as a café) with their earnings.

In reality, the maisons de passé were little more than open prisons. The girls that worked in them were given board and lodging in return for services rendered to their clients, but the fabulous earnings they had been promised never materialised. Worse still, once a girl entered a maison de passé, she found it extremely difficult to leave. Every prostitute in the house was watched closely at all times. They were not allowed out of the house unless chaperoned. In all probability, it was to such a house that Mary Kelly was taken.

Of course, the girls incarcerated in the maisons de passé dreamed of escape and the lucky ones (including Kelly) managed to run away, usually by enlisting the help of one of their clients, without whom they could not evade the beady eye of the chaperone. This obviously meant that a great deal of trust had to be placed on the integrity of the man and no doubt some girls were betrayed. However, if a good relationship existed between girl and client, it was possible to plan an effective escape. Once away from the brothel, most of the escaped girls were forced to rely again on the generosity of their client or the mercy of the British Consul in order to gain safe passage back to England.

Mary Kelly only stayed in the maison de passé for a few weeks before returning to London. However, once back in the capital, she considered it too dangerous to return to the West End for fear of bumping into one of the procurers. Consequently, she eschewed the comparative comfort and safety of Theatreland in favour of the rough, poor and dangerous East End Docks.

After staying at several addresses around St George in the East, Kelly became one of the girls at a house of ill-repute in Breezer's Hill; a mean side street just off the Ratcliffe Highway. The house at Breezer's Hill catered almost exclusively for sailors as it was within very easy walking distance of the north quay of the London Docks. The road it stood in was (and still is) very short and contained only four houses. The rest of the street was taken up with warehouses in which the goods from the ships were stored.

No records exist that reveal who was running the brothel at Breezer's Hill during the time Mary Kelly stayed there. However, by the time the national census was compiled in 1891, the head of the household was one John McCarthy, a 36-year-old dock labourer. McCarthy was living in the house with his wife Mary and three female boarders, all of whom are described as 'unfortunate', a Victorian euphemism for a prostitute.

The fact that Kelly had two landlords named John McCarthy over the period of approximately three years could, of course, be pure coincidence. Indeed, no conclusive evidence exists to confirm that both Johns were part of the same family. However, circumstantial evidence suggests that they were related, probably cousins and both working for the same 'firm'. Firstly, both John McCarthys were brought up in the mean alleys that ran off Borough High Street in Southwark. Secondly, they lived (or had lived) a ten minute walk away from one another in the Docks. Thirdly, both John McCarthys let (or sub-let) their properties to prostitutes. In addition to this, John (known as Jack) McCarthy of Dorset Street had several business interests in this part of town and it is quite possible that, in the mid-1880s, Breezer's Hill was one of them. Finally, as will become apparent very soon, Jack McCarthy's (of Dorset Street) behaviour towards Mary Kelly suggests that she was not a complete stranger to him.

As is still the case today, the profession of prostitution was peripatetic and during her time in St George's, Mary Kelly moved around, sometimes living with boyfriends, sometimes going it alone. During this time, there were two significant men in her life: a man named Morganstone, with whom Kelly lived near the Stepney Gas Works and one Joseph Flemming, a mason's plasterer who lived on Bethnal Green Road.

By early 1887, Kelly had left the brothel in Breezer's Hill and was plying her trade up and down Commercial Street, no doubt servicing the market workers that proliferated in that area. It was here that she met the man who was to become a significant figure in her life: Joseph Barnett was a fish porter at nearby Billingsgate Market. He had lived in and around Spitalfields all his life and evidently had few qualms about taking up with a girl who made a living from getting intimate with other men.

Barnett and Kelly's courtship was brief. When they first met in Commercial Street, Barnett took her for a drink in one of the local pubs and the pair arranged to meet the next day. Days later, they agreed that they should live together. This decision was most probably made out of necessity on Kelly's part; Barnett had a steady job with enough wages to allow her a break from prostitution. There is little doubt that lust was a deciding factor for Barnett.

The pair immediately took lodgings in George Street, the street that was also home to Margaret Hames and Emma Smith. Due to the proximity of their homes and the fact that these two women shared the same profession as Kelly, it is likely that the four were at least on nodding terms with one another.

For the remainder of 1887, nothing further is known of Kelly and Barnett's movements. No doubt they, like everyone else in the street, were shocked at the violent attack sustained by Margaret Hames that December. However, whether this precipitated their move to Dorset Street remains a mystery.

By the time Kelly and Barnett showed up on Jack McCarthy's doorstep, they had been living together for ten months. Although they were not legally married, they presented themselves as man and wife to keep up appearances. McCarthy had learned not to ask too many questions about prospective tenants anyhow. Barnett's steady job combined with Kelly's attractiveness and previous experience in prostitution made the couple a comparatively safe bet when it came to letting them a room. No doubt McCarthy reasoned that even if Barnett should lose his job, his 'wife' could raise sufficient funds to pay for the room herself. He may even have seen Kelly as a potential educator in the ways of the world for his fourteen-year-old son. Whatever, his reasons, McCarthy decided to keep Kelly and Barnett close to his own home at 27 Dorset Street. So close that he could see their comings and goings from the back room of his shop.

McCarthy offered Kelly and Barnett the back room of the house next door to his. This house (officially known as number 26 Dorset Street) had been built at the same time as number 27. Originally designed for the long departed silk weavers, its Mansard roof had large windows that threw light into the attic in which once stood the weaver's loom. When the silk weavers left in the early 1800s, the house had been home to a variety of people including locksmiths, painters, coal porters and slipper makers. In the 1860s, the house was purchased by a Jewish glass blower named Abraham Barnett.

Barnett worked hard and built up his business until he was able to move west to the leafier, more salubrious surroundings of Maida Vale. However, he kept hold of number 26 Dorset Street as an investment and by 1880, had let the property out to John McCarthy. When necessary, McCarthy used number 26 as an extension of his own home, allowing friends and family to stay there. In 1881, his friend and business associate William Crossingham's step-daughter Alice lived there with her first husband and children and ten years later, McCarthy's younger brother Daniel lived there with his new wife while they were waiting to move into their own home.

Whether McCarthy selected number 26 for Kelly and Barnett because he knew them is a moot point. The fact remains that early in 1888, the young couple moved into the back parlour at a rent of 4/6 per week. Their room was quite small, measuring little more than 10-foot square. Nowadays, letting agents would describe it as having character because it retained original features such as wall panelling and a working fireplace, complete with surround. Back in 1888, this room would simply be described as old. It had two windows, which overlooked what had once been the back garden but for many years had been two rows of cottages either side of a narrow alley known as Miller's Court. What had originally been the back door to the house was now the only means of access to the room because McCarthy had nailed up the interior door, thus blocking any means of escape for tenants who couldn't afford to pay their rent. Because the door to the room was down the alleyway, McCarthy decided to rename it 13 Miller's Court.

Like most of the rooms down Dorset Street, 13 Miller's Court was sparsely furnished, the main pieces of furniture comprising an ancient bed and two rickety tables. The fire was multi-purpose, acting as a room heater, a cooker, a storage cupboard and a clothes drier. Over the mantelpiece hung a cheap print entitled 'The Fisherman's Widow'. The floorboards were bare and clothing was hung at the windows in place of curtains. The door had a lock that was most probably a relic of better days; no one renting the room in 1888 would have possessed anything worth stealing. This was Mary Kelly and Joe Barnett's new home.

While Mary and Joe were settling into their new premises, events in their erstwhile home, George Street, took a turn for the worse. On 7 August 1888, John Reeves, a waterside labourer, left his room at 37 George Yard Buildings in the early hours of the morning. Like so many of his class, Reeves regularly left home at this time in order to join the queues of men at the Docks hoping to be picked to help unload the ships. As he reached the first floor landing, he came across a horrifying discovery. At his feet lay the body of a woman in a pool of blood.

Reeves immediately ran out into the street to find a policeman and quickly returned with PC Thomas Barrett who in turn sent for Dr Killeen, who lived nearby in Brick Lane. Dr Killeen arrived quickly, examined the body and pronounced life extinct. The woman had been victim to a frenzied knife attack, the like of which had rarely been seen before. In total the body had 39 stab wounds, one of which had pierced the heart. That wound alone would have been sufficient to cause death. God only knew what had been going through the perpetrator's mind as he had clearly lost all control when inflicting the wounds on the poor woman.

One of the saddest aspects of this horrific murder was that for some time, no one seemed to know who the victim was. Three women viewed the body but each one gave a different name. Eventually, the body was identified by Henry Tabram of River Terrace, East Greenwich, as that of his estranged wife, Martha. His wife had left him many years ago and he understood that she had long since been earning her living as a prostitute. Henry Tabram's identification was further confirmed by a Mary Bousfield, otherwise known as Mrs Luckhurst, of 4 Star Place, Commercial Road, who had been Martha's landlady for a period of time after she left her husband.

As time went on, Martha's final movements became known. Immediately prior to her death, she, like Margaret Hames, Emma Smith and, until recently, Mary Kelly and Joe Barnett, had been living in George Street (number 19). As her estranged husband suspected, when money was tight, she worked as a prostitute in order to pay the rent. Until three weeks before her death, she had been living with her long-term partner Henry Turner. Their reasons for splitting up are unclear, but it appears that Turner was the one that moved out. Police found him renting a bed at the Victoria Working Men's Home in Commercial Street; a popular residence for local men who were single. One would assume that Turner would be the major suspect in the murder enquiry, but it appears he must have had some sort of alibi as the police apparently spent very little time interviewing him.

As time went on, the police assigned to the murder inquiry despaired of ever finding the killer. Like the murderers of Emma Smith, Martha Tabram's assailant seemed to have vanished into the East End smog, leaving behind no clues to their identity. However, their despondency was temporarily lifted on 9 August when a prostitute named Pearly Poll (real name Mary Ann Connelly) appeared at the police station.

According to Pearly Poll, she and Martha had picked up two soldiers on the night of the murder. One was a corporal, the other a private. She did not know what regiment they belonged to but remembered they both had white bands around their caps. The foursome spent a short amount of time together and then each couple went their separate ways. Pearly Poll took her man up Angel Alley but did not know where Martha was planning to take her conquest. Either the soldiers never told the women what their names were or Pearly Poll had decided not to divulge them.

Spurred on by this new and important witness, the police hurriedly set up an identification parade at the Tower of London (the closest barracks to Spitalfields). In the line-up were all privates and corporals who were on leave on the night of the murder and the police were optimistic that they would secure a positive identification of at least one of the men. They were however to be disappointed. Pearly Poll decided not to turn up for the first parade and it took two days and the involvement of the CID before she was found. A second parade was organised and this time Pearly Poll did show up, but immediately discounted all the soldiers because they didn't have a white band around their caps.

Undaunted, the police tracked the uniform Pearly Poll described to the Wellington Barracks and organised another parade. This time Pearly Poll picked out two men. However, the two soldiers she identified had cast-iron alibis for the night of the murder. The police were back to square one and their unreliable witness fled to Dorset Street where she disappeared into one of the many overcrowded, anonymous lodging houses, never to be heard of again apart from a brief appearance at the inquest. Left with no clue, no motive and no other witnesses, the murder inquiry ground to a halt and the inquest jury were forced to return a verdict of wilful murder against some person, or persons unknown.

Pity the police of H Division. Not only did they have to contend with law enforcement of a district renowned for its lawlessness, they now had two unsolved, and particularly violent, murders to deal with. At a time when forensic science was in its infancy, the chances of bringing a murderer to justice when there were no witnesses and no clues left at the scene of the crime were virtually nil. But their already difficult and frustrating job was about to get worse. Much worse.

On 31 August, less than four weeks after the Tabram murder, a carman named Charles Cross was on his way to work along Buck's Row, just off the Whitechapel Road, when he noticed something lying across a gateway that looked like tarpaulin. As he got closer, he realised it was the body of a woman. As Cross approached the body, he was joined by another carman named Robert Paul who was also on his way to work. The two men knelt down by the body to get a closer look. It was still dark and difficult to see. Cross felt the woman's hand, which was cold and told Paul, 'I believe she is dead'. Paul put his hand over her heart and thought he could detect breathing, albeit very shallow.

After deciding against moving the body, the two men went to get help and soon found PC Mizen on his beat in nearby Baker's Row. The three men returned to Buck's Row and found another policeman, PC Neil, already there. PC Neil felt the woman's arm and noticed that it was still quite warm above the elbow, suggesting that the woman had not been dead long. Indeed, there was a very slim chance that she was still alive. Dr Llewellyn, who lived nearby on the Whitechapel Road, was fetched without further ado and came immediately. However, by the time he arrived, whatever little life may have been left in the woman was now extinguished and she was pronounced dead.

While arrangements were being made to move the body to the mortuary, PC Neil went to the nearby Essex Wharf to ask if anyone there had heard any sort of disturbance. No one had.

The woman's body was taken on an ambulance (in those days, a stretcher on wheels) to the mortuary, where Inspector Spratling from H Division took a description of the deceased and then began a thorough examination of the body in an attempt to find a clue to the perpetrator. As he lifted up the woman's skirts he made the most horrific discovery. The woman had been disembowelled.

Inspector Spratling's discovery made it clear that the murder was unlikely to be the result of a domestic dispute or a disagreement over payment for services rendered. Poor Martha Tabram's injuries had been horrific enough, but they paled in comparison to the damage inflicted on the latest victim.

Understandably convinced that no one could be disembowelled on a London street without anyone noticing, the police began an exhaustive search of the area surrounding the murder site. PC Thain was sent to examine all the premises close by while Inspector Spratling and Sergeant Godley searched the nearby railway embankments and lines and also the Great Eastern Railway yard. As with the two previous murder sites, nothing that looked even remotely like a clue could be found. Stranger still, no one in this densely populated part of the metropolis seemed to have seen or heard anything untoward. A policeman who had been on duty at the gate of the Great Eastern Railway yard, only about 50 yards away from where the body was found, had neither seen nor heard anything suspicious.

Emma Green, who lived opposite the murder site and was awake at the estimated time of the murder hadn't heard any sound. Neither had Mrs Purkis, a neighbour who had also been awake since the early hours of the morning. The employees of Barber's slaughter-yard, a mere 150 yards away from the murder site, had neither seen nor heard anything that could be described as unusual or suspicious. Even the police, who were still reeling from having to deal with the violent death of Martha Tabram, had failed to notice anyone or anything that might be connected with the terrible, savage attack.

With no witnesses and no clues left at the scene of the crime, the police turned their attention to the victim's identity, in the hope that it might help them catch her murderer. Items of her clothing bore the mark of the Lambeth Workhouse so the police made enquiries at this establishment and found out that the woman's name was Mary Ann Nichols, commonly known as Polly.

Polly's story echoed that of Martha Tabram. She had been married to a man named William Nichols, a machine printer, for some years. However Polly developed alcoholism and in consequence, the couple split up about nine years before she died. To begin with, her husband paid her an allowance but in 1882, he discovered she was working as a prostitute and so the payments stopped.

From that time on, Polly drifted through various workhouses throughout London until 12 May 1888, when she was offered a position below stairs at a house in Wandsworth. This new job, which later turned out to be Polly's last opportunity to get her life back on track, did not work out and on 12 July, she absconded from the house, taking £3-worth of clothing with her. Like so many of her kind, Polly then found herself in the rookeries of Spitalfields, taking nightly beds at common lodging houses in Thrawl Street and Flower and Dean Street.

On the night of 30 August, Polly was seen plying her trade on the Whitechapel Road, a popular haunt of streetwalkers. At around midnight, she visited the Frying Pan public house in Brick Lane for some liquid refreshment and then visited one of her preferred lodging houses at 18 Thrawl Street where she tried to secure a bed for the night unsuccessfully on account of the fact that she had spent all her money in the pub. The last time Polly was seen by anyone who knew her was at approximately 2.30am on the morning of 31 August when her friend and fellow lodger Ellen Holland encountered her on the corner of Osborn Street; pretty much the exact spot where Emma Smith had been fatally assaulted four months previously. Ellen Holland found Polly to be very drunk but determined to obtain the money for her bed and the two women parted company. Polly set off in the direction of Bucks Row. Just over an hour later, she was dead.

The police were once again baffled regarding both the killer and the motive. Polly had no money, so it was inconceivable that she was the victim of a violent robbery and all her friends and family said she was an affable person who had no enemies.

Clutching at straws, the police re-interviewed anyone who they considered to be the slightest bit suspicious. Suspects included workers at the nearby slaughterhouse in Winthrop Street and an odd character named John Piser, commonly known as 'Leather Apron'. Piser was well known among the Spitalfields prostitutes' fraternity because he regularly tried to blackmail the women and would assault them if they didn't comply with his requests. The press, who by now were beginning to see the opportunities for increased circulation in reporting on the murders, leapt on the Piser story and virtually convicted the man before he had even been interviewed by police.

Not surprisingly, Piser went to ground and when police eventually found him (on 10 September) it turned out that he had a cast-iron alibi for the night of the Nichols murder. The police were back to square one, this time with the added problem of unwanted attention from the press. Polly Nichols' inquest did not shed any further light on either murderer or motive, despite interviewing virtually anyone who had any sort of connection with the murder. The jury was forced to reach a verdict of 'wilful murder against some person or persons unknown' for the third time in little over four months.

The three murders that had occurred in Spitalfields during the first eight months of 1888 had brought a lot of unwelcome attention to the lodging houses and furnished rooms of the area. So far, most attention had been given to the residents of George Street, Thrawl Street and Flower and Dean Street because they were the roads in which the victims had resided prior to their untimely deaths. Consequently, the residents of Dorset Street had gone relatively undisturbed. Landlords McCarthy and Crossingham were no doubt relieved that this was the case as they would have benefited from the relocation of erstwhile residents of the victims' lodgings who were keen to avoid police interest at all costs. This is not to say however, that anyone who avoided the police did so because they were involved in the murders.

On the contrary, although Spitalfields was notorious for its lawlessness, murder (particularly that of a woman) was rare. The tenants of the lodging houses, although considered the lowest of the low by the chattering classes, were no doubt horrified that such violence was being perpetrated on their doorstep. In addition to this, their livelihoods were threatened by the murders; since the murder of Polly Nichols, the police were more vigilant than they had ever been before, thus making the crimes of theft and burglary more difficult. The prostitutes' job had become fraught with danger too and the women were more wary of strangers, until they were too drunk or desperate for a bed to care.

Throughout August 1888, Crossingham and McCarthy reaped the benefits of the migration away from the east side of Commercial Street, blissfully ignorant of the fact that within a matter of days, they too would become embroiled in what the press had now christened the 'Whitechapel Murders'.

At about 2am on 8 September, Timothy Donovan, the deputy in charge of William Crossingham's lodging house at 35 Dorset Street was visited by one of his regular lodgers. Annie Chapman (otherwise known as Siffey) was 45 years old. Like Martha Tabram and Polly Nichols before her, she had left her husband at the beginning of the

1880s, the break-up being precipitated by her addiction to alcohol. Since that time, Annie had wandered aimlessly through life (unknowingly with a potentially fatal disease of the brain) until she found herself on the streets of Spitalfields. Timothy Donovan was well acquainted with Annie. According to him, she had been working as a prostitute for well over a year and had become a regular at 35 Dorset Street some four months previously.

Annie's reason for seeing Donovan on the 8th was to try to blag a bed for the night, despite the fact that she had no money to pay for it. Donovan was well used to pleas for mercy such as this and refused. However, he did allow her to have a rest in the communal kitchen before resuming her hunt for punters. As she left, Annie told him not to let the bed as she would be back soon. It was the last time Donovan saw her alive.

About four hours after Annie had left Crossingham's lodging house, John Davis stepped out of the back door of a crowded, terraced house he shared at 29 Hanbury Street, Spitalfields and got the shock of his life. Lying at the bottom of the back steps was the body of a woman. Fearing the worst, Davis stumbled back through the house and out into Hanbury Street where he found two men on their way to work at Bailey's packing case factory, which was situated a few doors away. The two men followed Davis down the side passage of the house, took one look at the body and immediately went to fetch a policeman, telling several colleagues about their gruesome discovery on the way.

The men ran up Hanbury Street and soon found Inspector Joseph Chandler, who was on duty in Commercial Street. Inspector Chandler returned to the yard with the men. He found quite a few neighbours and passers-by loitering in the passage, but thankfully, all of them seemed too scared to approach the body in the yard. Seeing that the woman was either dead or dying, Inspector Chandler wasted no time in sending for the Divisional Surgeon, Dr Bagster Phillips, who lived in Spital Square.

Once the doctor was on site, it became obvious that the woman had been violently and ruthlessly assaulted. Her throat was deeply cut and she had been disembowelled, just the same as Polly Nichols. Unlike

Nichols however, her internal organs had been savagely hacked and strewn around her corpse. Following a closer examination, it was found that some organs, including her womb and part of her bladder, were missing, presumably taken away as trophies by the murderer.

Still reeling from the shock of this latest brutal slaying, the police set about attempting to identify and apprehend the perpetrator, hoping they would meet with considerably more success than last time. They interviewed all the residents of number 29 Hanbury Street and searched their rooms. When nothing incriminating was found, they widened their search to the surrounding houses and sent officers to all common lodging houses in the area to find out if any of the deputies had admitted anyone that morning who either looked suspicious or was acting strangely. Again, nothing. Usual suspects were rounded up and interviewed, prostitutes were questioned, statements were examined and re-examined. Nothing yielded any clue. The Whitechapel Murderer had claimed another victim. And this time, Dorset Street was right in the thick of the police enquiry.

Reasoning that it was probably best to be entirely cooperative with the police on this occasion, William Crossingham sent his deputy, Tim Donovan and his doorman (a man named John Evans), along to Annie Chapman's inquest with the instruction to be as helpful as possible.

Both men were questioned by the coroner and they agreed that it was inconceivable that anyone would want to harm Annie in such a vicious and horrific way. Donovan stated that he had never experienced any trouble with Annie and believed her to be on friendly terms with all the other lodgers at 35 Dorset Street. Evans was slightly less complimentary, saying that Annie had fought with another woman in the kitchen of the lodging house on the previous Thursday. That said, he had never heard anyone threaten Annie and was not aware that she was afraid of anyone. Various other witnesses were called, including policemen, residents of Hanbury Street and people who admitted to being in the street on the night of the murder. None of their testimonies revealed any incriminating evidence and once again, the inquest jury were forced to agree on the verdict 'wilful murder against some person or persons unknown'.

While the police were tearing their hair out trying to capture the murderer or murderers, the press were having a field day. Spitalfields, with its gross overcrowding and its volatile mix of cultures and ethnicities had long since been in a state of crisis. The appearance of the 'Whitechapel Murderer' had brought things to boiling point. The impoverished Huguenots blamed the Irish. The Irish blamed the Jews. The Jews (most of whom were relatively new to the area) kept their heads down and hoped to goodness it wasn't one of them.

The press fed off this mutual distrust and began publishing salacious stories concerning the murders, many of which were pure fantasy. A common theory was that an Englishman could never have committed such heinous crimes. Therefore, it was a foreigner that was to blame. *The Star* even went so far as to name John Piser (who was Jewish) as the killer. This frankly stupid move almost resulted in a costly legal battle for *The Star* when Piser quite understandably threatened to sue.

Rightly or wrongly, the police withheld a lot of information from the press and consequently, journalists began to speculate rather than report hard facts. Assuming the police were looking for just one man, the newspapers began to paint a disturbing picture of a spectral monster with an insatiable bloodlust who roamed the streets of Spitalfields searching for his prey. The fact that his victims were prostitutes gave journalists another angle and numerous valedictory articles appeared on the dismal plight of the fallen woman.

The spectral image of the murderer also gave rise to a number of press reports with a supernatural theme, the most famous being the myth that the image of the murderer was preserved, like a photograph, on the pupils of the victims' eyes.

This sensational style of reporting resulted in the residents of Spitalfields developing a morbid fascination for the dreadful crimes that were being perpetrated in their midst. As a subscriber to the *East London Observer*, Jack McCarthy kept himself up-to-date with the press's take on events. Meanwhile, his tenants in 13 Miller's Court also read the newspaper reports. Mary Kelly was no doubt greatly relieved that as long as she stayed with Joe Barnett, she wouldn't have to take her chances on the streets.

Annie Chapman's murder had brought things much closer to home. Chapman had been a long term resident of Dorset Street. Prior to her moving into Crossingham's lodging house at number 35, she had regularly stayed at McCarthy's lodgings at number 30. Therefore it is inconceivable that she was unknown to the McCarthy family and highly likely that she was acquainted with Mary Kelly and Joe Barnett. Annie Chapman was not some unknown, washed up unfortunate. She was a real person, possibly even a friend. As they read through the newspaper reports and dodged the increasing number of journalists that prowled Dorset Street for good copy, McCarthy, Crossingham and their tenants must have longed for the day that the miserable street they called home ceased to be front-page news on virtually every newspaper in Britain. That day would be a long time coming.

Three weeks after the murder of Annie Chapman, at 1am on the morning of 30 September, Louis Diemshutz drove his pony and coster barrow down Berner Street, just off the Commercial Road in Whitechapel. He was making for the yard of International Working Men's Educational Club, where he stored his goods. As Diemshutz turned to go through the gates by the side of the club, his pony shied to the left. Although it was very dark in the yard, Diemshutz looked down to his right to see what was obstructing the pony's way and saw a shape on the ground. Unable to make out what it was, he tentatively poked it with his whip, and then when it didn't move, he got down and lit a match.

The wind blew the match out almost immediately, but Diemshutz had enough time to see that the object on the ground was a woman, presumably in a state of inebriation. He went into the club and emerged again with a candle. This time, he could see that the woman was not simply drunk. There was blood. Wasting no time, Diemshutz went off to find a policeman. At first his search proved fruitless despite him shouting as loud as he could and he returned to the yard with another man he had met on the street. This man knelt down to look at the woman and gently lifted her head. It was then that to their horror, the two men realised her throat had been cut.

Eventually, Constable Henry Lamb was found on the Commercial Road and soon the police found themselves conducting yet another murder enquiry. The visitors to the Working Men's Club were interviewed, as were neighbours and passers-by. Once again, absolutely no clue was to be found, but this time, there was apparently a witness.

Israel Schwartz happened to be walking down Berners Street towards the Working Men's Club about a quarter of an hour before Louis Diemshutz arrived with his pony and barrow. As he approached the yard, Schwartz saw a man stop and speak to a woman who was standing in the gateway. He then watched as the man grabbed the woman and tried to pull her into the street. When she wouldn't move, he turned and threw her onto the ground. The woman screamed, though not very loudly.

Not wishing to become embroiled in what seemed to be a domestic dispute, Schwartz crossed over the road and while doing so, noticed a second man standing a short distance ahead of him lighting his pipe. The man who had thrown the woman to the ground then called out, apparently to alert the man with the pipe of Schwartz's presence. Alarmed at this rather strange series of events, Schwartz quickened his pace in order to get away from the scene but to his dismay, found that the man with the pipe was following him. Now quite afraid, Schwartz broke into a run but thankfully, the man did not follow him far.

Israel Schwartz's story was the biggest lead the police had received to date and they wasted no time in taking him to the mortuary where he identified the dead woman as the one he had seen outside the yard. He also gave detailed descriptions of the two men he saw: the first man was aged about 30, approximately 5'5" in height, with dark hair and a fair complexion. He had a small brown moustache, was broad-shouldered and had been wearing a black cap with a peak. The second man was about five years older than the first and about six inches taller. He had light brown hair and was wearing an old, black felt hat with a wide brim. The police immediately circulated the description of the first man to their officers. Strangely, they discounted the second man and no attempt seems to have been made to find him.

In addition to finding themselves a possible witness, the police also managed to identify the murdered woman. Her name was Elizabeth Stride, although she was commonly referred to as 'Long Liz', seemingly a reference to her face-shape, as she was not a particularly tall woman. She was about 38 years old and was originally from Sweden. Interestingly, Liz had more than one thing in common with the previous victims. In addition to being a prostitute, she favoured two lodging houses more than any others. One was in Flower and Dean Street (number 32) and the other was at number 38 Dorset Street – one of Jack McCarthy's properties and just three doors down from the lodgings used by Annie Chapman. As the police searched in vain for clues, a pattern seemed to be slowly forming, the epicentre of which appeared to be Dorset Street.

Although they feared that Elizabeth Stride had fallen victim to the 'Whitechapel Murderer', the police were puzzled that her body had not been mutilated. Some surmised that her killer had been disturbed by Diemshutz's pony and barrow. Indeed it was quite likely that the killer had still been at large while Diemshutz was in the pitch-black yard and had only made his escape when he went inside the club to get a candle. A disturbing thought, especially for Louis Diemshutz. However, within a matter of hours, it became glaringly obvious that Elizabeth Stride's killer had indeed been disturbed and he had left Berner Street to stalk prey elsewhere.

As Elizabeth Stride was being savagely attacked in Berner Street, a 43-year-old woman named Catherine Eddowes left Bishopsgate Police Station and walked down the street towards Houndsditch. Catherine had been locked up in the police cells at the station for a few hours after being found extremely drunk and rather amusingly impersonating a fire engine on Aldgate High Street. Seeing that she was temporarily incapable of looking after herself, the police decided to put her in a cell until she was sober enough to get herself home. By 1am the next morning, she had sobered up sufficiently to give the desk sergeant a false name and address (Mary Ann Kelly of 6 Fashion Street) and was allowed to go. As the gaoler let her out of the station,

Catherine asked him what the time was. When he told her it was 1am, Catherine responded by telling him that she would get 'a damned fine hiding when I get home'.

But Catherine never did go home. Although she began walking in the direction of the lodgings that she shared with her lover, John Kelly in Flower and Dean Street, she then changed direction and headed east, back towards the spot where she had been arrested.

At about 1.30am, Joseph Lawende and his friends Joseph Levy and Harry Harris, left the Imperial Club in Duke Street, a short distance away from Aldgate High Street. As they passed a small passage that lead to a quiet backwater called Mitre Square, Lawende noticed a man and a woman standing in the shadows. The woman had placed her hand on the man's chest. Thinking nothing of it, Lawende and his two companions continued their journey.

Less than a quarter of an hour later, PC Edward Watkins walked into Mitre Square on his usual beat and discovered the body of a woman who had been savagely attacked. Her throat had been cut, her face disfigured and her skirts were drawn up round her waist, revealing the fact that she had been disembowelled. Watkins raced over to a nearby warehouse to call for help.

Due to the location in which the body was discovered, Catherine Eddowes's murder fell under the jurisdiction of the City Police, rather than the Metropolitan Police (who had been responsible for the other murder enquiries). The City Police Officers were determined not to be outwitted like their Metropolitan colleagues and immediately launched an exhaustive search of the area. The Metropolitan Police were kept informed of developments and just before 3am, PC Alfred Long stumbled across the first real clue.

PC Long had been walking his beat along Goulston Street, a road that ran north from Aldgate, up towards the Dorset Street area. On passing a block of Model Dwellings, he noticed a blood-stained piece of material in the passageway. On picking it up, PC Long noticed that the blood was still wet. Above the spot where the material had lain was a chalked message that read 'the Juwes are the men that will not be blamed for nothing.' The material was promptly taken to the mortuary and it was found to have been cut from Catherine Eddowes's apron. After six murders and months of frustration, the police had their first clue.

The City and Met Police's confidence in their chances of apprehending the elusive murderer was temporarily boosted by the discovery of the piece of apron. They now knew that the assailant(s) had fled towards Spitalfields once they had committed the dreadful atrocities on poor Catherine Eddowes. The chalked graffiti on the wall of the Model Dwellings was another matter entirely. Both police forces were undecided as to whether it was pertinent to the murder enquiry or simply a racist message scrawled on the wall by a disgruntled local, intolerant of the area's newest immigrants. However, given the fact that race relations in the district were currently at boiling point, the Met police thought it best to wash the graffiti away before it was seen by the locals. Thus what could have been an indispensable clue was erased before it could even be photographed.

Concentrating their efforts on the discovery of the piece of apron, the police made their usual rounds of all the homes and businesses in the area to ascertain whether anyone had seen or heard anything suspicious on the night of the murder. Given the response from their previous enquiries, they might have guessed that nobody had noticed anything untoward.

As the police's frustration at the lack of progress in any of the murder inquiries grew, so did the frustrations of Londoners, particularly those living in the East End. Men in the area formed vigilante groups, the most well known of which was the East End Vigilance Committee, headed by a builder from Mile End named George Lusk. Soon after the murder of Catherine Eddowes, Mr Lusk was the recipient of a bloody parcel containing a portion of kidney that the sender claimed belonged to the murdered woman. Accompanying the kidney was a letter from the supposed murderer within which he admitted to eating the other half. The sheer sensationalism of this admission caused many people involved with the case to suspect that the letter was the work of either an enterprising journalist or a medical student with a fondness for sick jokes. However, it was never disproved that the kidney came from Catherine Eddowes.

The parcel containing the kidney was by no means the only piece of correspondence that was sent. The day before the murder of Elizabeth Stride and Catherine Eddowes, Tom Bulling of the Central News Agency passed a letter on to the police that had been received two days previously, on 27 September. The letter was addressed to 'The Boss' and had been posted in the EC (East Central) district of London. It read as follows:

> 'I keep hearing the police have caught me but they wont fix me just yet. I have laughed when they look so clever and talk about being on the right track. That joke about Leather Apron [Piser] gave me real fits. I am down on whores and I shant quit ripping them till I do get buckled. Grand work my last job was, I gave the lady no time to squeal. How can they catch me now, I love my work and want to start again. You will soon hear of me with my funny little games. I saved some of the proper red stuff in a ginger beer bottle over the last job to write with but it went thick like glue and I can't use it. Red ink is fit enough I hope ha. ha. The next job I do I shall clip the ladys ears off and send them to the police officers just for jolly wouldnt you. Keep this letter back till I do a bit more work then give it out straight. My knife's so nice and sharp I want to get to work right away if I get a chance, good luck.'

The police took especial notice of this particular letter due to the line about clipping the lady's ears off; a portion of one of Catherine Eddowes's ears had been severed and was subsequently found in the folds of her clothing. However, the extent of Catherine's facial injuries had been so great that it was quite possible that the cutting of her ear had not been intentional. Further, the severed portion of ear had been left at the scene and not sent to the police as promised in the letter.

Jack Sheppard's Farewell to Mr Wood.

Blueskin cutting down Jack Sheppard.

The body of Jack Sheppard carried off by the Mob.

The execution of Jack Sheppard at Tyburn, 16 November 1724. *Getty Images*

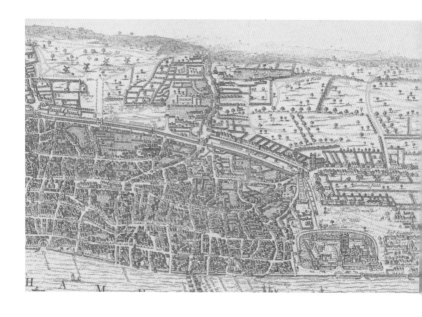

Above: The "Spittle Field" from Agas's *View of London* 1560. *By permission of the British Library*

Below: 17th century development shown on Ogilby and Morgan's map of London, 1677. *By permission of the British Library*

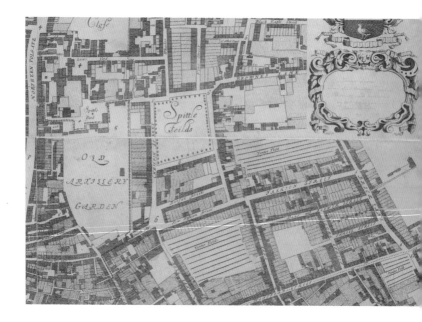

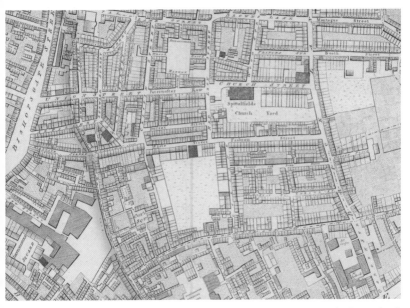

Above: Detail from Horwood's 'Plan of the Cities of London & Westminster, the Borough of Southwark and Parts Adjoining Shewing Every House' 1792 *By permission of the British Library*

Below: Detail from Charles Booth's 'Descriptive Map of London Poverty' 1898-9. Dorset Street is coloured black, defining the residents as the '…lowest class. Vicious, semi-criminal.' *By permission of the London School of Economics and Political Science*

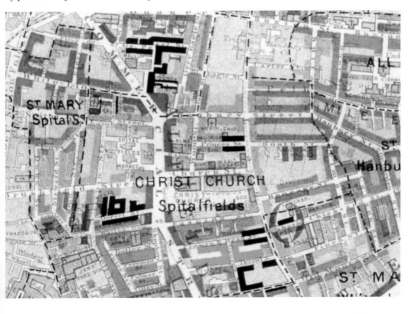

Above: Dorset Street circa 1900. *London, J. 'The People of the Abyss' (1903)*

Below: 18th century silk weavers at work. *Getty Images*

Above: Starving Irish congregate outside the workhouse gates during the mid-19th century potato famine. *Getty Images*

Below: Before 20th century state intervention, life for the poorest Londoners was exceptionally tough. *Getty Images*

Above: The sleeping quarters of a late-19th century common lodging house. *Getty Images*

Below: The communal kitchen of a late-19th century common lodging house. *Getty Images*

THE DISCOVERY OF THE SIXTH "RIPPER" MURDER.

Vol. II.—No. 13.

Thomas Bowyer, collecting rent, sees the body of Mary Jane Kelly through the broken window of the house at 13 Miller's Court, Dorset Street, Spitalfields. *Mary Evans Picture Library*

Above: Interior of a Victorian gin palace. *Getty Images*

Right: Customs officials examine the baggage of Jewish immigrants at St Katherine's Dock, 1904. *Getty Images*

While this letter turned out to be nothing more than yet another piece of correspondence to be considered by the police, to the press it was a gift from the heavens. Since John Piser had managed to prove his alibi for the nights of the Nichols and Chapman murders, the press had been forced to stop referring to the murderer as 'Leather Apron'. The letter gave them a name that, in journalistic terms, was simple, chilling and utterly appropriate. So much so that to this day it sends a shiver down the spine of children and adults alike. The letter was signed 'Jack the Ripper'.

Back in Dorset Street, the reportage of what was rapidly becoming known as 'the double event' had left the residents in shock. Elizabeth Stride had been a regular inmate at Jack McCarthy's lodgings at number 38 and her boyfriend Michael Kidney still lived there. No more than a month previously, long-term Dorset Street resident Annie Chapman had also fallen victim to the ghoul now referred to as the Ripper. The prostitutes that inhabited the lodging houses and courts along this Godforsaken street were literally in fear of their lives. However, many had no choice but to carry on working. They reasoned that it was better to take one's chances with a couple of punters each night than to sleep rough. That said, the night-times were terrifying for all the prostitutes that worked the streets of Spitalfields and Whitechapel.

The women sought regulars as much as they could, but not enough money could be earned from these men to pay for a bed for the night and obtain the alcoholic fix most of them required in order to function. Every new punter was treated with fear and suspicion. The murdered women had met their ends in close proximity to homes and places of entertainment but no one had heard them cry for help. There was no such thing as a safe place to take a punter. The vigilante groups were of little help as they couldn't be in more than one place at a time and the same went for the police.

In this atmosphere, it might be reasonable to assume that, in the absence of any other form of security, the prostitutes would have turned to each other for help. However there are no known reports of the women keeping an eye on one another. Being a prostitute in 19th century East London was indeed a lonely, dangerous profession.

At number 13 Miller's Court, things were not going so well for Joe Barnett and Mary Kelly. The catalyst for the breakdown in their relationship seems to be the fact that some time in the mid-summer of 1888, Joe lost his steady job as a porter at Billingsgate fish market. No contemporary documents give any clues as to why Barnett found himself out of work. However, he had been employed by the market as a licensed porter since the late 1870s so if he was sacked, it seems fair to assume that he must have committed a major offence.

The two main offences resulting in instant dismissal from Billingsgate Market at the time were theft or drunkenness. Given that no contemporary reports suggest Barnett had a drink problem, it is more likely that he was caught walking out of the gate with some of the stock in his pocket. That said, Barnett may not have been sacked at all. During the mid-to-late 1880s, the economy was in recession and therefore it is not inconceivable that Barnett was simply made redundant.

Whatever the reasons for Joe Barnett losing his job, the fact remained that he was jobless and he could not afford to provide for Mary Kelly. As autumn drew closer, Barnett and Kelly fell increasingly further behind with the rent. It might be reasonable to assume that their landlord Jack McCarthy would have been less than sympathetic to their plight. After all, he was in the business of letting rooms in return for money and could be forgiven for throwing out any tenants that could not pay their dues. In actual fact, Jack McCarthy was very sympathetic to Mary and Joe's impecunious situation and let them continue living in the room, despite the fact that their rent payments were at best erratic, at worst non-existent.

Jack McCarthy's behaviour towards Mary and Joe suggests one of three things: firstly of course, McCarthy may have felt sorry for them and charitably let them continue living in the room rent free. However, this is most unlikely. Secondly, he may have given Kelly more rope than other tenants because of a long association with his extended family. Perhaps, but in his line of work, McCarthy could hardly afford to be sentimental. Thirdly, and most likely, McCarthy saw the opportunity to make more money from the situation. In full knowledge of Kelly's erstwhile profession, he put her back on the streets, turning tricks in lieu of rent. This third option is backed up by the fact that by the end of the summer, Mary Kelly was indeed working as a prostitute once again.

Joseph Barnett was horrified that his longstanding ladyfriend was having to prostitute herself in order to keep a roof over their heads and the situation dealt a heavy blow to his already dented self-esteem. As the fear and hatred for the Ripper seeped through the once-safe streets and courts of Spitalfields, Mary and Joe's relationship began to fall apart. As Joe frantically looked for work in vain. Mary drank herself into the stupor necessary to pick up any man who would pay her for sex.

The drink made her loud and aggressive and the couple began to fight. In mid-October, they broke two panes of glass in one of their windows during an altercation, thus making them more indebted to McCarthy, who saw no reason to repair them until his tenants paid up. Consequently, the windows remained broken. As the weather got colder, Mary and Joe stuffed rags into the jagged holes in an attempt to keep out the bitter draught.

As Mary brought men home at all times of day and night, Joe Barnett became more and more uncomfortable living in 13 Miller's Court. In an attempt to bring in more money (and possibly to drive Barnett away) Mary brought other prostitutes into the room and also made no secret of the fact that she was seeing her previous beau, Joseph Flemming. As the situation came to a head, Joe Barnett saw all too clearly that he had to leave. On 30 October, he packed up what few possessions he had and paid for a bed at a lodging house in New Street, Bishopsgate. Without knowing it, Mary Kelly had lost the man who might have been able to save her life.

Although forced to leave, Joe Barnett was a stubborn man and refused to completely finish his relationship with Mary Kelly. While he continued his search for full-time work, he took whatever casual jobs came his way. Any money he had left after paying for his lodgings was given to Mary. It seems that Joe Barnett was reluctant to burn all his bridges regarding this relationship and no doubt hoped that one day he would be able to win Mary back.

On the evening of Thursday 8 November, Joe decided to pay one of his regular visits to 13 Miller's Court. He arrived at the room a few minutes before 7pm and found Mary with her fellow prostitute and occasional room-mate, Maria Harvey. The three chatted for about half an hour and then Maria left, giving Joe the opportunity to speak to Mary alone. Exactly what was discussed following Maria Harvey's departure will never be known, but whatever the topic of conversation, the erstwhile couple did not spend long alone together and Joe Barnett left the room at about 7.45pm. It was the last time he would see Mary Kelly alive.

After Joe's departure, Mary readied herself to go out. The November evening was cold and wet thus making it a bad night to pick up casual business on the street. This was the type of evening when the streetwalkers found trade most hard to come by. Few men were about in the streets and even less wanted to disappear down a dank back-alley for a knee-trembler. Girls like Mary, who had their own rooms in which they could entertain their 'guests' were a more popular choice on cold rainy nights, despite the fact that they cost more. The only down-side to this from Mary's point-of-view was that McCarthy would be able to see exactly how many tricks she turned that night because she had to walk right past the front door of his shop in order to get to her room.

At 11.45pm, Mary Ann Cox, a prostitute living at 5 Miller's Court, was making her way back to her room when she saw Mary Kelly and a man disappearing down the alley in the direction of number 13. As she followed, Cox noticed that the man was carrying a quart can of beer. She also realised that Mary Kelly was very drunk, having probably spent the best part of the evening in the pub. The couple closed the door to number 13 and almost immediately, Mary began to entertain her guest with a rendition of 'A Violet Plucked from Mother's Grave', a popular Irish folk song. Over the next hour, Mary Ann Cox passed through the court twice and noticed that Kelly was still singing. It seemed that her companion had eschewed the traditional services of a prostitute in favour of a vocal performance.

Shortly after Mary Ann Cox's departure from the court, Kelly's neighbour Elizabeth Prater returned home. However, before she made her way to bed, she went into McCarthy's shop and remained there for some minutes. There is little doubt that Elizabeth Prater was also a prostitute, so it is highly likely that, in a similar arrangement to Mary Kelly, McCarthy had put her to work on the streets until she could afford to pay her rent by more salubrious means. Her visit to the shop at this late hour was quite possibly to pay her landlord, thus avoiding being woken up by one of his rent collectors the next morning. During her time in and around the shop, (which amounted to about half an hour), Elizabeth Prater claimed she saw no one go in or out of Miller's Court. Neither did she notice any light coming from Kelly's room as she went upstairs to bed. As she heard no noise from Kelly either, Elizabeth Prater assumed that she had gone to bed.

But Mary Kelly had not gone to bed. Desperate for rent and/or drink money, she had left her room in search of more business. At 2am a man named George Hutchinson was walking down Commercial Street when he was accosted by Kelly, who wanted to borrow 6d. Hutchinson, who lived close by and knew Kelly reasonably well, had no money to spare and told her so. Unperturbed, Kelly went on her way and soon met another man who had been walking a short distance away from Hutchinson. The man tapped her on the shoulder, said something to her and the pair burst out laughing. He then put his arm around her and the pair made off in the direction of Dorset Street.

As he watched them, Hutchinson noticed that the man was carrying a small parcel secured by a strap. No doubt alerted by the newspaper illustrations of 'Jack the Ripper' carrying his knives in bags or packages, Hutchinson decided to follow the couple in order to make sure that Mary came to no harm. The couple turned into Dorset Street, stood at the corner of the court for a few minutes, then disappeared into room 13. Still worried, Hutchinson decided to hang around and watch for when the man came out. However, after waiting for three quarters of an hour, the inclement weather got the better of him and he went off in search of shelter.

Some time between 3.30 and 4am, Elizabeth Prater was awoken by her pet kitten. As she turned over to go back to sleep, she heard a woman cry out 'oh, murder!' However, cries such as these were as frequent along Commercial Street then as car alarms are today. Consequently, Elizabeth Prater ignored it and went back to sleep. Over at 2 Miller's Court, Sarah Lewis sat in a chair wide awake. She had come to the room about an hour before in order to seek sanctuary from her husband, with whom she had been arguing. 2 Miller's Court was rented by her friend Mrs Keyler and was only a short distance from her lodgings in Great Pearl Street. As Lewis tried to doze off in the cold, damp room, she too heard a cry of 'murder'. Like Elizabeth Prater, she ignored it.

What remained of the night passed by with little incident. Jack McCarthy shut his shop at around 2am and made his way to bed. By 5am, men began leaving Miller's Court on their daily trip to seek work at the Docks. A few hours later, their wives and partners began to stir. The shutters on McCarthy's shop windows came off and another day began. But this day was unlike any other. On this day, the names of Mary Jane Kelly, Jack McCarthy and Joe Barnett and the miserable thoroughfare of Dorset Street would be written into history and become forever linked with the squalor, depravation and hopelessness that was Spitalfields in 1888. As Jack McCarthy took the shutters from the windows of his miserable little shop on that rainy morning in November, little did he know that he and his hopeless, poverty-stricken tenants would become part of a mystery that would engross inhabitants of countries around the globe into the millennium and beyond.

At 10.45am, McCarthy gave up on Mary Kelly delivering her night's earnings personally and sent one of his rent collectors, a man named Thomas Bowyer, into Miller's Court to find her. Bowyer made his way through the narrow archway that ran between numbers 26 and 27 Dorset Street, into the mean little court. He turned and knocked on the door of number 13. There was no answer and no sign of movement inside the room. Bowyer knocked again, then walked around the side of the building to peer through the window.

The view through the first window was obscured by a thick, heavy piece of material so Bowyer put his hand through the pane of glass that had been broken some weeks previously and pulled it aside.

The cold November light fell into the ancient, squalid room and illuminated a small table upon which there seemed to be lumps of meat. Bowyer's natural impulse was to draw back. He let go of the makeshift curtain, and prepared to take a closer look. As he pulled back the curtain for a second time, the full horror of the contents of the room was revealed. The floor and walls were stained a deep, dark, blood red. Lumps of flesh and internal organs were strewn around the room, as if cast aside by some maniacal butcher.

On the ancient, vermin-infested bed lay what remained of Mary Jane Kelly. Unrecognisable now for her face had been mutilated with such ferocity that it was hard to believe that it had once represented youth and beauty. Her throat had been slit and her torso ripped open. Her breasts had been sliced off. A portion of her leg had been skinned. In a final sick, demented act, her butchered frame had been arranged in an appalling death-pose, the mutilated face turned towards the window with a blank, lifeless stare.

Bowyer drew back from the horrifying scene and ran to get Jack McCarthy who, after taking a cautious look through the window himself, sent Bowyer to the police station on Commercial Street. After composing himself (and possibly arranging for someone to stand guard lest Joe Barnett or one of Kelly's friends should return to the room), he followed Bowyer to the police station. Once at the station, McCarthy and Bowyer were seen by Inspector Beck, who immediately returned with them to Miller's Court.

Once the three men had arrived outside number 13, Inspector Beck sent for Dr George Bagster Phillips. The doctor duly arrived and attempted to enter the room, but found the door was locked. One would assume that as landlord, Jack McCarthy would have possessed a key, but if he did have one, he certainly did not reveal its whereabouts to the police. This led to the rather farcical situation of Dr Phillips having to look through the broken window to assess whether Mary Kelly required any medical assistance. However despite only being able to view the body from several feet away, the visible mutilations inflicted on Kelly were enough to convince Dr Phillips that she was dead.

Showing great presence of mind, Dr Phillips sent for a photographer so that the crime scene could be accurately recorded before being trampled over by the police. The four men then waited in the court for further instructions from more senior police officers. As more police arrived at the scene, word got around that two bloodhounds had been sent for. Dr Phillips rightly suggested that it was best to wait until the dogs arrived before attempting to gain access to the room. However, the dogs never materialised. Two hours passed before word came from Superintendent Arnold that since the key was still unforthcoming, McCarthy would have to break the door down.

Jack McCarthy went off to find the necessary tools for the job and soon returned with an axe. He set about chopping through the lock and the door fell open, revealing the full carnage inside the room. As the door swung ajar, it knocked against a small table that stood beside the bed. Dr Phillips entered the room and approached the corpse. He saw that Mary Kelly was dressed in her undergarments. Her throat had been slit. Thankfully, Dr Phillips believed the dreadful mutilation to her body had taken place after Mary was dead. He also noticed that the body had been moved after death so that it was lying on the left-hand side of the bed, facing out into the room.

Once Dr Phillips had completed his examination of the body, Inspector Abberline of the CID took an inventory of what was in the room. He noticed that a fire had been raging in the grate and had created such intense heat that the spout of a kettle had melted off. He also saw that articles of women's clothing had been burnt and assumed that this had been done to light the room as there was only one candle to be found.

By now, news of the latest murder had spread through Spitalfields like wildfire. Miller's Court had been sealed off and no residents were allowed in or out unless cleared by the police. Residents of nearby houses craned their necks out of windows to try and get a look at the court. Journalists rushed to the scene and began their own enquiries.

Once again, the police were baffled. No clues had been left at the scene. None of the residents of Miller's Court had seen anything suspicious. Only two had heard a cry of 'murder' the night before and had thought nothing of it. A large crowd gathered outside McCarthy's shop. By the time Mary Kelly's body was removed to the mortuary, the crowd had become so large and boisterous that a police cordon had to be formed before the flimsy, temporary coffin could be loaded on to the ambulance.

As he watched the mélée, Jack McCarthy knew that he was now embroiled in the most notorious murder enquiry the East End had seen for decades, perhaps ever. What he didn't realise was that over 100 years in the future, the mystery surrounding the deaths of Emma Smith, Martha Tabram, Polly Nichols, Annie Chapman, Elizabeth Stride, Catherine Eddowes and Mary Jane Kelly would still be discussed and ruminated over by thousands, perhaps millions of people, the world over.

The police never brought Mary Kelly's killer to justice. Her name was added to the list of the other women that had been killed and mutilated on the streets surrounding Spitalfields Market during the year 1888. After Kelly's dreadful death, the killings seemed to come to an abrupt halt, as though the perpetrator's mission was accomplished. This did not mean there were no more murders in the area. On the contrary, Spitalfields continued to be one of the roughest areas of London for nearly a century. But no more women were slain in such a brutal, shocking method.

The almost complete lack of clues to the murderer's identity naturally led to speculation. The first theories on the identity of 'Jack the Ripper' were banded about on the streets of Spitalfields even before the series of murders reached their conclusion. Since then, hundreds of theories have been put forward. 'Jack the Ripper' has become a man with a multitude of personalities and identities. He has been a poor immigrant, a middle-class school teacher, a wealthy businessman, a member of the Royal Family. He has worked as porter, a doctor, a sailor, a butcher. He has even been a she. His motive for perpetrating the murders has ranged from pure insanity to being part of a convoluted Masonic cover-up on behalf of royalty. The only certainty concerning the mysterious case of Jack the Ripper is that the perpetrator of these most heinous murders has long been dead.

However, his legacy was one of enlightenment within society. The massive amount of press coverage concerning the murders alerted people throughout Britain and abroad to the appalling living conditions residents of places such as Dorset Street had to endure. One might naturally assume that the Ripper's killing spree would prove to be the catalyst for change. Sadly it was not. If anything, during the years immediately following the murders, conditions in Dorset Street and its surrounds deteriorated even further.

After Mary Kelly's awful murder, it naturally took some while for Dorset Street and Miller's Court to return to normal. The police remained in Miller's Court for ten days after the murder. Initially, their presence was welcomed by the residents, who were understandably traumatised by the horrors that had been perpetrated in their midst. However, after a while, the police presence began to hinder the women's working practices and pressure was put on Jack McCarthy to get the police out of the court. Nothing would have pleased McCarthy more than seeing the back of them.

The publicity surrounding Mary Kelly's murder had attracted some very unwelcome attention. Morbid sightseers roamed Dorset Street, hoping to get a glimpse of the now notorious (and aptly numbered) Room 13. Seeing a money-making opportunity, a showman offered McCarthy £25 for the use of the room for one month and another wanted to purchase or even hire the bloodsoaked bed on which Kelly had been mutilated. To his credit, Jack McCarthy rejected both offers.

Wishing to put the whole tragic episode behind him, McCarthy complained to the police about their constant presence in the court and after ten days they left, leaving him to hastily tidy up number 13 in preparation for new tenants. Amazingly, he saw no reason to redecorate the room, despite the wall near the bed being covered with blood stains. Four years after Kelly's murder, a Canadian journalist named Kit Watkins visited Dorset Street while compiling a feature on the Whitechapel Murders. At Miller's Court, she met long-term resident Elizabeth Prater who took her to meet Lottie Owen, the room's current occupant. Lottie, (who was nursing a broken nose, inflicted by her husband's boot,) apparently showed no repugnance at living in a room with black bloodstains on the walls. Kit Watkins however, was less than impressed and left with the feeling that 'murder seemed to brood over the place'.

If the atmosphere seemed 'murderous' when Kit Watkins visited Dorset Street four years after the killings, tensions during the remaining weeks of 1888 must have been almost unbearable. The population were obviously ignorant of the fact that there were to be no further killings and so were understandably terrified. In the absence of any hard evidence, the press had created their own image of the Ripper as a tall, slim, menacing character wearing a top hat and carrying a black bag containing his weapons of choice. Consequently, any man walking alone in the East End carrying a black bag was regarded with great suspicion by the populace. Just after the Kelly inquest finished, a man carrying such a bag was accosted by a hostile crowd on Tower Street. The police were called and opened the bag, which was found to contain nothing that even vaguely resembled a murder weapon.

Kelly's funeral, which took place on 19 November turned into an event rarely witnessed in the East End. Since being removed from Miller's Court, her body had been kept in the mortuary attached to St Leonard's Church in Shoreditch. As Kelly was Catholic, it was arranged for her body to be buried at St Patrick's Cemetery some miles away in Leytonstone. The sexton of St Leonard's Church paid for the funeral with his own money as a mark of respect for those parishioners who lived destitute lives similar to that of Kelly.

As the bell of St Leonard's began tolling at noon, a massive crowd assembled at the gates of the church. The coffin was brought out on the shoulders of four men, who loaded it onto an open hearse. Atop the coffin were two wreaths from Mary's friends and fellow prostitutes and a cross made from heartsease. The appearance of the coffin had a huge effect on the crowd, who surged forward in an attempt to touch it as it went past. Women cried and men bowed their heads as the hearse pulled away on its journey to Leytonstone. Following it were two carriages of mourners. One contained a few of Mary's friends, the other carried Joe Barnett and an anonymous representative sent by Jack McCarthy (possibly his wife, Elizabeth). The crowd followed the cortege for some distance and then, as the roads became more open, they gradually fell away and returned to the slums and rookeries from whence they came.

Once Kelly's funeral was over, the press swiftly lost interest in the Whitechapel Murders and moved onto the next big news story. The residents of Dorset Street must have breathed a sigh of relief as they were finally able to return to their regular routines.

Part Four

A FINAL DESCENT

Chapter 18

The Situation Worsens

If Spitalfields had been a vile place to live before the Ripper murders in 1888, afterwards it descended even further into disrepair and destitution. Despite a huge amount of press interest in the deplorable living conditions endured by the residents, nothing was done to make things better for the very poor. An increasing number of people found themselves out of work and so were forced to share accommodation with others in order to pay the rent.

The East London Advertiser reported the tragic circumstances surrounding the death of a four-month-old baby. At the inquest, it transpired that the parents and seven children lived in one room approximately 12-feet square. One night, when the pitiful family were asleep, one of them accidentally rolled over onto the baby and suffocated the child. The jury returned a verdict of accidental death and recommended that the authorities address the overcrowding issued without further ado. As usual, nothing was achieved.

Of course, the chronic overcrowding in Spitalfields was good news for the landlords. Despite the stigma attached to properties in and around the now notorious Miller's Court, there were enough desperate people on the streets to ensure that any rooms vacated after the murder were quickly filled.

As residents attempted to recover from the terrible events that had overtaken Dorset Street during 1888, further trouble was brewing in the East End that would have a profound effect on the already traumatised and poverty-stricken community of Spitalfields.

Due to its proximity to the River Thames, many residents of Dorset Street and the surrounding roads regularly sought work in the Docks. Employment for these people was of a casual nature and involved walking to the Docks and then queuing with hundreds of other men hoping to be chosen to help unload one of the ships. There was absolutely no guarantee that work would be available and the majority of men were sent home each day with no money. Those that were lucky enough to secure work were usually only employed for a couple of hours.

The men that suffered the daily indignity of the 'call-on' really resented the way they were treated by the dock owners, who often abused their power and strode up and down the queues 'with the air of a dealer in a cattlemarket' picking out only the healthiest and strongest for work.

By the summer of 1889, a trade depression had led to fierce competition between the rival dock companies, each of which tried to offer the cheapest rates in a bid to attract more ships. Of course, the losers in this plan were the casual labourers, who quickly saw their bonuses for unloading ships considerably reduced. Things came to a head when the *Lady Armstrong* docked in the West India Docks in August 1889. The East and West India Dock Company decided to cut the casuals' bonus down to the bone, but still insisted that the ship was unloaded with great speed. This proved to be the final straw for the labourers and led by a man named Ben Tillet, the men walked out of the dockyard on 14 August, refusing to unload any more ships until management agreed to pay them a fair wage.

The mass walkout at the West India Docks caused a sensation as until that point, the dock owners had wielded complete control over their workforce, safe in the knowledge that if the men didn't work, they would starve to death. However, they began to feel a little uneasy as the Amalgamated Stevedore's Union (which included the highly skilled men that loaded the ships) joined the strike in support of the casual labourers.

By 27 August, the Docks were at a standstill as the stevedores and labourers were joined by many other trades such as firemen, lightermen, carmen, ropemakers and fish porters. In total around 130,000 men refused to work. The dockers formed a strike committee and demanded that they be paid the now famous 'dockers' tanner', which was 6d per hour instead of the previous 5d. In addition, they also demanded that the bonus system be abolished, that the inhuman 'call-ons' be restricted to only two per day and that the men chosen be employed for at least four hours.

The dockers' plight courted a great deal of sympathy from the press and public alike. However, the dock owners held their ground, banking on the fact that starvation would drive the men back to work before too long. In the meantime, the striking men became seriously concerned about how to feed themselves and their families. As the days without work turned into weeks, the men came under increasing pressure to find money for food and rent. Their landlords still demanded money each week, despite any sympathy they may have felt for the men's situation and, of course, the common lodging houses refused entry to anyone unable to pay in advance. Banners were hung along the Commercial Road, one of which summed up the moment perfectly. It read:

> 'Our husbands are on strike; for the wives it is not honey,
> And we think it is right not to pay the landlord's money,
> Everyone is on strike, so landlords do not be offended;
> The rent that's due we'll pay to you when the strike is ended.'

By the beginning of September things were, in the words of the

Strike Committee's press officer, 'very black indeed.' Despite huge public support, insufficient funds had been raised to maintain the strike for much longer and it looked increasingly likely that the dock owners would win the fight. However, news of the dockers' plight had now spread worldwide and their fellow workers in Australia began to raise money for the striking men. Before long money began pouring in, leaving the dockers free to concentrate on picket lines rather than scratching around for food.

The help from Australia caused great concern for the dock owners who realised that the strike could now go on indefinitely. Also, they were coming under increasing pressure from the ship-owners and wharfingers to resolve the dispute. The ship companies began discussing alternative ways for their ships to be unloaded and some wharfingers held separate talks with the strike committee in an attempt to get their wharves working. In a bid to resolve matters, the Lord Mayor of London formed a Mansion House Committee, which included representatives from both sides of the dispute. The Committee proved to be a success and eventually the dock owners conceded to virtually all the strike committee's demands. The dockers got their 'tanner' and returned to work on 16 September, five weeks after the first labourers had walked out of the West India Docks.

The Great Dock Strike of 1889 proved to be a turning point in the history of trade unions. Prior to the dockers' walkout, unskilled labourers had not possessed the confidence to join together in defiance of their employers. As more men and women saw the differences a united front could make to their lives, membership of trade unions soared. In 1888, 750,000 workers were members of a union. By 1899, that figure had reached two million.

The Great Dock Strike had an uneasy effect on anyone who exploited the poor and, of course, this included the Spitalfields landlords. Mindful of what could be achieved when men and women joined together with a common goal, the landlords adopted a policy of divide and rule. Tenants of lodging houses were encouraged to inform on their fellow lodgers and any disturbances were swiftly reported to the police. The following incident reported by *The Times* in June 1890, shows that their divide and rule policy was working well:

On the evening of 5 June, one of the Dorset Street lodging houses was the scene of a heated argument that broke out between Annie Chapman (obviously not the Ripper victim) and fellow lodger, Elinor French. The lodging house deputy made no attempt to nip the argument in the bud and soon the women were screaming at one another. Finally, unable to contain herself any longer, Chapman grabbed a broken pair of scissors and rushed at French, stabbing her in the face, just below her right eye. The police were summoned and French was encouraged to prosecute her attacker. Consequently, the two women appeared in court on 11 June. French appeared in the witness box with her head swathed in bandages, thus making Chapman look very much the villain of the piece. Annie Chapman was committed for trial and most likely enjoyed a spell in penal servitude as a result.

Chapter 19

A Lighter Side of Life

Although life in Dorset Street was tough, there were distractions and diversions available to even the poorest of inhabitants: drinking dens had been a feature of the area ever since it had been built. By the mid-1600s, local demand was such that William Bucknall opened a brewery in Brick Lane. In 1697, one Joseph Truman became manager and his family subsequently founded what was to become The Black Eagle Brewery – the largest brewery in London.

Back in the 17th century, pubs as we know them today did not exist. Instead, Spitalfields locals frequented alehouses and taverns. Alehouses were originally private properties belonging to individual brewers in which locals could purchase and consume the brewers' ale. Mention is made of their existence in England as early as the 7th century and it is highly likely that they were extant long before this. Over the following centuries, the population increased, the natural water supply became contaminated by industry and ale gained a reputation as a drink that was both safe to consume and had a pleasant effect on the imbiber's state of mind. The subsequent increase in demand led to ale houses evolving from informal, sometimes part-time affairs into profitable and efficiently-run businesses.

By the mid-16th century, improved transport and communication networks meant that foreign wines became increasingly accessible to the general public, particularly those with a reasonable amount of disposable income. As a result, taverns (a contemporary version of Roman 'tabernae') began to spring up in London and other major cities. Unlike the ale houses, which were very basic affairs designed purely for the consumption of alcohol, the taverns provided comfortable seating and tasty food alongside their selection of wines.

By the late 1600s, these forerunners of the modern public house catered for two, distinct types of customer. The ale houses tended to attract the labouring classes as although the surroundings were basic, prices were cheap. The taverns appealed to business-owners and the professional classes as they were an ideal venue in which to entertain clients, meet friends or simply relax after a hard day's work. The taverns were also a popular destination for the area's first prostitutes who found the drunk inhabitants a great source of income. As Spitalfields' population grew, the taverns and ale houses enjoyed a healthy trade and their owners sought ever-larger and more impressive edifices. However, their profits were soon to be severely affected by the arrival of the most pretentious of all watering-holes – the Gin Palace.

During the reign of William III (1689-1702), tensions between Britain and France led to a ban on French brandy and wine. The Huguenot silk weavers had traditionally drunk wine and brandies from their homeland and so sought illegal means of obtaining the drinks via smugglers. Illegal imports of French liquor were not just sought after in Spitalfields; throughout London and beyond, smugglers began to reap huge dividends by supplying the forbidden wines. Obviously, taverns could not serve French wines for fear of having their licence revoked and their trade inevitably went into decline. Realising that the ban was severely affecting the British alcohol industry, the authorities lifted all restrictions on distilling gin and soon the streets of every town and city in England were awash with gin shops. These shops replaced the older ale houses as places in which the poor sought shelter and temporary oblivion. They were designed purely for the consumption of drink and unlike the taverns, did not serve food or have any comfortable seating areas.

The cheapness and availability of gin made the spirit extremely popular with the poorer classes and by the 1720s, London was awash with the stuff. Londoners didn't necessarily have to sit in a gin shop in order to obtain their daily fix. Bottles of the spirit could be purchased virtually anywhere. Street vendors sold it from barrows along the city's major thoroughfares and there were even reports of employers giving gin to their workforce in order to keep them in a compliant state of mind.

Setting up as a gin vendor in the early 18th century was a relatively easy task. No licence was required and there were virtually no restrictions on where or how the commodity could be sold. In 1734, Joseph Forward stood trial at the Old Bailey accused of theft. He was found not guilty of the crime, but the report of the trial demonstrates just how simple it was to set up as a gin seller. Forward's accuser (his landlady, Mrs Ann Chapman) stated in court that a sheet, two candlesticks and a pair of tongs had gone missing from her house after the defendant and his wife took lodgings with her while working at the annual Bartholomew's Fair – a huge, annual extravaganza held in Smithfield over four days in August.

Chapman testified 'the Prisoner and his Wife hired a Room from me by the Week on the last Day of April. They staid till Bartholomew-tide, and then he set his Wife up in Bartholomew-Fair to sell Gin and Black-puddings.' Regrettably the Forwards' moneymaking scheme did not go according to plan. Mrs Chapman explained, 'some body stole (Mrs Forward's) Bottle of Gin, and then she was broke'. It was this misfortune that had apparently forced the Forwards into stealing Mrs Chapman's goods however, the jury did not believe her story and found in favour of the defendant.

Due to the excessive quantities of gin available, prices remained low and Londoners gradually became increasingly reliant on it to get through their day. Many poorer members of the populace would nip out for gin in the same way as we would pop out for a pint of milk today. Gin was an essential part of their daily diet and the resulting drunkenness began to have genuinely horrifying results. Sensational reports began appearing in the newspapers of drunken nurses mistaking babies for logs and putting them on the fire and inebriated mothers killing their children so they could spend more time in the gin shops.

By 1730, it became clear that the country (and London in particular) was in the grip of a gin epidemic and something had to be done to curb the public's insatiable appetite for the drink. A previous attempt to control public consumption of gin through taxation had achieved little so the Government decided to introduce more drastic measures. In 1736, the second Gin Act was passed through parliament. Ministers saw that those most addicted to gin were the poor and so they decided to raise the retail tax on the spirit to 20 shillings per gallon (it had previously run at 5 shillings per gallon). In addition to this, gin retailers were now required to take out an annual licence, at a cost of £50.

Generous rewards of £5 were to be awarded to anyone who informed the authorities of illegal trade. The idea behind the massive tax increase and annual licence fee was to make gin prohibitively expensive, thus stopping the masses from buying it. However, the retailers and distillers were not about to give up their lucrative businesses without a fight. Working on the (correct) assumption that very few members of the public would risk the wrath of their alcoholic neighbours by ratting on the gin suppliers, most gin shops continued to sell the spirit either under the counter or disguised as an exotically named 'medicinal' beverage. Popular brands at the time included 'My Lady's Eye Water' and 'King Theodore of Corsica'!

Unsurprisingly, the 1736 Act did little to stop the gin epidemic and if anything, consumption increased. Various solutions to the problem were discussed including an ill-advised campaign to encourage drinkers to switch to beer, using Hogarth's famous engraving 'Gin Lane' to illustrate the perils of gin drinking. In the end, it was an economic crisis that ended the gin epidemic rather than any Government influence.

During the 1750s, a series of poor grain harvests pushed the price of gin's basic ingredient to an alarming level. As the cost of grain soared, workers were laid off and farmers began supplying the food industry instead of the gin distillers whose alcoholic beverage was not considered as important a commodity as bread. With growing unemployment and higher food prices, the public had less disposable income and so gin consumption began to fall dramatically. Seizing the opportunity to kill off the epidemic for good, the Government passed yet another Gin Act, this time lowering the licence fees but severely restricting the number of outlets from which gin could be sold. This time, their efforts worked and by 1757 the gin craze was in its death throes.

However, gin never entirely disappeared from London's streets. Some gin shops survived the mid-eighteenth century recession in trade and by the dawn of the new century, London's burgeoning population was beginning to discover the delights of gin once again. As the city became increasingly overcrowded and living conditions deteriorated, the public sought escape through alcohol-induced oblivion. Seemingly oblivious to the horrors of the gin craze less than a century previously, the Government actively assisted the gin shop owners in attracting more custom by halving the cost of spirit licences and drastically cutting the duty payable on spirits. By 1830, around 45,000 spirit licences were being issued in Britain per annum and production of gin had increased by over 50% in little more than five years.

As business took off, the gin shop owners began to give their premises a makeover. Realising that their customers needed a respite from their often dark, squalid homes, they set about making their premises as light and bright as possible. Their interiors were brilliantly lit and large, etched-glass windows were fitted to the shop-fronts so passers-by were stopped in their tracks by the light flooding out onto the dark street. Inside, mirrors lined the walls to create a sense of space and reflect the light. To the poor, these gin shops, with their bright façades and glitzy interiors were like palaces and became known as such. Charles Dickens visited some of London's gin palaces while writing *Sketches by Boz* (1836) and described the one thus:

'All is light and brilliancy... and the gay building with the fantastically ornamented parapet, the illuminated clock, the plate-glass windows surrounded by stucco rosettes, and its profusion of gas-lights in richly-gilt burners, is perfectly dazzling when contrasted with the darkness and dirt we have just left. The interior is even gayer than the exterior. A bar of French-polished mahogany, elegantly carved, extends the whole width of the place; and there are two side aisles of great casks, painted green and gold, enclosed within a light brass rail, and bearing such inscriptions as "Old Tom, 459", "Young Tom, 360", "Samson, 1421" – the figures agreeing, we presume, with gallons...

'Beyond the bar is a lofty and spacious saloon, full of the same enticing vessels, with a gallery running round it, equally well-furnished. On the counter, in addition to the usual spirit apparatus, are two or three little baskets of cakes and biscuits, which are carefully secured at the top with wicker-work to prevent their contents being unlawfully abstracted. Behind it are two showily-dressed damsels with large necklaces, dispensing the spirits and "compounds".'

Dickens' description of a gin palace in the 1830s is surprisingly familiar. To this day, the Victorian gin palace survives throughout London and beyond and with it endure the myriad pleasures and problems associated with social drinking in Britain. The current alcoholic craze may not be for gin, but it presents the authorities with the same social problems as befell their predecessors. Despite the Government's best attempts, it appears that drinking to excess is an endemic part of British society and will never be eradicated.

While the gin palaces thrived, the old taverns were gradually being replaced by the forerunner of today's pub – the beer house. In 1830, the Beer Act lifted restrictions on producing and selling beer and just like the gin palaces before them, beer shops began to spring up on street corners. Trade was good and successful shop owners expanded their premises, sometimes dividing up the bars into 'Public' (for the workers), 'Saloon' (for management) and 'Private' (for their most influential patrons). The most favoured tipple at the beer shops and public houses of Spitalfields was Porter, a dark beer that had been developed in the eighteenth century. London Porter was strong and got the drinker in an inebriated state without them having to spend too much money. Consequently, it became extremely popular with the working classes: by 1835, The Black Eagle Brewery in Brick Lane was producing 200,000 barrels a year. Porter remained popular with the labouring classes until World War 1, when grain rations all but prevented the production of strong beers in England and the market began to be taken over by Irish brewers such as Guinness.

By the 1850s, there were literally thousands of pubs, beer houses and gin palaces in London. In working class areas like Spitalfields, there could be four or five down one street. Naturally, the sheer number of pubs, particularly in cities, made competition fierce. Publicans sought new ways to encourage more customers through the doors and once inside, to stay for as long as possible. One of the most successful strategies involved putting on entertainment. An ever-increasing variety of acts were booked and nineteenth century drinkers could expect to be entertained by singers, jugglers, magicians, comedians, contortionists, the list was endless. It was from these pub entertainments that one of the most popular of all Victorian pastimes was born – the Music Hall.

Music Halls were an integral part of the social lives of the working class. However, they vanished almost as swiftly as they arrived. Despite the valiant efforts of a few music hall groups and distant memories of a television programme called *The Good Old Days*, the British Music Hall is now obsolete. This is in a way unsurprising because it epitomised a moment in history that is now almost beyond living memory. However, in its heyday, the Music Hall was an incredibly important element of society.

Music Halls first began to emerge in the mid-nineteenth century.

In December 1848, a pub landlord named Charles Morton acquired the Canterbury Arms in Upper Marsh, close to Lambeth Palace. Morton had previously worked in theatre and decided to provide entertainment at his new pub in the form of 'harmonic meetings', where gentlemen were invited to come and listen to singers in an informal atmosphere. The harmonic meetings proved to be very successful and in order to increase business, Morton organised 'Ladies' Thursdays', which were so successful that he used the profits to build a new hall on the bowling green at the back of the old pub. The Canterbury Arms' motto was 'One quality only – the best' and Charles Morton worked hard to maintain a high standard of entertainment. He employed an in-house choir and regular soloists to perform operatic favourites and guests were provided with baked potatoes (for which The Canterbury became renowned) to soak up the alcohol. In addition to the musical entertainment, Morton operated a bookmaker's from the pub to satisfy his guests who enjoyed a flutter at the races.

In 1856, Morton ploughed his profits back into the business and rebuilt The Canterbury in a much larger and grander style. The new building comprised a main hall and a gallery and was decorated in a sumptuous, palatial style. The walls were adorned with paintings of such quality and value that The Canterbury was nicknamed 'The Royal Academy Across the Water' by one of its patrons. Out went the baked potatoes as the new hall had large tables at which visitors were served a more varied menu.

The increased size of the stage meant that more ambitious productions could be staged. *Gounod's Faust* was sung for the first time in England at The Canterbury and Morton was responsible for introducing Londoners to the work of Offenbach. Not all the entertainment in The Canterbury was so highbrow; interspersed between opera and ballet performances were displays of tightrope walking, bicycle tricks and animal shows. It was this variety that became the essence of Music Hall as a genre.

Landlords across London took note of the success of Charles Morton's Canterbury Music Hall and soon similar establishments were springing up all over the capital. In 1857, Edward Weston converted the Six Cans and Punch Bowl Tavern on High Holborn into Weston's Music Hall and a year later, the Royal Panopticon of Science and Art in Leicester Square was converted into the exotically-named 'Alhambra Palace' and promptly let to an American circus because the owner, one E. T. Smith, could not obtain a theatre licence. However, a year later, Smith managed to obtain a licence and promptly gave the circus their marching orders. He then set about converting the interior into a theatre. The circus ring became the dining area and the original Panopticon organ, which had loomed over the hall for decades, was sold to St Paul's Cathedral. In the gaping hole that was left, Smith built a stage. The Alhambra Palace Music Hall opened in December 1860 and one of its first major attractions was a trapeze act performed by Jules Leotard, the man who gave his name to the style of dancewear.

Following the success of his first venture across the river in South London, Charles Morton decided to go west and in 1861, opened the Oxford Music Hall on the site of an old tavern called the Boar and Castle Inn, close to the junction of Tottenham Court Road and Oxford Street. Morton used The Canterbury as a blueprint and The Oxford was an instant success. Spurred on by this, Morton decided to sell The Canterbury to a man named William Holland, who promptly redecorated the hall and invited patrons to come and spit on his new thousand guinea carpet! The sale of The Canterbury made Morton financially very secure, but this was to be short-lived as, a month after the sale went through, The Oxford was gutted by fire. Inadequately insured, Morton was forced to sell what remained of the building in an attempt to recoup his losses and never built another music hall.

By the 1870s, there were over 300 music halls all over London. Some were purpose built, like the Alhambra Palace and The Canterbury, others had been straight theatres in a previous life and others were literally the back rooms of pubs. The sheer diversity of the music hall venues meant that there was also a great diversity of talent. Obviously the established stars worked the larger halls almost exclusively while the less popular acts and artists still honing their skills were left to work in the smaller establishments.

This hierarchy provided a good training ground for would-be music hall stars and because the profession did not require any expensive qualifications it attracted a great many talented performers from less than privileged backgrounds. In fact, most of the stars from the heyday of the music hall were from Bethnal Green and Whitechapel rather than Kensington and Chelsea. The most famous star of all happened to be a cousin of Spitalfields landlord Johnny Cooney. Her name was Marie Lloyd.

Marie Lloyd was born Matilda Victoria Wood on 12 February 1870 in Hoxton. She loved performing in front of an audience from an early age and while still a child, toured with a minstrel group called the Fairy Bells. As she reached adulthood, Matilda realised that she wanted to make a career out of performing and thus began the laborious task of creating a fan base in the local music halls. Her first performance was at the Grecian Saloon in Islington where she sang a couple of songs under the exotic stage name of Bella Delamare. Matilda was paid nothing for this performance, but it did secure her a trial at Belmont's Sebright Hall in the Hackney Road. The proprietor was impressed enough to immediately offer her a week's engagement in return for the princely sum of 15 shillings.

Matilda worked hard at the Halls, sometimes appearing at three in one night and very quickly her career began to take off. The stage name Bella Delamare was dropped in favour of the simpler and apparently classier Marie Lloyd and a star was born. By the time she was 18, Marie Lloyd had married a part-time racing tout named Percy Courtenay and had begun to frequent Johnny Cooney's pub in Hanbury Street after performing at the local music halls such as the Royal Cambridge in Commercial Street. It was probably here that she and her fellow artistes first met Dorset Street landlord, Jack McCarthy and his son, John.

It is not hard to imagine the impression Marie Lloyd made on John McCarthy junior, who at the time was still in his teens. Determined to mirror Lloyd's success, John junior changed his stage name to Steve McCarthy (probably chosen because his mother's maiden name was Stevens) and worked hard on his comedy song and dance act in the smaller halls. It was at one of these halls that he met the girl who was to change his life. Her name was Minnie Holyome but on stage she called herself Marie Kendall.

When Steve McCarthy and Marie Kendall first met, both were struggling to make a name for themselves. Due to his father's burgeoning bank balance and local social standing, Steve possessed a fair degree of confidence that Marie lacked. Although considerably more talented than Steve, she was from a poor home and her parents had struggled to support her in her quest for fame.

Marie Kendall was born in Bethnal Green in 1873 to parents of Huguenot extraction. The unusual surname of Holyome was a corruption of the French Alyome and like so many of the original residents of Spitalfields, her family had originally been skilled silk weavers. However, by the time Marie was born, the silk weaving trade was all but vanished and the family had fallen on hard times. Her father tried a variety of jobs, from fish curing to wood carving, in order to provide for his family and there never seemed to be enough money to go round. However, despite their poverty, the family was close, happy and determined to support their children in their choice of career.

The music halls played a very important part in East End society. As we have seen, most working-class families endured exceptionally hard lives. By the time they entered their teenage years, they would be working up to six days per week for very little money. The lack of a good income meant that they were forced to live in dark, damp, cheerless homes that were often cold and overcrowded.

Like the gin palaces, East End music halls were designed to be the complete opposite of the audiences' homes. Bright lights illuminated their frontages and the interiors were warm and sumptuously decorated. These 'mini palaces' offered a much needed escape from life's daily grind at an affordable price (admission charges could be as little as 3d). Consequently, they were an extremely popular form of entertainment in Spitalfields and the surrounding areas.

Despite reasonable admission prices, a trip to the music hall was considered a treat for most families. In July 1886, little Minnie Holyome persuaded her mother Mary to take her to a local music hall to celebrate her twelfth birthday. Keen to give her daughter a night to remember, Mary Holyome scraped together the 12d needed for two seats in the front stalls at the Bow Music Hall on the Bow Road. On the bill that night were a turn called 'The Sisters Briggs' who entertained the audience with a song called 'Don't Look Down On The Irish' (a reference to the racist views held by some older members of the population.) Like most music hall songs of the period, this number had a simple, easily remembered chorus to which the audience were encouraged to sing along. Little Minnie picked up the melody quickly and sang along with such volume and enthusiasm that it stopped the Sisters Briggs in their tracks. After the performance, the Sisters came front of stage and told Minnie's mother that her daughter's exceptional singing voice could prove to be her fortune.

Mary Holyome took the Sisters Briggs' advice with a pinch of salt and took her daughter home, no doubt hoping she would forget what had been said. But Minnie didn't forget and pestered her parents to allow her to train as a music hall singer.

The style of singing in music halls was very different to popular singing today. Microphones were unheard of and artistes had to compete with noise from food and drink being served and an often boisterous and drunken audience. In addition, the songs' lyrics were often highly amusing satires on current affairs and so needed to be heard clearly. Consequently, music hall singers had to enunciate their words extremely precisely in order to be heard over the din of the auditorium. In addition to a good, strong voice and excellent diction, music hall singers had to be supremely confident.

Audiences were notoriously demanding and would regularly pelt artistes they didn't approve of with food, crockery or any other missiles they could lay their hands on. Terrified of the indignities their young daughter might suffer at the hands of the crowd, Mr and Mrs Holyome wisely packed Minnie off to J. W. Cherry's Music Hall Academy, Pentonville Road, for three months so she could learn the basics of performance. This act demonstrates how committed the

Holyome's were to their children; music academies were not cheap and at the time, the family had very little money to spare.

Happily, the Holyome's investment in their eldest daughter paid off. Almost as soon as she completed her course at the academy, Minnie secured her first engagement, by coincidence at the same venue as her encounter with the Sisters Briggs. The concert had been staged to raise funds for local tradesmen and Minnie appeared as a male impersonator (a very popular turn at the time), performing three songs written for her by Fred Bullen, the orchestra leader at the Sebright Music Hall. Minnie impressed the proprietor so much that he engaged her for the following week for 18s.

Following her stint at the Bow Music Hall, Minnie (who had temporarily changed her stage name to Marie Chester) practised her act in a number of small halls throughout the United Kingdom. She also went on tour to Europe, appearing in Germany and Holland. On her return to Britain, she changed her stage name to Marie Kendall and continued to secure work as a male impersonator, appearing quite low on the bills. She also often took the role of Principal Boy in pantomime.

As she approached her twentieth birthday, Marie began to despair of her career ever taking off. She had little trouble getting work in the small halls, but was badly paid and those close to her felt her talent was being underused. In October 1892, she met up with her friend Flo Hastings and complained that her career was not going as well as she had initially hoped. Flo listened intently and then suggested that Marie should dispense with the male impersonation act in favour of 'going into skirts' (performing as a woman). In later years, Marie admitted that she didn't like Flo's advice but took it, feeling that she had nothing to lose. It was to be the best move she ever made.

Early in 1893, Marie secured a role in a drama called *After Dark*, which was playing at the Bedford Music Hall in Camden Town. A singer named Charlie Deane was also working at the Bedford, performing his hit song *One of the Boys*, a laddish ditty that the male half of the audience loved. Marie and her mother heard the song and thought it would be wonderful if they could persuade Deane to write a female version. One morning, they bumped into Deane at York Corner and Mary asked him if he would write the song for her daughter. 'She's a decent little turn,' said Deane, 'and if I can help her I'll be happy to do so'. So it was that Charlie Deane wrote *One of the Girls* and Marie Kendall got her first hit.

Over the following year, Marie's fortunes turned around. She secured herself a new agent and was soon earning £2 10s per week and playing to packed audiences at halls up and down the country. It was at one of her many engagements that she met Steve McCarthy.

Marie Kendall and Steve McCarthy were married on 5 February 1895. Due to their Huguenot roots, Minnie's parents were understandably dead against her converting to her husband's Catholic faith, so the couple were wed at St Mary's, Spital Square; a Protestant church. Steve's sister Margaret and a friend named Robert Buxton acted as witnesses. Steve listed his father John as being a general dealer, a reference to their shop at 27 Dorset Street. Marie cheekily stated that her father William was a 'gentleman'.

By the time of their marriage, Marie Kendall was rapidly becoming one of the country's most successful music hall stars, while Steve had to content himself with having his name much further down the bill. At a time when very few married women enjoyed anything remotely resembling an independent career, Marie's success must have been a bitter pill for Steve to swallow. To his credit, Steve did his utmost to further his wife's career, even being responsible for the discovery of what was to become her biggest hit. However, privately he resented her success and the financial independence it afforded her and his resentment often turned to violence. Even on their wedding day, Steve attacked Marie in the back of a Brougham, cutting her forehead open; an incident that was to repeat itself throughout their married life.

Chapter 20

The Landlords Enlarge their Property Portfolios

As Steve and Marie embarked on married life, Jack McCarthy senior had to contend with marked changes in the way he ran his Dorset Street property. In 1894, the police handed control of common lodging houses over to the London County Council. This handover heralded a sea change in the way that this particular business was run. The police had long since regarded common lodging houses as the resorts of criminals rather than homes. Consequently, any inspections concentrated more on the list of inmates than the sanitary conditions therein. This had meant that landlords like Jack McCarthy were under absolutely no pressure to keep up any standard of cleanliness or hygiene.

Once the LCC took over inspections, everything changed. The council officials demanded that all walls in the common lodging houses had to be lime-whited and cleaned every six months 'to remove the evidence of vermin around the beds, etc.' In addition, the makeshift bunk-beds and oilskin mattresses were abolished in favour of proper beds and new, clean bedding. The mixed-sex lodging houses (known colloquially as 'doubles') were also banned since they had long been recognised as being thinly disguised brothels. Most importantly, the new, cleaner lodging houses would be inspected on a regular basis by council officials.

This dramatic change in the way common lodging houses were run had a dramatic effect on the entire business. Many of the smaller lodging house keepers, especially those who rented the properties, simply could not afford to make the changes and gave their businesses up. Others saw a dramatic decline in revenue as their 'doubles' were closed down in favour of single-sex accommodation.

Jack McCarthy gritted his teeth and made the necessary changes, no doubt treating the council inspectors with the utmost reverence whenever they appeared and giving them the two-finger salute on their departure. He even used left-over lime-white to give Miller's Court a facelift. Whether or not he covered up the bloodstains on the wall of Room 13 remains a mystery.

The arrival of the council inspectors in Spitalfields resulted in many of the older lodging houses being abandoned by their previous lessees. Never one to miss an opportunity, Jack McCarthy used the situation to his advantage and started buying up more property. The lease on a massive lodging house on the corner of Thrawl Street and Brick Lane came up for sale in the spring of 1894, which was duly snapped up by McCarthy. This huge old property could hold up to 141 lodgers and so represented a sizeable revenue. Jack McCarthy presented this new acquisition to his brother Daniel and continued his search for more bargains.

For many years, he had coveted the two houses next door to his shop at 27 Dorset Street, which had been run as a lodging house by Alexander McQueen and his wife for over 20 years. The McQueens had been reluctant to relinquish control over the property, but the new legislation (no doubt coupled with further pressure to sell from Jack McCarthy) finally forced them to reach a decision. McCarthy bought the leases of number 28 and 29 Dorset Street in 1884 and by June, had registered the two houses in his name. These two properties were even more ancient than number 27 Dorset Street and had probably been built in the first half of the 18th century. They had mansard roofs and tiled attics, in which a silk weaver's loom had once worked. Back in the 1840s, the ground floor of one of the houses had been used as a shop by one of the first Jewish immigrants to the area.

By 1894, the houses were a shadow of their former selves. At some stage, their gardens had been built over and now two mean cottages stood where once there had been trees, grass and flowerbeds. The ground floor of one of the cottages served as the kitchen for all the lodgers, thus making the tiny court a very busy place at mealtimes. In total, the two houses plus the two cottages at the rear were capable of accommodating 50 lodgers.

McCarthy's Dorset Street neighbour William Crossingham, took advantage of the new council legislation too and bought up more property. By this stage, McCarthy and Crossingham owned or let virtually the whole of Dorset Street and the Courts that ran off it. And despite the recent expense of refitting their lodging houses to meet the new council requirements, both men continued to make a lot of money.

Chapter 21

The Worst Street In London

By the 1890s, Spitalfields was one of London's most crime-ridden areas and Dorset Street was its worst thoroughfare. Charles Booth's researchers described it as the 'worst street in London' and many local people, including tough, well-built men, were scared to go there. Even policemen only ventured into the street in pairs. It appears that Jack McCarthy and William Crossingham did very little to improve the image of the street they virtually owned. This was with good reason.

Dorset Street's near-mythical notoriety meant that the residents could carry out their business relatively undisturbed, and that made the dilapidated properties that lined the street ideal venues for illegal gambling dens, brothels, and the storage of stolen property. The courts served as makeshift rings for bare-knuckle boxing bouts and could be fenced off for illegal dog fights. McCarthy and Crossingham's property empire opened up possibilities for all manner of business activities. The trouble was, few of them were legal.

Despite the remarkable control McCarthy and Crossingham had over Dorset Street, they were becoming increasingly isolated. By

1895, this little street was a gentile ghetto in an area that had become overwhelmingly Jewish. That year, one of the last surviving silk weaving firms left Spitalfields for leafy Braintree in Essex, taking sixty weavers and their families with them. Later in the year, a map of Jewish East London was compiled. What it revealed was startling: three quarters of the area immediately north of Dorset Street was populated by Jews and 95% of the households immediately south were Jewish. In contrast, less than 5% of Dorset Street inhabitants were Jewish.

Most of the Jewish immigrants that now populated Spitalfields were honest, hardworking, law-abiding people who did their level best to maintain peace with their non-Jewish neighbours. However, the sheer numbers of immigrants that flooded into this relatively small area during the latter part of the 19th century meant that some new residents would cause trouble.

The 1890s saw the arrival of the first organised gangs of Eastern European immigrants. Once settled in Spitalfields, these gangs set about organising protection rackets. They generally picked on their fellow immigrants, particularly those who had set up small shops and demanded money in return for 'protection'. Although plenty of Spitalfields residents were involved in many nefarious activities such as prostitution and illegal gambling, there is no evidence to suggest that they ever harassed shopkeepers. Therefore quite who the new gangs were protecting the shop keepers from remains unclear and it must be surmised that the 'service' was purely an attempt at extortion.

The most notorious gang to emerge from the area in the 1890s were the Bessarabians, otherwise known as the 'stop at nothing' gang. The gang was made up of Eastern Europeans and Greeks who, in addition to running protection rackets, forced respectable Jewish families to pay them hush money. If the family refused, the Bessarabians could ruin a family's reputation within the Jewish community by spreading rumours about them.

The Bessarabians also ran prostitution rings and operated illegal gambling establishments. Within a short space of time, their criminal activities had won them quite substantial rewards and more than a modicum of local influence. However, their nemesis was about to materialise in the form of another Eastern European gang called the Odessians.

Over in Brick Lane, there was a restaurant called the Odessa, which was owned by a Jew named Weinstein. One day, the Bessarabians turned up at the restaurant demanding protection money. Weinstein, who was a big man with gangland connections of his own, refused to give in to their demands and attacked the gang with an iron bar, putting several Bessarabians in hospital. Word got around the Brick Lane area about Weinstein's heroism and a group of Russian youths formed the Odessian gang in a bid to put a stop to the Bessarabians' rackets. Before long, the Odessians were inundated with requests from shop and pub owners who were being intimidated. One such man was the owner of the York Minster Music Hall, just off the Commercial Road. The owner told the Odessians that the Bessarabians planned to sabotage that night's performance because he hadn't paid their protection money.

That evening, the Odessians lay in wait for their rivals, who showed up during a Russian dancing act. A vicious fight broke out, the police were called and several members of each gang were arrested. Once in custody, some gang members decided to talk, which resulted in the gang leaders becoming so sought-after by the police that they had to go into hiding. With no leaders available, their 'businesses' disintegrated. However, some of the original gang members managed to escape on ships bound for America, where legend has it, they became instrumental in shaping the now notorious Chicago underworld of the 1930s.

Gang warfare did little to improve the atmosphere of Spitalfields and, as the end of the 19th century approached, Dorset Street and its surrounds reached their lowest point. This once proud, prosperous street had been reduced to a den of iniquity, where prostitutes openly plied their trade, thieves fenced their pickings and violence was an everyday occurrence. The arrival of the Eastern European Jews had made an already bad situation worse as non-Jews created their own ghetto in the mean street and courts that had escaped population by the immigrants. The redevelopment of the once dreadful Flower and Dean Street pushed even more of the dregs of society into this little street. Locals humorously referred to the road as Dossett Street due to the fact that it was comprised almost entirely of doss houses. Soon this small, seemingly insignificant thoroughfare began to attract the attention of the press once again.

Local clergyman and social reformer Canon Barnett, referred to Dorset Street in a letter to *The Times* in 1898. He described the residents as men and women who seemed to 'herd as beasts' and declared the road to be the 'centre of evil.' During the same year, a researcher ventured into Dorset Street on behalf of the social investigator Charles Booth. Accompanied by a policeman, he made his way around the doss houses, courts and alleyways and later described what he found:

'The lowest of all prostitutes are found in Spitalfields, on the benches round the church, or sleeping in the common lodging houses of Dorset Street. Women have often found their way there by degrees from the streets of the West End. He (the policeman accompanying him) spoke of Dorset Street as in his opinion the worst street in respect of poverty, misery, vice – of the whole of London.'

Chapter 22

The Murder of Mary Ann Austin

It appears that by the turn of the century, the police had all but given up attempting to maintain any sort of public order in Dorset Street and had pretty much left the road to police itself. An explanation for their defeatist attitude can be found in the events surrounding the death of a young woman named Mary Ann Austin, an inmate of William Crossingham's lodging house at number 35, in May 1901.

At about 10.30pm on Saturday 25 May, Mary Ann Austin arrived at Crossingham's lodging house with a man purporting to be her husband. Despite the fact that the lodging house was supposed to be reserved for women only, the deputy let the couple a bed after the man produced 1/6d (an exceptionally large amount of money to pay for such accommodation.) The couple were shown to bed number 15 on the third floor of the lodging house and promptly retired for the night. At approximately 8.30am the next morning, a female lodger came rushing into the deputy's office claiming that Mary Ann had been viciously attacked. The deputy's wife (one Maria Moore) went immediately to the third floor to find Mary Ann groaning in agony from several stab wounds. Her erstwhile male companion was nowhere to be seen. Mrs Moore sent for a doctor immediately but instead of also calling the police, she summoned William Crossingham's brother-in-law, Daniel Sullivan, who ran another of Crossingham's lodging houses just round the corner in Whites Row. On arriving at the scene, Sullivan decided against summoning the police and set about destroying any useful evidence before the doctor arrived.

First, he dressed the dying Mary Ann in another lodger's clothes and arranged for her own clothing to be burnt. He then moved her downstairs to a bed on the first floor, presumably so the murder site could be cleaned up. By the time that the doctor arrived, any incriminating evidence had been successfully removed but poor Mary Ann was in a very bad way. The doctor immediately arranged for her to be taken to hospital but it was too late to save her. Mary Ann Austin died of her injuries on Sunday 26 May.

The subsequent inquest into the murder of Mary Ann Austin proved to be frustrating and baffling for both the police and the coroner. The man that took the bed with Austin on the Saturday night was found and identified himself as her husband, William, a stoker by profession of no fixed abode. However it seems more likely that he was simply a casual acquaintance of Mary Ann, who had promised her a bed for the night in return for sexual favours. William was promptly arrested for her murder; a crime he vehemently denied committing. Whether William Austin really did kill Mary Ann is a moot point. However, the subsequent fiasco at the inquest clearly shows the complete lack of respect the inhabitants of Dorset Street had for the authorities.

At the start of the murder inquiry, all witnesses lied about the circumstances surrounding Mary Ann's death including the fact that the body was moved and evidence destroyed. They only changed their story in court when alternative accounts of what happened proved they were lying. Daniel Sullivan's account of events was so inconsistent that the coroner was moved to conclude that he had 'run as close to the wind as you possibly could'. Despite the best efforts of the police to find reliable witnesses, the coroner was forced to conclude that there was no reliable evidence to convict William Austin of the murder and the prisoner was released.

The fatal stabbing of Mary Ann Austin joined the long and ever-growing list of unsolved crimes perpetrated in Dorset Street at the turn of the century. However, the inquest fiasco shows conclusively that by this time, Dorset Street was run exclusively by its inhabitants. The lodging house keepers and their employees took on total responsibility for dealing with any crimes committed within the walls of their establishments and any outside interference was to be avoided at all costs.

Despite the residents' dislike of outside interference, Mary Ann Austin's murder prompted yet more unwelcome attention for Dorset Street from press and well-meaning members of the public alike. Two months after the murder and subsequent cover-up, Dorset Street received its most damning indictment to date when one Fred. A. McKenzie wrote about the street in the *Daily Mail* under the heading 'The Worst Street In London'. Mr McKenzie trod the same path as many 'social investigators' before him, taking an uneducated and frankly snobbish stance against the street's beleaguered residents, laying much of the blame at the feet of the dreaded lodging house keepers and resorting to sensationalism in order to drive his point home. Nonetheless, his article does paint a clear picture of the depths to which Dorset Street had sunk by the turn of the century and illustrates that the social deprivation that had first come to the public's attention during the Ripper murders had most definitely not been addressed. Under the heading 'Blue Blood', Mr McKenzie wrote:

> 'The lodging houses of Dorset Street and of the district around are the head centres of the shifting criminal population of London. Of course, the aristocrats of crime – the forger, the counterfeiter, and the like do not come here. In Dorset Street we find more largely

the common thief, the pickpocket, the area meak, the man who robs with violence, and the unconvicted murderer. The police have a theory, it seems, that it is better to let these people congregate together in one mass where they can be easily found than to scatter them abroad. And Dorset Street certainly serves the purpose of a police trap. If this were all, something might be said in favour of allowing such a place to continue. But it is not all… Here comes the real and greatest harm that Dorset Street does. Respectable people, whose main offence is their poverty, are thrown in close and constant contact with the agents of crime. They become familiarised with law breaking. They see the best points of the criminals around them. If they are in want, as they usually are, it is often enough a thief who shares his spoils with them to give them bread. And there are those who are always ready to instruct newcomers in the simple ways of making a dishonest living. Boy thieves are trained as regularly and systematically around Dorset Street to-day as they were in the days of Oliver Twist.'

While there was undoubtedly some truth in what Fred McKenzie wrote, his overdramatic prose, combined with ludicrous exaggeration (according to him, Dorset Street 'boasts of an attempt at murder on an average once a month, of a murder in every house, and in one house at least, a murder in every room') really got the goat of both the lodging house keepers and their tenants. In response, Dorset Street resident Edwin Locock convened a protest meeting. The initial date for the meeting was set for Wednesday 17 July (the day after the article had appeared) but the room was not large enough to accommodate the sizeable crowd that attended and so it was adjourned until the following Monday. In the meantime, bills were posted throughout

Spitalfields stating that the new meeting would be held at the Duke of Wellington pub in Shepherd Street. The sole speaker at this protest would be none other than Jack McCarthy, described by the local press as 'a gentleman who holds a considerable amount of property in the neighbourhood'.

On the evening of the meeting, a sizeable crowd arrived at the pub including numerous Dorset Street residents, a handful of representatives from local charities and, quite bravely, the writer of the article that had so inflamed the inhabitants – Mr McKenzie. Jack McCarthy's response to the article was both eloquent and lengthy. According to press reports, he spoke for two hours, taking McKenzie's article apart in a manner fit for a courtroom rather than the back room of an East End pub. Suffice to say, McCarthy refuted every indictment made by McKenzie but the picture of Dorset Street painted throughout his long diatribe is probably as inaccurate as the one imagined after reading Fred McKenzie's article.

Even knowing that he was largely preaching to the converted, Jack McCarthy's speech leaves the impartial observer with the impression that Dorset Street was inhabited almost solely by cheeky cockney types who would not look out of place in a production of *Oliver!*, presided over by altruistic landlords only too willing to sacrifice their rental income in order to provide shelter for the needy. One suspects that the truth lay somewhere between these two gentlemen's colourful descriptions.

Despite the best efforts of Jack McCarthy, speeches in local pubs (however impassioned) were no match for the massive publicity machine that was the national press. Dorset Street retained its dubious reputation as 'The Worst Street In London' and the authorities continued to leave the inhabitants to their own devices. However, the notoriety that Dorset Street and its surrounds suffered did add certain kudos to the already shady reputations of the men that ran the streets. In their little patch of London, the Spitalfields landlords enjoyed a huge amount of power and this power afforded them status. Men such as Jack McCarthy, Jimmy Smith and Frederick Gehringer were very well known around the area and due to the amount of control they wielded, they were generally respected by their dependents.

By the turn of the century, the landlords had reached the peak of their success. Unbeknown to them, the property empires they had worked so hard to build up were about to go into a slow but unstoppable decline. However, the first few years of the 20th century were probably the most financially stable that any of the landlords had previously experienced. All owned a sizeable chunk of property by this stage, there was no shortage of tenants and the authorities continued to ignore the squalid conditions that prevailed. Consequently, the landlords earned a lot of money and they quickly developed a taste for showing it off in most eccentric ways. Jimmy Smith had long since established himself as the 'Governor of Brick Lane', particularly in the eyes those who participated in his illegal gambling activities. However, one night Jimmy had too much to drink and fell into a fire, severely burning himself.

The burns were so deep that they destroyed a great deal of muscle on one side of Jimmy's body, leaving him partially paralysed and no doubt in a lot of pain. However, once recovered, Jimmy did not let his disability stop him from going about his daily business. He employed a minder to lead him along as he patrolled his 'manor' and was one of the first people in the East End to own a motor car, in which he was ferried around by a chauffeur in a chocolate-coloured uniform.

Jack McCarthy also enjoyed spending his money on the latest fashions and was described by contemporaries as looking most 'gentlemanly' despite his rough background in the slums of Southwark. He was well regarded by the workers at nearby Spitalfields Market who referred to him as a 'real pal'. The local costermongers also enjoyed a particularly close business relationship with McCarthy, who allowed them to store their barrows in a shed next to 26 Dorset Street thus preventing them from being stolen overnight. In contrast, Arthur Harding, a local lad who wasn't beholden to McCarthy for anything (and was probably envious of his status) dismissed him as a 'hard man' and a 'bully'.

Frederick Gehringer was also well-known to the costermongers as he ran a barrow-hire business from one of his properties in Little Pearl Street. This sideline was to grow into a full-time business in later years as Gehringer progressed from barrows to horses and carts and finally motorised lorries. The Gehringer family was in the haulage business until well into the 20th century. Like Jimmy Smith, Frederick Gehringer enjoyed being flash with his new-found wealth and rumour has it that he enjoyed parading around his properties on a sedan chair.

The landlords' families also benefited from their increasing wealth and began to live a distinctly middle-class existence. Men who had been raised in slums found they could give their own children a vastly superior start in life. In a bid to keep them away from the daily horrors of Dorset Street, Jack McCarthy sent two of his younger daughters (Annie and Ellen) to boarding school in Battle, Sussex. This small school was run by Mrs Fanny Lambourn, the wife of the preceptor tutor at Battle Town Grammar School. Here the girls were taught the 'three R's', learned how to sew and cook and also acquired a command of the French language; a skill that was not in much demand around Dorset Street since the Huguenots had departed.

However, as the new century unfurled, subtle changes in how and where Londoners lived and worked were underway. These changes would have a profound effect on Dorset Street, its surrounds and the way McCarthy and his fellow landlords made their money.

By 1900, better transport links in and out of the capital meant that it was no longer necessary for men and women to live within walking distance of their work. Spitalfields had for decades been a popular residential area not just for the destitute, but also for low paid workers whose employment was found in the City or along the banks of the Thames. As transport links improved, developers began to build new estates of affordable housing in parts of Middlesex, Kent and Surrey that until recently had been impossible to commute from. Suddenly it became possible for workers to move out to the new suburbs such as Charlton, Norwood, Wembley, Finchley, Ilford and still retain their jobs in central London. This sea change in the way people lived and worked would eventually have a devastating effect on the fortunes of the Spitalfields landlords.

While the very poor remained in the area, those who had once relied on their furnished rooms and two-up, two-down cottages were lured away to the suburbs, never to return. This economic change was coupled with the fact that many of the houses the landlords let out were literally falling to pieces. The once middle-class properties had been in a pretty bad state when the landlords had acquired them twenty years previously. Since then, they had been ill-used by the tenants and neglected by their owners – remember that McCarthy didn't even bother to paint over the bloodstained wall in Mary Kelly's room, let alone embark on any serious renovation work.

In addition to the population changes and the dilapidated state of many properties in Spitalfields, traffic around Spitalfields Market was still causing increasing problems. On market days, there were so many carts, vans and barrows around that the streets became impassable. Market customers complained that they couldn't get close enough to the market to pick up their goods, non-market related shops moaned that their customers couldn't get through the mêlée (thus losing custom) and thefts from unattended vehicles were commonplace.

By the 1890s, the newly-formed London County Council could clearly see that widening the streets around the market would solve two problems in one fell swoop. Firstly, wider streets would ease traffic congestion considerably, and, secondly, it would give them the opportunity to get rid of the dreadful courts and alleys that surrounded the market for good. The only problem was that the market did not belong to the council.

Undeterred, the LCC began introducing bills in Parliament that they hoped would give them the power to purchase the freehold on Spitalfields Market. In 1902, their wish was granted and the freehold was bought from the trustees of the Goldsmid family (the current owners). The leaseholder, Robert Horner (who had run the market since the 1870s), proved a more difficult nut to crack. After much negotiating, Horner reluctantly agreed to relinquish control of the market for £600,000 – a massive sum in those days. However, his agreement contained many caveats and for the next ten years, the situation at Spitalfields Market remained the same as the LCC and Robert Horner battled it out.

The landlords and residents of Dorset Street realised that it was only a matter of time before their lives and businesses would be seriously affected by the proposed redevelopment around the market. However, the daily struggle to simply stay alive prevented most of the residents from worrying too much about the fact they may soon be made homeless. Jack McCarthy and William Crossingham didn't lose too much sleep over the proposed expansion either. By the beginning of the new century, they were reaching retirement age and their thoughts were inevitably turning to more leisurely activities than the hard and sometimes violent profession of slum landlord. In addition to this, running common lodging houses was getting to be an increasingly frustrating business.

By 1903, all lodging-house keepers were required to register their properties every year (previously one, initial registration had been sufficient). In addition, each lodging house had to be equipped with certain facilities. For example, a lodging house accommodating between 60 and 100 people had to provide one water closet for every 20 people and all lodgers had to be provided with towels. Previously, landlords had got away with one or two water closets for the entire house so the provision of extra toilets meant that space had to be converted for the purpose.

The provision of towels also proved a headache. Most of the lodgers were not too interested in personal cleanliness and many were infested with lice and other creepy crawlies. In 1908, the council had to pay for 32 women lodgers from the Salvation Army Women's Shelter in Hanbury Street to be washed at the Poplar Cleansing Station. Consequently, the towels they were given quickly became infested and the lodging house keepers were faced with the old problem that laundries refused to take them. Washing usually fell to some of the local women who, in the absence of appropriate washing facilities, usually made the towels dirtier than they had been before they were washed.

The new laws also made it illegal for lodging houses to be unattended between the hours of 9pm and 6am. This may have proved problematic for the more rural establishments, but the nature of the Spitalfields residents had long since made it necessary for a deputy to be on-site constantly while the house was in use.

The new laws attached to common lodging houses prompted the writer Jack London to investigate them while researching his book *The People of the Abyss*. Instead of asking local policemen about conditions and touring the area with an armed escort, London decided to experience the lodging houses from the inside. His comments following his research prove that he learnt far more about the problems associated with the lodging houses than any councillor could ever hope to. At the time of Jack London's research, there were 38,000 registered common lodging houses in London. London noted: 'There are many kinds of doss-houses, but in one thing they are all alike, from the filthy little ones to the monster big ones paying 5% [to investors] and blatantly lauded by smug middle class men who know nothing about them, and that one thing is the uninhabitableness.'

Jack London went on to describe one of the lodging houses he stayed in, in Middlesex Street, Whitechapel:

> 'The entrance was by way of a flight of steps
> descending from the sidewalk to what was properly the
> cellar of the building. Here were two large and
> gloomily lit rooms, in which men cooked and ate. I had
> intended to do some cooking myself, but the smell of
> the place stole away my appetite... A feeling of gloom
> pervaded the ill-lighted place.'

London beat a hasty retreat from the kitchen and decided to go and pay for his bed. After surrendering his money, he was issued with a 'huge, brass check'; his ticket, which had to be surrendered to the doorman upstairs before venturing to the sleeping quarters.

Once upstairs, he gave a brilliantly observed description of what a typical lodging house bedroom looked like at the turn of the century: 'To get an adequate idea of a floor filled with cabins, you have to merely magnify a layer of the paste-board pigeon-holes of an egg crate till each hole is seven feet in height and otherwise properly dimensioned, then place the magnified layer on the floor of a bar-like room, and there you have it. There are no ceilings to the pigeon-holes, the walls are thin and the snores from all the sleepers and every move and turn from your nearer neighbours come plainly to your ears.'

By the beginning of the 20th century, changes to lodging house regulations showed that the powers that be were at least making some effort to improve the lot of the very poor. However, many of the streets in which the lodging houses stood had gained such a nefarious reputation over the years that mere mention of their name caused a sharp intake of breath. In a rather desperate bid to rid the worst streets of their appalling reputation, a council official suggested that a name change might help and so it was that, in 1905, Dorset Street changed overnight into Duval Street. No explanation exists as to why the name Duval was chosen, although it may have been selected to evoke memories of the long departed Huguenot silk weavers that populated the street during happier times. Not surprisingly, the name change did little to improve the general ambience of the street.

In addition to the more stringent lodging house regulations and Dorset Street's name change, the council also attempted to improve the surrounding area. For decades, the churchyard of Christ Church (which was opposite Duval Street, across busy Commercial Street), had been the unofficial meeting place for numerous local drunks and prostitutes. At some point in the past, benches had been placed along the pathways, the intention being that the churchyard could be used as a place of quiet reflection. By the turn of the century, Christ Church churchyard was anything but. Violent rows broke out among the gravestones. Monuments were used as makeshift privies. The benches were used as al fresco beds and those that reclined on them were so filthy and verminous that the churchyard was known locally as 'Itchy Park' – a reference to the constant scratching undertaken by its users.

The problems associated with Itchy Park were raised at a London County Council meeting in July 1904. A few months previously, a children's playground had been laid out to the rear of the churchyard. However, parents had complained that in order to gain access to the play area, they and their children had to run the gauntlet of drunks and prostitutes that lined the pathway. The rector of Christ Church (one Reverend W H Davies) was consulted and his representative at the council meeting reported that 'young girls openly ply their prostitution in the churchyard and fights between women are frequent. The people who monopolise this garden are not ordinary poor people, but of the class who habitually refuse every opportunity of improving their circumstances. The result is that the garden which might be of so much use in this densely crowded neighbourhood is a veritable plague spot.'

In its wisdom, the council decided that Itchy Park should henceforth be only accessible to children under 14 years old (and their guardians) during the summer months and that anyone designated to patrol the park should wear a uniform. It is not recorded whether or not this ruling was successful in the short term. However, it should be noted that decades later, musician Steve Marriott wrote about Christ Church churchyard in the Small Faces classic song *Itchycoo Park*. Even if the council managed to rid the park of its verminous visitors, it seems that it failed to erase its nickname.

While the LCC tried its best to begin erasing all traces of the Duval Street area's seedy reputation, subtle changes in the way the street was run were also taking place. On 28 February 1907, landlord William Crossingham, who owned a considerable amount of property in Duval Street and the neighbouring Whites Row and Little Paternoster Row, died of kidney disease at his home in Romford. All property was passed to his wife, Margaret but tragedy struck a second time, when just four months later, she succumbed to breast cancer. The Crossinghams' deaths resulted in all their property being taken over by a builder named William Hunnable. Hunnable continued to run the properties as lodging houses, but Jack McCarthy had lost his long-term neighbour and closest ally.

Chapter 23

The Beginning of the End

William Crossingham's death marked the beginning of the end for Duval Street. Increased regulations and regular inspections from the LCC meant that lodging houses were no longer cheap to run and any lodgers that were halfway decent had deserted the area for the suburbs. The only tenants left were those who lived on the very margins of society. Circa 1908, H. A. Jury described the frequenters of women's lodging houses for a council meeting:

'A good proportion are prostitutes, but others are street-vendors and perhaps charwomen, but they all have some vice, even if it is no worse than laziness. It is clear they do not like work. Many pay others to wash their clothes for them and cook their food.'

This aversion to work caused many problems for the landlords as the number of lodgers with the means to pay for a regular bed got smaller and smaller. The area became utterly destitute. Any visitor to the area would never have believed that Duval Street was once the lively centre of a thriving weaving industry. Women lolled around outside the doors of their lodgings, men drank from morning till night and children ran around the streets in little more than rags. The area looked more like the Third World than part of one of the planet's wealthiest cities. Young men continued to prowl the area in gangs and violence between rival groups remained commonplace. However, by the beginning of the twentieth century, gang warfare took on a deadlier twist as guns became more freely available if you knew where to look.

Local gang member Arthur Harding remembered being involved in a confrontation in Duval Street circa 1907. An associate named George King had been arguing with Duval Street resident Billy Maguire and asked for Arthur's help: 'He [King] took me down Dossett [Duval] Street because he wanted to do a fellow named Billy Maguire… I fired at him but Kingie got the blame of it, not me.' Guns were rapidly replacing knives as the gang members' weapons of choice and Duval Street would echo with gunfire intermittently until its final demise.

The criminal fraternity that populated the lodging houses and furnished rooms of Spitalfields was also changing as the new century began. Jewish families that had fled to Spitalfields from Eastern Europe during the closing decades of the nineteenth century had now firmly settled themselves in the area. However, in a bid to escape the grinding poverty endured by their parents, some of the children of Jewish immigrant families resorted to exploiting their neighbours.

Crime throughout the city was gradually becoming more organised and the way was slowly being laid for the likes of the Kray and Nash families to follow. Like many young men before them, Jewish lads from Spitalfields soon found that good money could be made from illegal gambling, extortion and prostitution. Jews that made a living from running prostitution rings were referred to as 'shundicknicks'. Probably the most fascinating and well known shundicknick of the era was one Isaac Bogard, known colloquially as 'Darky the Coon' on account of his curly hair and dark complexion.

Bogard was born in Mile End Old Town in the early 1890s to Russian parents. Contemporary reports suggest that he possessed a quick brain and a courageous nature and no doubt would have excelled in legitimate business, had he been given the opportunity. However, like so many poor East Enders before him, he found criminal activities were much more widely available. By the time he was in his late teens, Bogard was known for inflicting violent assaults on those who wronged him and was described by rivals as vicious. However, despite his obvious flaws, Bogard was also one of the most flamboyant characters of his era. Long before Westerns were popular, he styled himself as a Cockney urban cowboy and patrolled the streets dressed in a shirt open to the waist and a wide-brimmed hat, with a gun stuck down his belt. Contemporaries even claimed that he cultivated an American accent.

It wasn't just Bogard's apparel that was eccentric. News reports of his exploits also reveal unconventional behaviour. In 1914, the *East London Observer* reported that after violently attacking a man with a hammer, Bogard bent down and kissed him before running off. A later article tells of how he attempted to ward off police who were trying to arrest him by climbing onto the roof of a nearby outhouse and pelting them with tiles. There is no doubt that Isaac Bogard was unruly and involved in various criminal activities. However, his fearlessness was invaluable during World War 1, where he was allegedly awarded a medal for outstanding bravery.

Chapter 24

Kitty Ronan

Criminals like Isaac Bogard tended to stick with their own and generally pestered only Jewish stallholders and shopkeepers for protection money. Behavioural studies also suggest that the brothels they ran were primarily aimed at Jewish men. Therefore, the landlords of the other lodging houses were largely unaffected by the rise of the Jewish underworld. The world of Duval Street continued as normal, in more ways than one.

One day a young woman marched into McCarthy's shop and asked if he had any rooms to let. As it happened, the upper room of number 12 Miller's Court was available and so the woman paid her deposit and moved her meagre amount of belongings in. Little did McCarthy know that this woman would be at the centre of the most strange and terrible coincidence within a matter of weeks.

Kitty Ronan was a young woman of Irish descent and the daughter of Andrew Ronan of Antill Street in Fulham. Like most girls of her station in life, Kitty received virtually no education and by the age of 14, went into service. However, this mundane way of life proved not to suit Kitty and by her early 20s she had found her way to the East

End where she tried her hand at a number of jobs including flower selling and clothes laundering. When Kitty was unable to earn enough money to pay the rent, she took to prostitution.

By the time Kitty Ronan appeared on McCarthy's doorstep, she had taken up with a man named Henry Benstead, a news vendor who sold his papers on the main thoroughfares of Spitalfields. She and Henry moved their meagre possessions into the top floor of one of the now crumbling cottages in Miller's Court and tried to enjoy their new life together as much as was possible in such dreadful conditions. However, money was always short and soon Henry's paltry earnings from selling newspapers was not enough to cover the rent. In desperation, Kitty took to the streets.

In the early morning of 2 July 1909, Henry Benstead left his drinking partner at Spitalfields Church and walked across the road into Duval Street and then turned into the narrow alley that led to Miller's Court. On arriving at the front door of number 12, he noticed it was ajar and as he reached the top of the rickety staircase, he realised that the door to his shabby room was also open. Henry pushed the door and stepped inside the room. Due to the absence of any artificial light in the court, it was pitch black. He quickly lit a lamp and noticed that Kitty was lying on the bed, fully clothed. He greeted her but received no response. It was then that he noticed a thick swathe of blood around Kitty's neck that had flowed down into the bed linen.

Henry Benstead shot out of the room, through the court and into Jack McCarthy's shop screaming 'someone has cut Kitty's throat!' In a scene almost identical to that 21 years previously, Jack McCarthy calmly sent for the police, no doubt cursing the fact that this latest murder would attract unwanted attention to his business affairs yet again.

Henry Benstead's histrionics had woken a good few people in Miller's Court and morbid curiosity got the better of many, who climbed the stairs of number 12 to get a look at the body before McCarthy could stop them. Once inside, they found a small penknife, the blade of which was quite blunt, lying on the floor soaked in blood. John Callaghan, a stableman living at Mary Kelly's old address, picked it up to save for the police.

Early in the morning of 2 July, an ambulance arrived to take away Kitty's body. As they had after Kelly's murder, the police interviewed everyone in and around the court. As usual, no one had seen or heard anything untoward. However, two witnesses did come forward and told police that they had seen Kitty go into her room at about midnight with a stranger. About twenty minutes later, the stranger came out of the cottage and, after looking about him in a rather furtive manner, walked out of the court in the direction of Commercial Street.

Despite having a couple of vague descriptions of a suspect and a possible murder weapon, the police's enquiries quickly went cold and many officers assumed that this, like the murder of Mary Kelly in 1888, would go unsolved. However, 16 days later, events took an unusual turn.

On 18 July, a man calling himself Harold Hall walked into a police station in Bristol claiming to be the killer of Kitty Ronan. Naturally suspicious, the police asked him why he should want to do such a thing and Hall told them the following story. On the evening of 1 July, he had gone to the Shoreditch Empire for an evening's entertainment. After the performance finished, he came out of the theatre and began to walk down Commercial Street, where he met Ronan plying her trade. She suggested they go back to her room and Hall agreed. Once inside, Kitty asked Hall to light a candle and, while his back was turned, busied herself with rifling through his pockets.

As Hall turned with the lit candle, he caught Kitty with her hand in his jacket pocket and immediately grew incensed as not long before he had been robbed of £30 whilst in a similar situation. According to Hall's story, he grabbed his pocket knife and plunged it into Kitty's neck, killing her almost instantly. Realising what he had done, he fled the cottage leaving the bloodstained murder weapon lying on the floor beside the bed. That night, he walked to Limehouse where he got a bed at the Sailor's Rest lodging house under the name of Johnson.

The police felt that Hall knew an awful lot of details about the story and decided it was worth remanding him in custody and sending him to London. Once back in the capital, Hall was put into an identity parade and one of the witnesses picked him out as the man he saw with Kitty on the night of the murder. Hall was charged with murder and imprisoned pending the trial.

The police were no doubt relieved to have seemingly solved this dreadful murder but by the time of the trial, they had grave doubts as to whether they had the right man. Under cross-examination by the defence counsel, the witness who had picked Hall out in the identity parade admitted that he had been suffering from a severe hangover at the time and was now unsure that Hall was the man he had seen with Kitty. Another witness was called who claimed that the penknife allegedly used in the murder was exactly the same as one that he and Hall had found whilst working in a paper sorting warehouse. The man claimed the blade was distinctly damaged and this was how he could identify it without doubt. The only problem with this testimony was that it was never conclusively established that the penknife was indeed the murder weapon.

Despite very flimsy evidence, Hall was found guilty. The judge sentenced him to death but the sentence was never carried out and it is unknown what eventually became of Harold Hall. Miller's Court was once again the venue for a murder for which the motive and the perpetrator would be unclear. At the trial it was discovered that Harold Hall was a lonely drifter without friends or close family who had been deserted by his parents at an early age. Did he really kill Kitty Ronan or was he a troubled, lonely man desperate to gain acknowledgement through notoriety?

Despite Duval Street's terrible reputation, the fact that the crumbling properties stood on land in such close proximity to the City meant that they were still worth a considerable amount of money to their owners. In 1910, the Government decided to assess the capital appreciation of real estate by individually surveying every property in every street in every town. This mammoth undertaking was known as 'Lloyd George's Domesday' and never got completely finished. However, the vast majority of London was surveyed and Duval Street was no exception. By this time, Jack McCarthy owned or leased huge tracts of the road including numbers 2, 3, 4, 8 on one side and numbers 26, 27 (including Miller's Court,) 28, 29, 30, 31 and 31a on the other. In total, these properties were valued at £6,170 – a very substantial sum of money despite the fact that most of them were falling to pieces. It transpired that the Valuation Survey was timely. In 1914, the City of London (Various Powers) Act was passed which granted the Corporation of London the power to finally widen the streets around Spitalfields Market that had been causing problems for so many years.

The freeholders and leaseholders of properties in Duval Street were all contacted to ascertain whether or not they were in favour of the proposed extension even though there was a good chance that their property would be subject to a compulsory purchase. Jack McCarthy voted in favour of the extension. This might on the surface sound surprising because of his long-standing business interests in the area, not to mention that fact that Duval Street had been his home for nearly 40 years and the place in which he had raised his children. But Jack McCarthy was not a stupid man. He realised that trade was in decline and that the market expansion would go ahead despite any reservations he may have had. His decision to support the expansion was finally cemented when, on 18 February 1914, his wife Elizabeth succumbed to bronchitis and died at home in the upstairs rooms of 27 Duval Street.

Elizabeth's death marked the end of an era for Jack McCarthy. His children were grown up and able to look after themselves and his old friend and colleague William Crossingham was dead. He was also getting old himself and in his mid-60s, no longer had the energy to assert the constant control one had to wield over the unruly ruffians and gangs that proliferated the area. It was time to retire and Duval Street was about to lose its most influential resident.

Jack McCarthy's retirement from the day-to-day running of his businesses was swiftly followed by an event that would have a much greater effect on Duval Street than any number of gangs or town planners could ever hope to achieve. On 4 August 1914, the Prime

Minister announced that German troops had invaded Belgium. A bloody and devastating world war was about to begin that would change the face of Duval Street, Spitalfields, London and all the towns beyond forever.

Chapter 25

World War 1

Following the declaration of war, it soon became clear to the Government that more men were needed to fight. In August 1914, the British Army comprised approximately 250,000 regular troops. In contrast, the German Army had 700,000 soldiers and was considered the most efficient war machine in the world.

On 7 August, the War Minister, Lord Kitchener, began a massive recruitment campaign where he tried to persuade male civilians between the ages of 19 and 30 to join up. Keen to defend their country from the fearsome Hun and ignorant of the horrors that war could inflict, many young men complied with Kitchener's request and by mid-August, an average of 33,000 men were joining the army every day. This initial flurry of enthusiasm was encouraged further when, at the end of August, the age limit was raised to 35 and by mid-September, half a million men had volunteered.

The casual labourers and market workers that resided in Duval Street and its surrounds were extremely keen to sign up as it offered them an opportunity to do something far more constructive with their lives than their current employment could ever offer them. However, at first many were thwarted in their attempts to join the army, which had certain regulations regarding who could enlist. All new recruits had to be at least 5'6" tall with a chest measurement no less than 35 inches. Many of the poor Spitalfields dwellers had been raised on a very bad diet and consequently were undernourished and small in stature. However, they received a second chance when, in 1915, volunteers began to reduce so the army relaxed its regulations to allow men over 5'3" to sign up.

The age limit was also raised to 40 and by July 1915, the army decided to create what were colloquially known as 'Bantam Battalions', which consisted of men measuring between 5' and 5'3" in height. Many men from Spitalfields and the surrounding areas joined battalions of the City of London Royal Fusiliers. Local boy Arthur Harding later remembered seeing inebriated new recruits gathering at Columbia Road Market before marching off to Waterloo Station bound for training camps in Aldershot. Many of these men were destined never to return.

Although Spitalfields became caught up in the fervent patriotism that was universally prevalent during 1914 and the early months of 1915, there were many men who did not rush to join the queue at the recruitment office. These men had many reasons for not joining their friends and colleagues. Some were fearful of fighting, others objected to war in principle. Most thought it irresponsible to leave their families as they were often the sole wage-earner whose job it was to care not only for their young families, but also for elderly and sick parents. This reluctance by a large proportion of eligible men to join up was country-wide and so the Government hatched an elaborate plan to change these men's views.

The War Propaganda Bureau was set up and amongst other tasks, was assigned the job of persuading more civilian men to join the army. The Propaganda Bureau responded with a highly sophisticated PR campaign that centred on the promotion of fervent patriotism combined with dissemination of terrible stories citing the horrific barbarism of the German army. Popular writers of the time were invited to produce pamphlets that were distributed around the streets. This resulted in the production of persuasive tracts from eminent authors such as Rudyard Kipling, Sir Arthur Conan Doyle and Arnold Bennett. A highly effective poster campaign was also launched and large businesses were encouraged to set up their own recruitment drives. The *Manchester Guardian* newspaper for example offered the following privileges to employees who decided to sign up:

> Four weeks' wages from date of leaving.
> Re-engagement on discharge from service guaranteed.
> Half pay during absence on duty for married men from the date when full pay ceases, to be paid to the wife.
> Special arrangements for single men who have relatives entirely dependent on them.

Most of the recruitment drives organised by the Propaganda Bureau were successful but some of their schemes were heavily criticised. One such scheme was the creation of the Order of the White Feather. This organisation was set up in August 1914 by Admiral Charles Fitzgerald who believed that he could shame men into signing up. Young, attractive girls were encouraged to patrol the streets and hand out white feathers (signifying cowardice) to any man who looked the right age to fight. The main problem with the concept of the Order of the White Feather was that the young girls had no idea of their victims' backgrounds. Many men that were given white feathers had previously failed the army physical. Many others had resisted joining because of personal tragedy, for example the death of a wife or child. The delivery of the white feather simply added to their misery by making them feel guilty.

Of course, these recruitment drives and PR campaigns cost money and with a hugely increased number of new soldiers to pay, the Government coffers soon began to look decidedly depleted. In a bid to significantly increase their funds, the Treasury introduced the War Loan scheme, a savings plan designed to prop up the economy for the duration of the war. Local businesses, unions, friendly societies, clubs and even private individuals were encouraged to invest money in the scheme. Following a national appeal, the Costermongers' and Street Sellers' Union, whose headquarters were in Spitalfields, generously invested virtually all its funds – £800 – in the fund. However, not all Spitalfields workers were quite as keen to help the war effort. Some time later, Joseph Goldberg, Joseph Coen and Abraham Applebrook were summoned before a judge accused of selling potatoes at a rate above the fixed price. It is not clear whether the three men were members of the union.

The army recruitment drives also had their detractors. In August 1917, Myer Gritzhandler Smerna, a 27-year-old warehouseman from Spitalfields, was arrested with two associates for using 'insulting words and behaviour'. *The Times* reported that, 'The evidence of two constables was that the men formed part of a crowd of 150 outside the Aliens' Registration Office in Commercial Street at 10 o'clock on Tuesday night.' Mr Smerna's friend cried '**** the army, I am not going to join' and Smerna concurred loudly and enthusiastically. The crowd didn't take too kindly to the men's outburst and in the words of *The Times* reporter, 'became very hostile towards the prisoners. The Police had considerable trouble getting them to the station.' Smerna and his associate were subsequently bound over to keep the peace, the judge sagely noting that they could have found themselves in a very dangerous situation had the police not intervened.

Following the massive recruitment drives of 1914 and 1915, London's demographic changed considerably. A vast number of men aged between 19 and 40 vanished from the streets. In some areas, the entire male population vanished. Consequently, businesses that relied on these men suffered considerably and none more so than the common lodging houses.

The average age of a male common lodging house resident in Spitalfields before 1915 had been 35. By 1916, the lodging houses had been emptied of virtually all their labouring clientele and were left with older men and women. The landlords tightened their belts and hoped that the war would soon be over.

In Spitalfields, the landlords were not the only people to be affected by the sudden disappearance of the younger men. The prostitutes also found their trade was severely affected. They had no choice but to lower their prices and find trade where they could. Now with much more time on their hands, they sat and drowned their sorrows in the pubs alongside the lodging-house deputies, the old men and the wives and girlfriends of men away at the front.

As pubs increasingly became a place of refuge for those affected by the sudden disappearance of all the younger men, the Government became concerned at the level of alcohol consumed by the remaining proletariat. Work at munitions factories (which were essential to the war effort) was being constantly disrupted as the beleaguered workers turned up either drunk or severely hung over.

The amount of alcohol consumed by women was of particular concern: A survey of four London pubs revealed that in one hour on a Saturday night, alcohol was consumed by 1,483 men and 1,946 women. Keen to resolve this growing problem, the Government announced in October 1915 several measures they believed would reduce alcohol consumption: A 'No Treating' Order meant that pub visitors could only buy drinks for themselves. Taxes on alcohol were raised significantly and pub opening times were reduced to 12pm – 2.30pm then 6.30pm – 9.30pm. Previously, pubs had been allowed to open from 5am until 12.30am.

These new measures had a huge effect. In 1914, Britain consumed 89 million gallons of alcohol. By 1918, this figure had fallen to 37 million. The number of people arrested for being drunk and disorderly also decreased dramatically. While this was good news for the Government and the local police force, it spelt more bad news for the lodging-house landlords, many of whom (such as Gehringer and Cooney) owned pubs and relied on drunkenness and alcoholism to fill their beds each night.

Although Londoners' drinking habits were forcibly changed during World War 1, the food they ate remained much the same despite the German navy's attempts to starve Britain into submission. By 1916, German U-Boats were patrolling the seas and destroying about 300,000 tons of shipping per month. In response, Britain became much more self-sufficient and for a while this worked very well indeed although potatoes, sugar and meat proved hard to obtain. This was the one piece of good news for men such as Jack McCarthy who subsidised their losses in the lodging houses by hiking up the prices of the food and household essentials they sold in their shops. They also made a point of being publicly pessimistic about how long Britain could cope with having so much imported food destroyed by the Germans, thus creating panic buying.

Panic buying was not just a feature of London's poorer streets. By the end of 1917, most civilians were genuinely fearful that Britain would soon run out of food. Their panic buying created a food shortage in itself and so in January 1918, the Ministry of Food introduced rationing on sugar and meat.

By this stage, many of the poorer families who had relied on their young husbands and brothers for an income were becoming desperate. As thousands of men died in bloody battles fought across French fields, thousands of families back in Britain lost their only source of income for good. Others received their once healthy menfolk back home having been discharged through injuries, some of which were horrific. For poor families, this was worse than receiving the dreaded telegram that informed them of a death as they now had to care for another person, who was often severely disabled.

Many thousands of Londoners suffered terrible injuries from bullets and shells during their time at the front. However a significant number of servicemen also endured the effects of a deadly new weapon that came in the form of gas. One man who witnessed the horrors of a gas attack was Jack McCarthy's only son, who had been doing his bit for the war effort by entertaining the troops in France.

In April 1915, the German army stationed at Ypres began firing chlorine gas cylinders at French troops. At first the soldiers noticed yellowy-green clouds of smoke coming across the battlefield. Next they noticed a curious smell that seemed reminiscent of pineapples mixed with pepper. Seconds later, they experienced severe chest pains and a burning sensation in their throats. Once the gas had invaded their respiratory systems, it quickly attacked their lungs and the men slowly asphyxiated. Chlorine gas was used numerous times by the German Army and despite frantic efforts to save the victims, doctors could not find any successful treatment. By the end of the war, nearly 2,000 British soldiers had died from the effects of chlorine gas and over 160,000 had been injured by it.

Following the 'success' of chlorine gas attacks, the German Army looked for an even deadlier gas to unleash on the Allies. They found it in mustard gas and in September 1917, they launched their first attack with this devastating weapon. Mustard gas was the most lethal chemical weapon used in World War 1. It was very difficult to detect as it had no odour and took 12 hours to take effect. However, it was devastating for those who breathed it in. Soldiers exposed to mustard gas experienced blistering skin and very sore eyes. Soon after, they were violently sick. As the effects of the gas took hold, they experienced internal and external bleeding followed by the slow stripping of the mucus membrane from the bronchial tubes. Death could take up to five weeks and the soldier's decline was slow and utterly agonising. Many had to be strapped to their beds to stop them thrashing about and their horrific death throes proved highly distressing for the medical staff caring for them, many of whom were young girls.

As the war raged on, those left in Britain began to despair of ever seeing an end to the conflict. London had been surrounded by a ring of barrage balloons in mid-1918, which effectively halted any aerial assaults from German Gothas because it was very difficult to fly the planes over the top. However, the people were becoming increasingly dispirited. Hardly any families escaped the despair of receiving a telegram telling them that a loved one had been killed. Many others were trying to cope with caring for their husbands and sons crippled from war and unable to work. Life had been tough before 1914. The outbreak of war had made it almost unbearable. As usual, those who suffered the most were the very poor. They tried to remain upbeat for their boys still at the front, but for many it was difficult, especially when they received word from the soldiers who themselves were becoming very dispirited. Charles Young, who served in France, told an interviewer in 1984:

'One day I was in the trench and we'd been under attack for days. Well, two blokes with me shot themselves on purpose to try and get sent home and out of the war. One said to me "Chas, I am going home to my wife and kids. I'll be some use to them as a cripple, but none at all dead! I am starving here and they are at home, so we may as well starve together." With that, he fired a shot through his boot. When the medics got his boot off, two of his toes and a lot of his foot had gone. But injuring oneself to get out of it was quite common'.

While self-inflicted injuries were not unusual, some men took an even greater risk – that of desertion. Deserting the Army during World War 1 was dangerous to the point of being foolhardy. Firstly, most men were in a foreign land where they did not speak the language, know the geography or understand the culture. Secondly, they not only had to escape from their army, but also from the enemy. Finally, if they got caught, they would most likely be court-martialled and shot. Despite these risks, some men did run away and a few actually managed to get away for good, although the fact that they had left their mates in the trenches must have severely played on their conscience for many years afterwards. In total, 304 British soldiers were caught and, after a court martial, were executed by firing squad.

Henry Morris, a bookmaker's clerk from Spitalfields, had a lucky escape from the death penalty. At some time during the course of the war, Morris had deserted and found his way back to London where he probably would never have been discovered had it not been for his failure to resist his criminal tendencies. Late in 1918, Morris attempted to steal a pocket book from Walter Stacey while riding on an omnibus down Kingsway in Holborn. Unfortunately for him, he was caught red-handed and promptly arrested. Had Morris been arrested one year previously, it is highly likely he would have faced the firing squad. However he was extraordinarily lucky and despite being found guilty, was only sentenced to three months' hard labour.

Desertion was not the only offence punishable by death. As the war became more hellish, officers became less tolerant of their subordinates. Seventeen men were shot for cowardice, four for disobedience and two were executed for falling asleep at their posts. Some men escaped the death penalty only to suffer Field Punishment Number One, a terrifying ordeal whereby the offender was tied to a post or tree for up to two hours a day, sometimes for months on end. Often, the post to which they were tied was within range of enemy fire.

Horror stories from the battlefield made their way back to Britain and by the early months of 1918, soldiers and civilians alike were desperate to find an end to the conflict. Little did they know that a new horror was on the horizon that would do more damage to civilians than the Germans and their allies could ever have hoped to achieve.

In spring 1918, large numbers of soldiers serving in France started to suffer from headaches, sore throats and high fever. This virus was extremely infectious but only lasted about three days. Doctors decided the soldiers had flu and the illness became known throughout the trenches in France as Spanish Flu (although it probably originated in the US).

For a few months, this new strain of influenza did not make much of an impact on the battlefield. However, as summer approached, the symptoms suddenly got a lot worse and victims began to develop pneumonia, septicaemia and heliotrope cyanosis; a condition where the face turns blue. Nearly all the men that developed heliotrope cyanosis died within a few days.

Of course, soldiers carrying the influenza bug returned to Britain and in May 1918, the virus appeared in Glasgow. It soon spread south and in the next few months, it killed more people than the cholera epidemic of 1849. The poorer areas of the country were particularly affected by the flu epidemic and Spitalfields was no exception. Panic spread among an already exhausted population as the Government took preventative measures in an attempt to halt the virus. Streets were sprayed with chemicals designed to kill the bug and people began wearing masks outside. Some factories waived their no-smoking rules as they thought that tobacco smoke might kill the virus. The newspapers offered bizarre advice on how to avoid catching it. On 3 November 1918, the *News of the World* told its readers: 'Wash inside nose with soap and water each night and morning; force yourself to sneeze night and morning, then breathe deeply; do not wear a muffler; take sharp walks regularly and walk home from work; eat plenty of porridge.'

Unsurprisingly, the newspaper's advice had no effect on the spread of the disease and 228,000 people throughout the UK died.

As Britain was in the grip of the flu epidemic, some hopeful news arrived via Woodrow Wilson, the President of the United States. On 4 October, the German government appealed to Wilson for a ceasefire. In response, Wilson produced the 'Fourteen Points Peace Plan', which set out the conditions under which the Allies would accept a surrender from the Central Powers (namely Germany, Austro-Hungary, Bulgaria and Turkey). An agreement was finally reached on 11 November 1918 and all territories occupied by the Central Powers were abandoned.

News of the war's end was received in London with huge relief. Crowds danced in the streets and families eagerly awaited the return of their boys. However, the servicemen would return to a very different place to the one they had left. London had changed forever. In some streets, one whole generation of men had been wiped out by war. In others, soldiers returned to find their wives and children dead from the flu epidemic. Many ex-soldiers found that although they had left the battlefield, the battlefield refused to leave them. They suffered from anxiety attacks, mood swings and nightmares. In total, 908,371 British soldiers were killed or injured during World War 1. Far more bore psychological scars that would haunt them for the rest of their lives.

Chapter 26

The Redevelopment of Spitalfields Market

Back in Spitalfields, the residents and landlords of Duval Street had known their days were numbered ever since the LCC saw the benefits of widening the roads around Spitalfields Market. World War 1 brought a temporary halt to any development works but it didn't stop council inspectors from slapping condemned notices on the derelict cottages in Miller's Court in 1914. As the war progressed, these notices became largely ignored as no one from the council was around to enforce them. However, as Britain began to recover after the end of the war in 1918, the redevelopment of the market streets resumed.

Just before Christmas 1921, notices concerning the redevelopment of Spitalfields Market were sent to all owners, lessees and occupiers of properties in Duval Street. As part of the redevelopment programme, the Corporation of London proposed that Duval Street be widened so lorries and carts could have better access. In order to do this, the whole of the north side of the street (including Miller's Court) would be demolished and Little

Paternoster Row (a narrow alley leading to Brushfield Street) would, in the words of the Corporation, be 'stopped up'. Time passed by as the Corporation of London and the LCC discussed how best to approach the proposed redevelopment. As meeting after meeting was arranged, the common lodging houses and furnished rooms in Duval Street continued to attract the same class of people they always had. This did not escape the notice of the council officials who were keen not to make the same mistakes as their predecessors. They wanted to change the identity of the area surrounding Spitalfields Market for good, not just move the undesirable residents across the road to the south side.

Finally, after much deliberation, the Corporation of London began work on a western extension of the market in 1926. For Jack McCarthy, the writing was on the wall and it was only a matter of time before he would have to vacate the mean, vicious little street in which he had made his fortune, brought up his family and become a truly powerful influence. Despite its dreadful reputation, Duval Street was Jack McCarthy's home and it held as many good memories as bad. In addition to this, McCarthy was now an old man and it was with a heavy heart that, in 1927, he locked the doors of his properties, loaded his belongings into a van and headed for a new home near his son in Clapham, South London.

Since his encounter with mustard gas, Steve McCarthy had experienced chronic problems with his health. His marriage to Marie Kendall had been destroyed through a combination of Steve's liking for members of the fairer sex and several violent assaults on his wife; on more than one occasion, he had threatened to kill her. Consequently, the couple had lived apart on a semi-permanent basis since around 1910. Jack McCarthy's arrival in Clapham meant that father and son could care for one another, which is precisely what they did until Jack's death in 1934.

Virtually as soon as Jack McCarthy had left Duval Street, the demolition crew moved in and the north side of the little street that had gone through such a long decline finally felt its death throes. The once-proud eighteenth-century silk weavers' houses had their hearts torn out as workmen ripped away the ornate fire surrounds, flagstone floors and slate roofs. The fine oak panelling that lined their rooms was dismantled and carted away. The elegant front doors were removed and the sash windows, some of which contained the original glass were taken out. The bloodstained walls of Mary Kelly's old room were reduced to rubble as were the walls within which poor Kitty Ronan's body was discovered.

As the demolition crew worked their way through they destroyed the last remaining evidence of generations – the hard-working, optimistic Huguenot silk weavers' homes; the grounds of Thomas Wedgwood's china showroom; the shop belonging to Miller the butcher, who had built the fated court; The Blue Coat Boy Pub, which had provided refreshment and warmth for over 100 years; William Crossingham's huge lodging house at number 35 from which Annie Chapman had made her last fatal journey and Mary Ann Austin met her fate. All were razed to the ground. So much history and so many memories reduced to rubble.

Although only one side of Duval Street was actually demolished, the Corporation of London saw to it that the entire street was changed. Out of the rubble on the north side rose a huge structure housing auction rooms, offices and fruit stores. On the south side, the ancient furnished rooms and many of the remaining lodging houses were closed down and cold stores, offices, warehouses and factories took their place. Duval Street had come full circle. It had started life as a place of industry, had slowly declined into a resort of loafers and now resembled its industrious past as market and office workers walked in and out of the street that, just a few years previously, policemen had been scared to visit.

The demolition of the north side of Duval Street also marked the end of an era for the underworld that inhabited its dilapidated buildings. As half the street disappeared to make way for new business and property, so many of the landlords that had controlled life on Spitalfields' streets over the previous fifty years retired from active service, thus clearing the way for more organised individuals to take over. After World War 1, the entire social landscape of Duval

Street and Spitalfields began to change. Large numbers of Eastern European Jews continued to settle in the area throughout the first years of the twentieth century and by the 1920s, evidence of the Ashkenazi culture could be seen on virtually every street.

In November 1928, a journalist from *The Times* ventured into the neighbourhood and noted that 'There are foreign names over three shops out of five... here and there a poster, across which run those strangely picturesque Hebrew characters which one instinctively associates with astrologers, magicians and other mysterious people.' The reporter was also fascinated with the unfamiliar languages he heard while exploring the area. 'Stand at [Aldgate East] station entrance and watch and listen. You may hear Russian or Polish spoken. You may hear that strange language of the Jewish proletariat of Eastern Europe, a corruption of the German of Frankfurt, half drawled, half chanted mingled with Hebrew words and written in Hebrew characters, which some call "Jargon" and others "Yiddish".'

By the 1920s, the local street markets were run almost exclusively by Jews, their Irish and English predecessors having either moved out of the area or switched to alternative employment. The costermongers and hawkers who once made up a huge proportion of Duval Street residents had also disappeared, much to the regret of the markets that once supplied them. An article in *The Times* in 1930 mourned the loss of street selling in East London with a salesman at Billingsgate lamenting 'before the War the hawkers came with their barrows about 9 o'clock in the morning, when the main business of the day at Billingsgate was finished, and bought up surplus consignments at prices that enabled them to sell cheaply in a street and house-to-house trade. Today the hawkers have been reduced to a small number and the wholesale salesmen are often at a loss to dispose of the occasional gluts which keep them standing at their stalls.'

The demand for fruit and vegetables by hawkers had not diminished quite as much as fish, although the once flourishing weekend trade had all but disappeared by 1930. *The Times* reporter noted 'in the case of fruit and vegetables... there was the casual hawker, who took out his barrow only on Saturdays and Sunday mornings… They no longer present themselves at Spitalfields [Market] to look around for cheap lines.'

The main reason behind the sharp decline in hawking in the first quarter of the twentieth century was almost certainly the establishment of unemployment benefit in 1911. Prior to its introduction, the out-of-work poor were largely left to fend for themselves. Consequently, hawking became a popular temporary means of income until more steady employment could be found. Setting up as a hawker was cheap and easy. The only piece of equipment needed was a barrow and set-up costs comprised just a small amount of cash to buy stock. In many ways, hawking benefited everyone. The wholesale markets got rid of unwanted goods, the poor got the opportunity to purchase food at knockdown prices and the hawkers earned themselves a living.

Indeed, the salesmen at Billingsgate wished for a return to the old days. 'Billingsgate would like to see the hawker come back with his barrow… a resumption of street sales would benefit the fisherman, the poorer class of consumers, and the hawker himself.' Regrettably, this was not to be. The concept of 'signing on' to receive state money gradually increased in both popularity and social acceptability. The economic downturn that resulted from expenditure during World War 1 pushed more workers onto the benefit system and by 1921, over two million people in Britain were receiving 'dole'.

It wasn't just the hawkers who were disappearing from the streets of Spitalfields. Casual labour and home-working schemes were beginning to be abandoned in favour of steadier work in the manufacturing, construction and service sectors. In 1928, the London Advisory Council for Juvenile Employment analysed the employment pattern of young people living in the capital. One in three of the female working population were employed in either hotels, restaurants or as domestic servants while the largest proportion of men were employed in either the manufacturing or construction industries.

For the men of Spitalfields, the biggest local employers were the furriers in Stepney, the furniture factories in Bethnal Green and the new electric cable, wire and lamp manufacturers slightly further north in once rural districts such as Leytonstone. The communication industry was also making its mark; Spitalfields got its own automatic telephone exchange with capacity for 5,000 lines in 1928.

For Jack McCarthy, things were never quite the same again. While the council had destroyed half of Duval Street, a combination of the war and the increasing prevalence of Eastern European Jews in the area effectively destroyed his trade in lodgings for the destitute. Many young men who may have used his rooms were now lying dead on the battlefields of France. In their place came the Jews who, being enthusiastic proponents of the extended family, saw little need for the isolation and loneliness of a single bed in a common lodging house. Jack McCarthy's reign as one of the most influential and powerful men in Spitalfields was over.

Jack McCarthy died on 16 June 1934, having suffered for some years with heart problems. He was 83 years old. He was buried alongside his wife Elizabeth, in St Patrick's Cemetery, Leytonstone, a few yards away from the grave of his most tragic and notorious tenant – Mary Kelly. Prior to his death, he had asked that his funeral cortege pass down Duval Street one last time. His funeral was well attended by family, friends and the few colleagues that survived him. The *East London Observer* published a lengthy obituary, giving much emphasis to the deceased's charitable donations and ignoring the less salubrious aspects of his life. Thus, Jack McCarthy – a child of the ghetto, slum property magnate and landlord to the most infamous murder victim of all time – departed this life for the hereafter taking his secrets, stories and memories of a truly extraordinary life to his grave.

But what a legacy he left behind. Following Jack McCarthy's death, his two eldest daughters and their husbands continued to run lodging houses, overseen by Steve (who was by now in failing health) and his son, John. Steve's other son took up a career on the stage, forming an act with his younger sister Patricia. While performing, he met a dancer named Gladys Drewery and the couple wed in 1923. Soon after, a son (Terry) was born, followed by a daughter (Patricia Kim) in 1925. Two years later, Terry and Gladys McCarthy's third and final child was born. The baby was a girl and the couple decided to name her Justine (in reference to Terry's real name of Justin) Kay. Justine developed the family flair for entertaining and in her adult life found massive fame under the stage name of Kay Kendall, starring in several Hollywood films and marrying the actor Rex Harrison before succumbing to cancer at the tragically young age of just 32.

Jack McCarthy's son Steve died in 1944 of pneumonia. His now ex-wife, Marie Kendall (they were divorced in the 1920s) continued to work until well past retirement age, and is one of the few music hall stars to be recorded on film. After Steve's death, her eldest son John invited her to take one of the family properties overlooking Clapham Common and it was here that she died in 1964, a few days before her ninety-first birthday.

Back in Duval Street, the once thriving lodging-house business was finally winding down but the criminal underworld of Spitalfields showed little sign of disappearing. Instead, it evolved into something more organised and potentially dangerous than ever before.

Ever since Jimmy Smith had set up his illicit rackets in the late nineteenth century, illegal gambling had been a popular pastime in the courts and alleyways of Spitalfields. Even the intervention of World War 1 failed to bring activities to a halt and as the new century progressed, police found themselves dealing with ever more sophisticated operations. On 18 September 1917, Robert Kenny from White's Row appeared at Old Street Police Court charged with 'being concerned in the management of a gaming house' in Old Montague Street.

Police had raided the house, which had previously been used as a tailor's workshop, the previous Saturday and had been surprised to find that the once commercial interior had been completely refitted as a gaming saloon, complete with 'incandescent' lighting over the tables and refreshment facilities. It appears that the police took the gamblers completely by surprise and consequently they fled, leaving their cards and money strewn across the tables. On searching members of the management, an astonishing £371 was found on the men – at the time, almost enough money to buy a house on Duval Street. On further investigation, it was discovered that the gaming house was owned by Edward Emanuel from Bethnal Green, a known proprietor of illegal gambling dens, who was duly fined £300; a paltry sum when it had already been established that he could take over that in one night.

As Spitalfields became riddled with gambling dens, the police struggled to keep the new crime wave in check. Unsurprisingly, some were only too happy to turn a blind eye if a bribe was offered. However, little did they know that their lackadaisical attitude to illegal gambling and more importantly, towards the men who ran the establishments, would contribute to the evolution of underworld characters whose exploits would make the activities of their nineteenth century predecessors look like playground antics.

As we have already discovered, 1920s Spitalfields was largely divided into two distinct groups of residents – the newly arrived Eastern Europeans and the English/Irish. The Eastern Europeans had been forced to leave their homeland and came to a country that was foreign in both culture and language. Having very little money at their disposal, they had no option but to live in the poorest areas of London in often squalid and overcrowded conditions. The existing population felt threatened by the new immigrants whose language and practices were different to their own. Consequently, divisions appeared and with those divisions came animosity, contempt and violence. The young of both factions went about in groups and learnt at a young age that there was safety in numbers. Unfortunately, these groups quickly evolved into gangs and began to create disturbing new problems for the area.

Gangs causing trouble in Spitalfields was certainly not a new phenomenon. There had been serious problems with group violence since the silk weavers' insurrections in the eighteenth century. However, the twentieth century gangs were the first to realise that intimidation and the threat of violence would not only cultivate fear and a certain twisted prestige. It could also earn them a living.

By the end of World War 1, the Eastern European gangs had begun to demand protection money from the traders at Petticoat Lane street market. No doubt playing on the social divides that existed at the time, they would scare the traders into parting with ridiculously large sums of cash. In return, they would 'keep an eye' on the traders' stalls and make sure that nothing happened to either them or their stock. In reality of course, the only threat that existed was from the gang offering protection. Protection rackets were the first rung of the criminal ladder for many young Spitalfields men. Following success in this field, they would inevitably move on to the well-established and extremely lucrative illegal gambling circuit and from there to all manner of illegal activities from robbery to murder.

One of Britain's most famous gangland bosses learnt his trade on the streets of Whitechapel and Spitalfields. Jacob Comacho was born in Myrdle Street, Whitechapel, in 1913, the son of Polish immigrants. Known from an early age by his nickname 'Jack Spot' (due to a distinctive mole on his cheek) the young lad soon embarked on a criminal career pinching lead from a local scrap dealer and selling it back to him. On leaving school, Jack tried out a few straight jobs including a spell in the Merchant Navy. However, a law-abiding life proved to be uninspiring and soon he was back with the local gangs in Whitechapel, this time working the protection rackets along Petticoat Lane.

During his late-teens, Jack Spot earned a reputation as both a competent worker and a fierce fighter and his exploits soon came to the attention of older, more experienced members of the criminal fraternity. He began working for various local bookmakers (quite possibly including Jimmy Smith) and became a trusted member of their team, even managing a local club for one of them. Because the local police had long since washed their hands of the illegal gaming and drinking clubs in the area, evenings at these establishments were regularly disrupted by rival gangs from other parts of London keen to get in on the action.

The most feared mob was the Italian gang from Clerkenwell, headed by the enigmatic Darby Sabini. Sabini's gang had first emerged just before World War 1 and after hostilities ended, they quickly asserted themselves as the pre-eminent mob in London, specialising in both street crime and racecourse bookmaking. They were a constant threat to their East End adversaries and continued to be a thorn in their side until World War 2.

As part of his work for the bookmakers, Jack Spot was regularly sent to racecourses and dog tracks where he earned his keep practising betting scams on race-goers and intimidating rival bookmakers into relinquishing their pitches. During this period, Spot also developed a talent for self-promotion. Keen to offset his criminal activities with seemingly good works, he began to style himself as a defender of the East End's much-persecuted Jewish contingent. In the autumn of 1936, an incident occurred that was to improve his public profile immensely.

On 4 October, Oswald Mosley's British Union of Fascists planned to march through the largely Jewish neighbourhood of Stepney. This march, which was ostensibly organised to mark the fourth anniversary of the foundation of the party, was also designed to strike terror into the heart of the Jewish community. The Stepney branch of the Communist Party were horrified at the prospect of the march going ahead and were determined to stop it taking place. They began to whip up support from the local community and on the morning of the march some 15,000 anti-Fascists blocked the Commercial Road chanting 'They Shall Not Pass'.

Sensing that there could be a bloodbath if the two factions met head on, the police commissioner insisted that Mosley's men (who totalled a rather pathetic 2,000 in number) march in the opposite direction. The commissioner's last-minute decision probably averted a catastrophe. Even though there was not a head-on collision of the two rival groups, several major scuffles did break out. However, the police managed to maintain order for the majority of the day. Rightly proud of the fact they had scuppered Mosley's plans, the East End residents returned home full of enthusiastic tales and soon stories of the confrontation became exaggerated.

What in reality had been a series of isolated incidents became known as 'The Battle of Cable Street'. Seizing the opportunity to develop his reputation, Jack Spot quickly disseminated tales of his pivotal role in the battle, even claiming that he had been sentenced to six months in prison for assaulting one of Mosley's men. In truth, Spot was never imprisoned as a result of fighting the Fascists but his tale helped to cement his reputation as defender of his people.

Three years later, the outbreak of World War 2 proved to be a turning point in the fortunes of not only Spot but also dozens of other underworld characters as they made a small fortune out of the wartime black market. In addition to this, as the war progressed, the ensuing hostilities with Italy resulted in many members of the Sabini gang being interned, thus leaving the way clear for other gangs to take over their business interests. Together with fellow gangster Billy Hill, Jack Spot capitalised on the lack of competition and asserted control over much of the criminal underworld on the north side of the Thames. For nearly ten years after the end of the war, Spot and Hill were the self-proclaimed leaders of London's criminal fraternity.

Enjoying his new-found wealth and success, Spot left his native Whitechapel and moved up west, renting a spacious Edwardian apartment in Hyde Park Mansions, minutes away from the West End. However, his newly found opulent lifestyle was destined to be short lived. By 1953, Jack Spot was rapidly losing control of his empire. His bookmaking operations were being seriously threatened by the larger betting companies and once-loyal allies were beginning to turn against him. The final nail in the coffin came when safebreaker Eddie Chapman began to spread rumours that Spot was an informer after allegedly obtaining a copy of his police file. In 1956, Jack Spot was made bankrupt. Now with few friends left in the criminal fraternity, he retreated into obscurity and lived out the rest of his life in highly reduced circumstances, finally passing away in 1995.

Back in 1953, Spot had made a last-ditch attempt to protect what remained of his bookmaking pitches by employing the services of two rising stars of the underworld who operated close to his old manor of Whitechapel and Spitalfields. The surname of these two men was Kray.

Much has been written on the criminal careers of the Kray twins and many debates have taken place as to why they chose to embark on a life of crime. While Ron battled with mental illness as he grew older, it seems that Reg possessed both the intellect and business sense to have made a success of himself without resorting to unlawful activities. However, a close look at the men's heritage reveals characteristics that perhaps make the twins' choice of career less surprising. It also reveals that both their maternal and paternal grandparents had close links to Spitalfields.

Ronald and Reginald Kray were born on 24 October 1933 to Charles David Kray and his wife Violet Lee. Charles Kray spent most of his life earning a precarious living from hawking any goods he could get his hands on and spending the proceeds either in the pub or the bookies. Despite the unstable nature of the work, he enjoyed the freedom that self-employment gave him. During World War 2, he deserted the Army and spent the following years constantly on the run from the police. This meant that he was rarely at home when the twins were young. Desertion from the Army does however seem to be the only major crime Charles Kray ever committed, despite the fact that he regularly mixed with the East London criminal fraternity.

In the late 1960s, he boasted to the writer John Pearson, 'I was brought up with most of the famous villains in the old East End. Knew 'em all in my time, 'specially when I was on the trot.' However when Pearson asked why he didn't get involved in his neighbours' criminal pursuits he replied, 'I couldn't see anything in it. Say you get caught for doin' a grand and get ten years for it, I ask you, what does it represent? How much a week? Too much like hard work for me.'

While Charles Kray's avoidance of the criminal life seems to be due to laziness, the same could not be said for his father James. Charles Kray told Pearson, 'My father was a tough old boy, very good looking but wild. Same type as Ronnie. He was known as "mad Jimmy Kray".'

James Kray was also remembered by old East End villain Arthur Harding who recalled:

'The Krays came from a great hawking family, one of the biggest in London. Old Jim Kray, he had the next door to me in Brick Lane, next to the "Princes Head" so I knew him quite well. He was a wardrobe dealer, but more a rag-and-bone bloke years ago – they used to call 'em "totters"… They had a way of going to the tailoring shops, where there'd be a lot of cuttings… and they're only too glad to get someone to take 'em. Then they'd take them down Radgies' – they bought all rags and that.'

James Kray and his parents originated from the Old Nichol, which at the time was one of the worst slums in London, controlled by the infamous 'Old Nichol Mob' so it is unlikely that Charles Kray was exaggerating when he claimed to have known many of the area's most notorious criminals in his youth.

The Kray twins' mother's heritage was little better than their father's. Violet Lee came from a family who also had strong links with Spitalfields. In fact her grandfather had rented a shop in Brick Lane during the late nineteenth century. It was this man who may be responsible for the mental illness that plagued Ron in adulthood. Violet's father, music hall entertainer and part-time pugilist, Jimmy 'Southpaw Cannonball' Lee, told John Pearson that his father, a butcher by trade, was a violent man and a heavy drinker. One night while fuelled with alcohol, his mind finally caved in and he savagely attacked his wife and children. Following this terrifying incident, he was committed to a lunatic asylum, where he died. His father's drunken attack left a deep impression on young Jimmy, who remained a strict teetotaller throughout his life and wouldn't even allow alcohol in his home.

As World War 2 commenced, the Spitalfields recalled by Jimmy Lee and Charles Kray had almost completely disappeared. The story of the worst street in London was nearly over. However during the war years, the location of Duval Street and the surrounding area made it a centre for the storage of black market goods, from stockings to tobacco. Once again its proximity to the Docks and network of ancient tenements and warehouses made it the perfect place for the likes of Jack Spot and his cronies to hide contraband. Luckily for them, their stock remained largely undamaged despite heavy bombing of the East End during the Blitz.

The Blitz began on 7 September when the German Luftwaffe launched a ferocious airborne assault on London. The planes' initial targets were the Beckton gas works, the docks and the Royal Arsenal factory at Woolwich. However, World War 2 bombing campaigns were not precise and consequently many civilian areas were hit. East London was an overcrowded, densely populated place and the residents found few places to shelter as the bombs rained down. In total, 430 people were killed on the first night of the Blitz and over three times that number were seriously injured.

The London Blitz continued for 76 nights with only one night of respite. Unlike many of their West End neighbours, most East Londoners did not have the necessary funds to escape to the safety of the British countryside and so were trapped at the centre of the action. Quickly recognising the need to devise shelters if they were to survive the nightly raids they commandeered any underground structures in the locality and made them into makeshift dormitories. Tube stations became a popular destination during air raids, as did the crypts of churches.

For the remaining residents of Duval Street, the closest air raid shelters were at Aldgate underground station – a short walk down Commercial Street or the crypt of Christ Church, which was just ' at the top of the road. Although many East Londoners regularly used the underground shelters, many families stayed in their own homes during air raids, deciding it was better to take your chances above ground than risk being buried alive if the underground shelter took a direct hit.

The East End took such a battering during the Blitz that it might be reasonable to assume that Spitalfields suffered severe damage. However, this was not the case. Thrawl Street, Flower and Dean

Street and Fashion Street escaped virtually unscathed, as did Spitalfields Market and the roads directly adjacent to it. Of all the streets close to the market, Whites Row fared the worst when houses at the western end suffered a direct hit. The resulting explosion also damaged five properties in Duval Street, rendering them uninhabitable. After the war, these buildings were turned into warehouses and offices for traders at Spitalfields Market.

The remaining part of Duval Street staggered on. However, the publication of a paper by economist Sir William Beveridge in 1942 was to have a profound effect on Duval Street's depleted residents and would also inadvertently signal the final destruction of this squalid but tenacious little thoroughfare.

In December 1942, the coalition Wartime Government published Beveridge's paper under the title 'Social Insurance and Allied Services'. The message conveyed by the paper of state support 'from the cradle to the grave' was widely published and to many people's surprise, the public's response to the 'Beveridge Report' (as it became widely known) was extremely favourable. This positive response showed just how much the public's attitude to the poor had changed since the beginning of the century. Back in Victorian times, the prevailing attitude towards the poor was that they should help themselves (temperance and attending church regularly being the main routes to redemption). However, as the Labour movement became more powerful and the catastrophic loss of life during World War 1 eroded many families' religious faith, the public gradually began to see that state intervention might be a better way to help those in need.

Prime Minister Herbert Asquith had begun to put the concept of a welfare state into action during the early years of the twentieth century by introducing the Old Age Pensions Act in 1908 and the National Insurance Act three years later. However, both these acts were reminiscent of the philanthropic housing schemes of the previous century in that they only benefited those who had been in regular (and legal) employment. It wasn't until the end of World War 2 that life for the chronically poor was changed for the better.

In 1946, the National Insurance Act created a system of benefits to help those unable to work due to ill-health, redundancy, pregnancy or old age. Two years later, the National Health Service began providing free diagnosis and treatment. Finally, the long-suffering residents of Duval Street (and hundreds of other streets like it) could see a light at the end of a very long tunnel.

As we have previously seen, most residents of Duval Street, from the 1880s onwards were only there because they had nowhere else to go. Many were unable to work because they were either too old or mentally or physically sick. The creation of the NHS meant that these people could finally be correctly diagnosed and/or effectively helped. If treatment was not possible, then benefits were available to enable them to keep a decent roof over their heads and food in their stomachs. The mere fact that hospital beds were now free meant that many could finally leave the dreadful common lodging houses and seek medical help.

Of course, the creation of the welfare state did not completely solve the problem of the destitute poor. The common lodging houses still took in nightly lodgers and local prostitutes still required furnished rooms in which to ply their trade. However, the number of people requiring the services offered by the lodging-house keepers declined dramatically from the mid-1940s onwards.

By the 1950s, former common lodging houses that had been bursting at the seams during the winter months no more than 15 years previously, now had just a handful of tenants. The ever-enterprising landlords changed the usage of their property to adjust to the times. Former 'thieves' kitchens' became tea rooms for office staff. Upstairs dormitories became brothels thinly disguised as private 'gentlemen's drinking clubs'. It was in one of these private establishments that a nightclub manager and possible descendant of landlord Johnny Cooney met with an ignominious end, thus bringing this story of the worst street in London back to where it began.

Selwyn Cooney was an ex-boxer who managed the Cabinet Club in Soho for gangland boss Billy Hill. A few days before the incident at the Pen Club in Duval Street described in the opening chapter, it is alleged that Cooney was involved in a fracas with North London gangsters the Nash brothers after an altercation with one of their girlfriends. Unfortunately, it seems that the fight did not clear the air and a few days later, Cooney ran into Jimmy Nash at the Pen Club. This time, it seems that Nash let his temper get the better of him and he pulled a gun on Cooney, shooting him at point blank range. In the ensuing mêlée, club owner William Ambrose (known as 'Billy the Boxer') was also shot at and wounded. Selwyn Cooney managed to stagger down the stairs and out into the street but collapsed on the cobbled, rain-soaked roadway.

Selwyn Cooney was the final person to die in Duval Street. Soon after his shooting, plans were drawn up by the council to create parking and loading bays for market lorries along the south side of the road and the remaining, squalid houses were served with demolition notices. Like the residents of the Flower and Dean Street rookery over 100 years before, the last residents of Duval Street disappeared into the shadows as silently and anonymously as they had arrived. By the mid-1960s, night-time in Duval Street was eerily quiet.

The London County Council changed their plans for the lorry park and erected a singularly unattractive, multi-story car park where the south side of Duval Street once stood. It is still there today and holds the dubious but fitting local reputation of being the most crime-ridden car park in London. As for Duval Street itself, the roadway still exists but all traces of 'the worst street in London' have been erased. The foundations on which once stood proud silk weavers' homes, lively pubs and beer houses and squalid hovels like 13 Miller's Court now lie under warehouse shutters and twenty-first century tarmac. Spitalfields as a whole is now a vibrant and fashionable place to live, work and play; the home of artists and artisans, just as it was when the Huguenots settled there.

Indeed, many of the streets and buildings that would have been familiar to the silk weavers are still standing. Hawksmoor's masterpiece Christ Church still stands proudly at the top of Brushfield Street. Opposite, Spitalfields Market continues to trade albeit in fashion, jewellery and house wares rather than the previous commodities; the fruit and vegetable market moved out to larger premises in Leyton and is now the biggest horticultural market in the UK. Down in Brick Lane, the old Truman Brewery has suffered a similar fate as Spitalfields Market. It is now a complex of retail outlets, food stalls and event spaces. During the day, the area is bustling, hectic and colourful. However, as dusk falls, the streets take on a more sinister air, particularly the narrow alleyways that lead off the main thoroughfares. The seemingly indelible, sordid side of this fascinating part of London emerges from the darkness as the unknowing descendants of Mary Kelly, Mary Ann Austin and Kitty Ronan begin to ply their trade around the hallowed walls of Christ Church. Duval Street may have disappeared but its legacy is too powerful to ever be entirely erased.

Part Five

A WALK AROUND SPITALFIELDS

Time: Approximately one hour, allowing for a refreshment stop at the Ten Bells pub.

Start/End: Liverpool Street Station (Metropolitan, Circle, Central and Hammersmith & City Underground Lines and Network Rail.)

NOTE: To make the most of your walk, book a tour of 18 Folgate Street and Christ Church. Contact details and further information can be found on the web at www.dennissevershouse.co.uk and www.christchurchspitalfields.org. Details of the different market days at Spitalfields Market can be found at www.visitspitalfields.com.

Start at Liverpool Street Station (Liverpool Street exit).
This station was opened in 1874, replacing the old Bishopsgate Station. It was built by the Great Eastern Railway's chief engineer, Edward Wilson, and occupied a site where the Hospital of St Mary

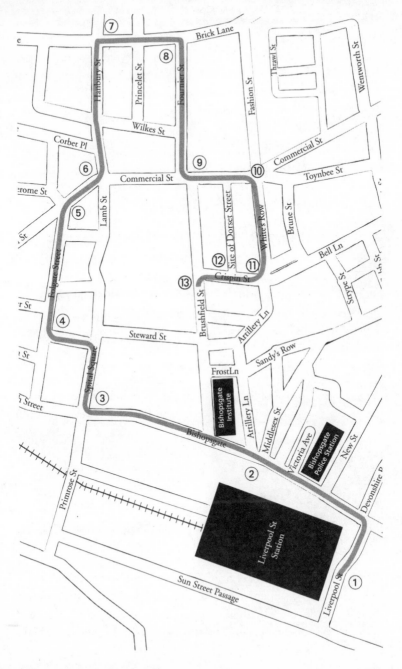

Bethlehem – Britain's first psychiatric asylum – once stood. The chaotic and sometimes disturbing scenes witnessed by visitors to the hospital gave rise to the use of the word 'Bedlam' (a corruption of Bethlehem) to describe an uproarious scene. The hospital moved to Moorfields in 1676. Turn left out of the station, then left into Bishopsgate. Walk past the police station and the Bishopsgate Institute (on your right.)

Cross the road and turn left into Spital Square.
This is where William Brune built his hospital in 1197. The Spital Field backed onto the grounds and was used by inmates as a source of pleasant views and fresh air. Today it is difficult to imagine this highly developed area as a rural retreat.

Turn left round Spital Square to Folgate Street.
Number 18 belonged to artist Dennis Severs until his death in 1999. Dennis came to London from the US in the 1970s and fell in love with Spitalfields. He managed to scrape together enough money to purchase this house and set about restoring it to reflect various periods in its history. The result is a truly unique experience where visitors feel they have stepped back in time. The exterior is a fine example of how the house would have looked when the Huguenot silk weavers populated the area. Tours of this fascinating house are available – go to www.dennissevershouse.co.uk for booking information.

Turn right into Folgate Street.
On the right is Nantes Passage, named after the revocation of the Edict of Nantes in 1685, which prompted the Huguenot silk weavers to come to Spitalfields.

Out onto Commercial Street.
The opposite side of the road was once a warren of streets that formed the northern edge of the 'wicked quarter mile' in the late 19th century. Much of the slum housing was demolished between

1922 and 1936 to make way for a massive tobacco factory, built for Godfrey Phillips and Son who had been trading in the area since the 1860s. The Royal Cambridge Theatre was also demolished during the redevelopment works. This theatre, known colloquially as the Cambridge Music Hall, was once a popular venue for performers such as Marie Lloyd and Marie Kendall. It stood roughly two thirds of the way down the factory façade. The building has now been divided up into retail, office and residential units.

Turn right and cross the road into Hanbury Street.
Many of the Spitalfields lodging housekeepers mentioned in The Worst Street in London also kept pubs. Johnny Cooney ran the Sugar Loaf at 187 Hanbury Street (a regular patron was his cousin, the music hall star Marie Lloyd) and the Weavers Arms at number 17. Prostitute Annie Chapman was murdered by Jack the Ripper in the backyard of 29 Hanbury Street (now demolished).

Walk along Hanbury Street to the corner of Brick Lane.
To the left is the Truman Brewery. The Truman family were associated with the area from the 1660s onwards. By the 19th century, the brewery was a major employer. It closed in 1988 and is now an office, shop and event complex.

Turn right down Brick Lane.
This was the home of Jimmy Smith, lodging house landlord, illegal bookie and police "fixer" who lived at 187 for much of his life. During the late 19th century, Jimmy was an influential resident responsible for bribing the local constabulary to turn a blind eye to illegal boxing bouts and dog fights. Jimmy evidently enjoyed his status as he would later tour his 'manor' in a chauffeur-driven Rolls-Royce – at the time, most Spitalfields residents rarely saw a motorcar, let alone one of such quality. Brick Lane was at the centre of battles between Eastern European Odessian and Bessarabian gangs at the turn of the century and was also the location of work premises kept by Jimmy Kray, grandfather to the infamous twins.

Stop at the corner of Brick Lane and Fournier Street.

The building on the right-hand side of the road was built by Huguenots in the early 18th century as a Protestant chapel. In 1898, it was converted into a synagogue, which closed in the 1970s and is now a mosque. This building provides a perfect example of the area's constantly evolving social structure.

Turn right into Fournier Street.

There are some particularly good examples of 18th century silk weavers' homes along this street. Look up to see the garrets where the looms once stood. There were many windows in the garrets so weavers could take advantage of the dimmest amount of light. Number 14 Fournier Street was built in 1726. The silk for Queen Victoria's wedding dress was reputedly woven here. Fournier Street was known as Church Street until the end of the 19th century when the council saw fit to change the name in honour of George Fournier, a wealthy silk weaver, who had left a large bequest for the Spitalfields poor in his will.

Continue to the top of Fournier Street.

On your left is Christ Church, built by Wren's protégé, Nicholas Hawksmoor, between 1714 and 1729. The church suffered a rather savage rehash of its interior in the 1850s and by the mid-20th century, it was in a very poor state of repair. However, in 2004, the church underwent a massive restoration project and now looks much as Hawksmoor had intended. Guided tours of the church are available – go to www.christchurchspitalfields.org for details.

To your right is the Ten Bells pub. Go inside and have a look at the original 19th century tiles on the walls, including a frieze showing 18th century silk weavers. By the late-19th century, this pub was at the epicentre of the 'wicked quarter mile' and was frequented by lodging house residents, market porters and prostitutes. Opposite the Ten Bells is Spitalfields Market. The market occupies what was originally the eastern edge of the Spital Field. There has been a market on this site since 1638 and the current building was opened in 1887. Spitalfields Market ceased to be a wholesale fruit and vegetable market in 1991. It is now a popular fashion and lifestyle market with numerous shops, cafés and specialist stalls. For full details of the different market days go to www.visitspitalfields.com.

Turn left along Commercial Street.
This road was built in the 1840s to relieve traffic going to and from Spitalfields Market. Many ancient rookeries were demolished in the process and the displacement of their residents caused serious overcrowding in the nearby roads such as Dorset Street, Flower and Dean Street and Fashion Street. On the far side of Christ Church is what remains of Itchy Park – for centuries a popular recreation ground for tramps and prostitutes. Musician Steve Marriott remembered playing hooky from school in the park during the 1960s in the Small Faces hit *Itchycoo Park*. Note: the 'park' is actually Christ Church's graveyard.

Continue to Fashion Street (one of the worst roads in the area by the late 19th century) then on to what was once the entrance to Flower and Dean Street. This road has now been completely obliterated. It was once filled with lodging houses and rivaled Dorset Street in its notoriety. Many of the houses were knocked down after The Cross Act came into power. However, the empty sites were rejected by developers and stood empty for years until the Rothschild family built Rothschild Buildings (on the right hand side of the street) and Nathaniel Buildings (on the left) in the late 1880s.

Cross the road and go back towards Spitalfields Market.
This part of Commercial Street is historically a popular place for prostitutes to ply their trade. After dark they can still be seen today, often trying to persuade unwitting drinkers to give them a cigarette.

Turn left into Whites Row.
This road was originally a path across the Spital Field. There is a very fine master weaver's house halfway down this street (identified by a steep flight of steps to the grand front door). By the 1880s, both sides of this street mainly consisted of common lodging houses and furnished rooms, many of which were run by William Crossingham of Dorset Street. In World War 2, a bomb exploded at the bottom of Whites Row, which helped the council push through plans to demolish the north side of the street along with the remaining south side of Dorset Street.

Turn right into Crispin Street.
On the left hand side of the road is what was once the Providence Row Night Refuge. Opened in 1868, it took in destitute men, women and children and was a popular shelter for the local prostitutes, who pretended they had seen the error of their ways in order to get a bed for a couple of nights.

Walk up Crispin Street and look right.
This small, unassuming service road was once the worst street in London. The street was originally built for silk weavers. The houses would have looked similar to those in Fournier Street. Looking up the street from Crispin Street, there was a pub on the left-hand side (on the corner) called The Horn of Plenty. Halfway up on the left stood the Blue Coat Boy, one of the area's oldest pubs. At the Commercial Street end was the Britannia, a gin palace-type affair.

By the 1880s, this street was almost entirely comprised of lodging houses and furnished rooms. About a third of the way up on the left lay Little Paternoster Row, which led to Brushfield Street. The lodging house where Mary Ann Austin was killed was on the corner of this street. Just over half way up on the left was the notorious Miller's Court where both Mary Kelly and Kitty Ronan were murdered. Jack McCarthy lived in a house at the entrance to Miller's Court, the downstairs of which was a general shop.

The north side of Dorset Street was demolished in 1929 to make way for the present building (offices and a flower and fruit auction room). The road was narrowed during development. The south side of the street was demolished in the 1960s to make way for Whites Row car park. The walk is now at an end. To return to Liverpool Street Station, continue along Crispin Street, and then turn left into Brushfield Street. At the end of the road, turn left into Bishopsgate. Liverpool Street Station is a short distance away on your right.

Bibliography

Ackroyd, P., *London – The Biography*, 2000, Chatto & Windus

Acton, W., *Prostitution Considered in its Moral Social and Sanitary Aspects*, 1857

Anonymous, *My Secret Life*, 1974, Ballantine, New York

Archer, T., *The Terrible Sights of London*, 1870, Stanley Rivers

Arnold, C., *Necropolis – London and its Dead*, 2007, Pocket Books

Asbury, H., *The Gangs of New York*, 2002, Arrow

Barnett, C., *The Great War*, 2003, BBC Worldwide

Beames, T., *The Rookeries of London*, 1852, Thomas Bosworth

Booth, C., *Survey Notebooks of Life & Labour in London*, 1898, LSE

Booth, W., *In Darkest England and the Way Out*, 1890, The Salvation Army

Cantlie, J., *Degeneration amongst Londoners*, 1885, Leadenhall Press

Cullen, C., *Autumn of Terror*, 1966, Fontana

Dickens, C., *Dickens's Dictionary of London 1888*, 1993, Old House Books

Dickens, C., *Sketches by Boz*, 1995, PenguinDillon, P., *The Much Lamented Death of Madam Geneva*, 2003, Review

Evans, S. P. & Skinner, K., *The Ultimate Jack the Ripper Sourcebook*, 2001, Robinson

Evans, S. P. & Skinner, K., *Jack the Ripper and the Whitechapel Murders*, 2002, Public Record Office

Fishman, W. J., *East End 1888*, 1988, Hanbury

Fishman, W. J., *The Streets of East London*, 1979, Gerald Duckworth

Fraser, F., *Mad Frank's London*, 2002, Virgin Books

Golden, E., *The Brief, Madcap Life of Kay Kendall*, 2002, University Press of Kentucky

Goldman, W., *East End – My Cradle*, 1940, Faber & Faber

Greenwood, J., *A Night in the Workhouse*, 1866, Pall Mall Gazette

Hollingshead, J., *Ragged London*, 1861, Smith, Elder & Co

Hyde, R. (intro), *The A-Z of Georgian London*, 1981, Harry Margary

Hyde, R. (intro), *The A-Z of Victorian London*, 1987, Harry Margary

Inwood, S., *A History of London*, 1998, Macmillan

Jakubowski, M. & Braund, N., *Jack the Ripper*, 1999, Robinson

Jones, S., *Capital Punishments*, 1992, Wicked Publications

Laslett, P., *The World We Have Lost – Further Explored*, 2000, Routledge

Lillywhite, B., *London Coffee Houses*, 1963, George Allen & Unwin

Linnane, F., *London's Underworld – Three Centuries of Vice and Crime*, 2003, Robson

London, J., *The People of the Abyss*, 2001, Pluto Press

Mayhew, H. & Quennell, P. (ed), *London's Underworld*, 1950, Hamlyn

Morrison, A., *A Child of the Jago*, 1994, Academy, Chicago

Morrison. A., *Tales of Mean Streets*, 1997, Academy, Chicago

Morton, J., *Gangland*, 1992, Time Warner Books

Morton, J., *Gangland Today*, 2002, Time Warner Books

Morton, J. & Parker., *Gangland Bosses*, 2004, Time Warner Books

Nicholson, D., *The Londoner*, 1946, Adprint

O'Neill, G., *My East End – Memories of Life in Cockney London*, 1999, Viking

Orwell, G., *Down and Out in Paris and London*, 1999, Penguin

Paterson, M., *Voices From Dickens' London*, 2007, David & Charles

Pearson, J., *The Cult of Violence*, 2002, Orion

Perry Curtis Jr, L., *Jack the Ripper and the London Press*, 2001, Yale University

Phillips, W., *The Wild Tribes of London*, 1855

Picard, L., *Dr. Johnson's London*, 2000, Weidenfeld & Nicolson

Picard, L., *Restoration London*, 1997, Weidenfeld & Nicolson

Picard, L., *Elizabeth's London*, 2003, Weidenfeld & Nicolson

Preston, W. C., *The Bitter Cry of Outcast London*, 1969, Cedric Chivers

Ritchie, E., *Days and Nights in London*, 1880, Tinsley Bros

Samuel, R., *East End Underworld – Chapters in the Life of Arthur Harding*, 1981,
    Routledge & Kegan Paul

Sandford, J., *Edna the Inebriate Woman*, 1976, Marion Boyars

Schama, S., *The History of Britain Vol III*, 2003, BBC Books

Severs, D., *18 Folgate Street*, 2002, Vintage

Sims, G. R., *How the Poor Live*, 1889, Chatto & Windus

Sinclair, I. (ed), *London – City of Disappearances*, 2006, Hamish Hamilton

Smith, S., *Underground London – Travels Beneath the City Streets*, 2004, Little, Brown

Tames, R., *City of London Past*, 1995, Historical Publications

Thomas, D., *The Victorian Underworld*, 1998, John Murray

Thomson, J., *Victorian London Street Life*, 1994, Dover Publications, New York

Trench, R & Hillman, E, *London Under London – A Subterranean Guide*, 1993, John Murray

Waller, M., *1700 – Scenes From London Life*, 2000, Hodder & Stoughton

Weightman, G., *Bright Lights, Big City*, 1992, Collins & Brown

White, J., *Rothschild Buildings*, 2003, Pimlico

Victorian Ordnance Survey Collection – London, 2006, David & Charles

Journals Consulted:

All Year Round

The Builder

Daily Mail

Daily News

East London Advertiser

East London Observer

Entr'Acte

Era

Express

Illustrated London News

Illustrated Police News

Household Words

The Lancet

Pall Mall Gazette

Penny Illustrated Paper

Punch

Strand

The Times

INDEX

Ale houses 147-148

Alhambra Palace............................155

Ambrose, William 9, 216

Armstrong, John and Mary 36

Artillery Ground............18-19, 25, 46

Austin, Mary Ann..........168-170, 202,

....217

Balch, John 25

Barnett, Abraham 112

Barnett, Joseph..............110-114, 123,

....129-135, 139

Barnett, Reverend.............90, 92, 167

Bartholomew Fair 149

Bedford Music Hall 159-160

Beer houses 152-153

Benefit of Clergy 39-40

Benstead, Henry 185

Bessarabians 165-166

Beveridge Report, The.................214

Billingsgate Market................203-204

     Stolen goods from 79

     Joe Barnett and 110, 130

Black Eagle Brewery 147,

....153, 217

Blue Coat Boy pub 50, 101, 202

Bogard, Isaac...........................182-184

Bohun, George 26

Booth, Charles 164, 167

Boxing prize fights 99

Breezer's Hill...........................109-110

Brick Lane 57, 113

     Jimmy Smith and.................99, 173

     Polly Nichols and 117

     Black Eagle Brewery ..147, 153, 217

     Jack McCarthy and 162

     Gangs and 166

     The Krays and 212

Britannia pub, Commercial Street ....

....101

Brune, William (Walter) and Rosia ..

....17

Brushfield Street........24, 89, 201, 216

Bucknall, William 147

Cable Street 210

Calico 44-45

Canterbury Arms pub 153-155

229

Captains of the Artillery Garden ..19
Chandlers' shops.........................78-79
Chapman, Annie 119-123, 125,
....129, 137, 202
Christ Church 10-11, 26, 46,
................................53-54, 64, 216-217
   Nicholas Hawksmoor and 46
   Churchyard 178-179
   Air raid shelter 213
Commercial Road 63, 113, 123,
....144, 166, 209
Commercial Street ..9-10, 26, 46-47,
.........................114, 119-120, 133, 186
   Roads leading off 12
   Creation of 54-55
   Prostitution on 96-97
   Britannia pub..............................101
   Mary Kelly and ..110-111, 133, 135
   Royal Cambridge Music Hall 156
   Kitty Ronan and 186
Aliens' Registration Office............193
Common lodging houses ...12, 51-52,
............................56, 71, 75, 167, 201
Common Lodging Houses Act 1851
....70-72
Customers 74, 78-79, 91
Landlords........................74-75, 78-81
   Prostitutes and 78-80
   Thieves' kitchens....................89, 215
   Smith family and 97
   Overcrowding in 102
   Polly Nichols and 117
   1889 Dock Strike and 144
   London County Council and ....
....161-163
   Registration of............................176
   Jack London and 177-178
   World War 1 and 193
   Jack McCarthy and 205

The demise of 215
Cook, Lieutenant James..................42
Cooney, John 98, 101, 194, 215
   Marie Lloyd and 156
Cooney, Selwyn.............9, 16, 215-216
Corporation of London 188, 201-202
Cox, Mary Ann 132
Crispin Street 23, 101
Cross Act, The 82-84, 98
Crossingham, William 12, 99, 112,
...............................163, 176, 188, 202
   Annie Chapman and 119-121
   Mary Ann Austin and..........168-169
   Death of 179-180
Culpeper, Nicholas...........................20
Deane, Charlie 159-160
Dickens, Charles 152
Diemshutz, Loui 123-124
Docks, Th.................16, 67, 113, 134
   Irish and 68-69
   Prostitution and............................87
   McCarthy family and 110
   1889 Strike 143-145
   World War 2 212-213
Donovan, Timothy 119-121
Dorset Street 10, 12-13, 16, 48, 82,
........88, 101, 125, 140, 143, 146, 166
   Creation of.....................................24
   Silk weavers and 46-47
   Thomas Wedgwood and 48-49
   Pubs 49-50
   Overcrowding in 55, 84, 96
   Irish and.....................................58, 64
   Common lodging houses 69
   Collapse of a house 72
   Furnished rooms 75
   Description of a typical tenant ....
....78-79
   Landlords 80, 89

Prostitution 88

   Jack McCarthy and 98-99, 108,
......110-112, 119, 122-123, 134, 156,
................................161-163, 172-174

   Steve McCarthy and 160

   Jews and..............................102, 165

   Mary Kelly and 108, 111-113,
....133-134, 138

   Pearly Poll and 115

   Annie Chapman and 119-120,
....122-123, 129

   Elizabeth Stride and 125

   Kit Watkins and 138-139

   Charles Booth and......................164

   Mary Ann Austin and..........168-170

   Fred McKenzie and 170-172

   Redevelopment 176

   Change of name 178

Duke of Wellington pub 172

Dutch weavers......................19, 27-28

Duval Street 178, 181, 200-202,
....212-215, 217

   Arthur Harding and 182

   Kitty Ronan and..................184-186

   1910 Valuation Survey 187-188

   Jack McCarthy and 188, 205

   World War 1 188-189

   London County Council,
Corporation of
      London and 200-202, 216

   Demolition of, ...202

   World War 2 212-214

   Selwyn Cooney and 215-216

East End Vigilance Committee 127

East India Company..................28, 44

East London Dwellings Company 90

Eddowes, Catherine 125-128, 137

Edgworth Bess 31-32

Fashion Street.............................23, 55

   Catherine Eddowes and 125

Fencing 31-32, 78-79, 101, 166

Flemming, Joseph..................110, 131

Flower and Dean Street 23, 82, 84,
....167, 216

   Rothschild Buildings 90-91

   Jimmy Smith, John Cooney and......
....97-98

   Polly Nichols and 117, 119

   Elizabeth Stride and 125

   Catherine Eddowes and......125-126

   World War 2 213-214

Forward, Joseph 149

Fossan, Thomas and Lewis 23

Fournier Street............................29, 53

Fraternity of the Artillery................18

Gambling..78, 164-165, 182, 206-208

   Horses 73

   Jimmy Smith and............97, 99, 173

   Boxing 99

Gehringer, Frederick 97-98,
....172-174, 194

George Street 107, 111, 113-114, 119

Gin craze 148-152

   Gin palaces..........101, 148-152, 157

   Gin Acts......................................150

Goulston Street 84, 90, 126

Hall, Harold 186-187

Hames, Margaret 106, 111, 114

Hanbury Street................................22

   Hanbury family and 22

   John Cooney and..................98, 156

   Murder of Annie Chapman and ......
....120-121

Salvation Army Women's Shelter
176

Hanging 34, 37

   Jack Sheppard and 33-34

Harding, Arthur ....
........................97, 173, 182, 191, 211

Harrison, Rex 206

Harvey, Maria 132
Hayes, Catherine 37-38
Hill, Billy 9, 210, 215
Horn of Plenty pub 101
Horner, Robert 175-176
Huguenots 27-29, 46, 53, 95, 122,
......................148, 174, 178, 202, 216
   Marie Kendall and..............157, 160
Hunnable, William 180
Hutchinson, George......................133
Irish Potato famine 58-63
   In London 65-67, 70
   Professions 68-69
   Landlords.....................................98
   Jews and 101-102
   Jack the Ripper and 122, 132
Islington 20, 36
   Slums 82
   Marie Lloyd and 156
Itchy Park 179
Jack the Ripper 10-13, 34, 57,
....97, 106-140
Jews
   Anti-Semitism 85-86, 94
   Rothschild Buildings and 90
   Immigration 93-95, 203
   Spitalfields and...................101-102
   Abraham Barnett 112
   Jack the Ripper and 122
   Bessarabian and
Odessian gangs 165-166
   Crime and 182, 184, 209
   The Battle of Cable Street 209-210
Kelly, Mary 108-114, 122-123,
....129-140, 217
Kendall, Kay 206
Kendall, Marie 157
   Career...........................159-160, 206
   Steve McCarthy and 160, 201

Kray family 182, 211-212
Lee family 212
Lewis, Daniel 98, 101, 106
Lloyd, Marie.............................98, 156
London County Council ....
....82, 91-92, 101
   Common lodging houses and ..161
   Street development and 175, 179,
....200-201, 216
London, Jack...........................177-178
Lusk, George 127
McCarthy family.........................67-68
   Daniel.......................................67-68
   Daniel Jnr 99
   Jack 98-101, 161-164, 172-176,
..............................180, 188, 201, 205
   Mary Kelly and....108-113, 130-139
   Jack the Ripper and....119, 122-123,
....125, 129
   Marie Lloyd and 156
   Steve 156-160, 195, 205-206
   Kitty Ronan and..................184-186
McKenzie, Fred 170-172
McQueen, Alexander 162
Maisons de passé....................108-109
May Laws 94
Mayhew, Henry..68, 70, 73, 79, 85-86
Mearns, Reverend Andrew..............89
Metcalf, Edward 25-26
Metropolitan Board of Works ..82-84,
....90, 92
Miller's Court 55, 136, 216
   School room in 84
   Prostitutes in 88
   Jack McCarthy and 98, 112-113,
....122, 162, 188
   Mary Kelly and 129-137
   Kit Watkins and 138-139
   Kitty Ronan and..................184-187

Demolition of 200, 202

Mitre Square....................................126

Morton, Charles 153-155

Mosley, Oswald 209

Music hall 98, 153-160, 166

Marie Kendall and..............160, 206

The Krays and 212

Nash family............................182, 216

National Health Service................215

Newgate Calendar 37-38

Newgate Gaol 32-33, 37

Nicholas, Edward and Cooke,

George 23-24

Nichols, Polly 117-120, 137

Odessians 166

Old Bailey, The............35-36, 40, 149

Jack Sheppard and 33

Old Nichol, The 87-88, 212

Osborn Street..........................107, 118

Paternoster Row................................24

Little Paternoster Row 179,200-201

Peabody Buildings 91

Pearl Street, Great 97, 134

Pearl Street, Little 97, 174

Pearly Poll..............................114-115

Petticoat Lane (Middlesex Street) 27,

....177, 208

Philip, Arthur 43-44

Piser, John......................118, 122, 128

'The Boss' letter and 128

Pogroms 93-94

Porter (beer) 153

Potato famine 58-66

Prater, Elizabeth 132-134, 138

Priory of St Mary Spital 17-18

Prostitution..............................12, 215

The Black Lion and......................31

Spitalfields and 52-53, 75, 78, 86-

............88, 96, 129, 165-167, 178-179

Prostitutes' lodgings ..75, 79-80, 86,

......................................100, 110, 181

Crime and 79, 101, 166, 182

The poor and................................82

Street gangs and 87-88, 102, 106,

....165

Alcoholism and 88, 106

Emma Smith and 106-107

Mary Kelly and ....

........................108-111, 122, 130-139

Jack McCarthy and 110

Martha Tabram and 113-114

Polly Nichols and............... 117-118

Jack the Ripper and 119, 121-122

Annie Chapman and 119-120

Elizabeth Stride and............124-125

Taverns and 148

Kitty Ronan and 185

World War 1 194

Red Lion Inn 20

Ringer's Buildings..........................101

Ronan, Kitty 184-187, 202, 217

Rothschild Buildings..........90-91, 102

Rothschild family 90, 92, 95

Sabini, Darby 208-210

St Leonard's Church, Shoreditch .. ....

....36, 139

St Patrick's Cemetery, Leytonstone ...

....139, 205

Schmidt, Frederick..........................35

Schwartz, Israel 124

Sheppard, Jack............................30-35

Shoreditch 36

Mortuary 139

The Empire 186

Silk weavers 11, 28, 54, 112, 178,

..............................201-202, 207, 216

Weavers' Company and 20

Huguenot weavers......................27

Calico and 44-45

Wages 47

Insurrection 47-48, 207

Silk imports 52-53

Destitution....................................70

Marie Kendall and.....................157

Sims, George 89

Smith, Emma 106-107, 111, 114,

....118, 137

Smith, Jimmy ....

.......................57, 97, 99, 172-174, 208

Smith, John 56-57

Spital Field.....................17-21, 27-28

Sermons...18

Roman burial ground 19

Market licence 20, 25

Development of 19-26

Spitalfields Market ..9, 10, 64, 87, 97,

................................137, 214, 216-217

Creation of..............................25-31

Traffic problems 54

Redevelopment 88, 200-201

London County Council and....101,

....175-176

Jack McCarthy and 173

Corporation of London and......188,

....201-202

The Blitz and...............................214

Spot, Jack 9, 208-210, 213

Stride, Elizabeth ..124-125, 127, 129,

....137

Tabram, Martha 113-117, 119, 137

Taverns 147-148, 152

Ten Bells pub 11, 47

Theft 35-36, 52, 130, 149

Animal theft....................................35

Punishment for 39

Spitalfields and 30, 175

Thrawl Street 98, 106, 117, 119,

....162, 213-214

Transportation 40-44

Treason 37-38

Truman, Joseph 147

Valuation Survey (1910) 187-188

Watkins, Kit 138-139

Wedgwood, Thomas.........48-49, 202

Wentworth Street.....................90, 97

Weston, Edward............................154

Wheler, William 22-24

Daughter Katherine 25

Wheler Street 46

Whitechapel Road 106, 115-117

White's Row 55, 89

Prostitutes in 97

William Crossingham and 169, 179

World War 2 bombing 214

Wild, Jonathan 32-33

World War 1 ....183, 190-200, 204,

....209, 214

Lord Kitchener and....................190

War Propaganda Bureau 191-192

Alcohol consumption during 194

Gas attacks 195-196

Desertion during 197-198

Influenza and 198-199

World War 2 ....209, 212-214

THE
WORKS 2

Brian Moses spends much of his time touring his poetry and percussion show around the UK's schools, libraries and festivals. He has written or edited over 200 books, the latest of which are *A Cat Called Elvis* and *Brian Moses' School Report*. Find out more about Brian at www.brianmoses.co.uk and on his blog: brian-moses.blogspot.com

Pie Corbett – poet, storyteller and educator – was a primary teacher and head teacher. He worked in teacher training and was English inspector in Gloucestershire. Author and editor of over 250 books, he was made a Doctor of Letters in 2009 by the University of Winchester for services to poetry, storytelling and creative education. Pie works across the country running research and development projects with schools.

Also available from Macmillan Children's Books

The Works
Chosen by Paul Cookson

The Works Key Stage 1
Chosen by Pie Corbett

The Works Key Stage 2
Chosen by Pie Corbett

Brian Moses' School Report
Very Funny Poems about School

Evidence of Dragons
Poems by Pie Corbett

A First Poetry Book
Chosen by Pie Corbett and Gaby Morgan

THE
WORKS 2

POEMS ON EVERY SUBJECT
AND FOR EVERY OCCASION

Chosen
by **BRIAN MOSES**
and **PIE CORBETT**

MACMILLAN CHILDREN'S BOOKS

Pie and Brian would like to dedicate this book to all the teachers and children that they have worked with – those who set alight the creative spark, fan the flames of imagination and celebrate our unique ability to wonder.

Mol an óige agus tiocfaidh sí.

Celtic Proverb: Praise the young and they will flourish.

First published 2002 by Macmillan Children's Books

This edition published 2014 by Macmillan Children's Books
a division of Macmillan Publishers Limited
20 New Wharf Road, London N1 9RR
Basingstoke and Oxford
Associated companies throughout the world
www.panmacmillan.com

ISBN 978-1-4472-7483-4

A

Printed

This

by

or oth

in a

it is p

co

Contents

Introduction   xvii

Art and Design

First Art Lesson	James Kirkup	3
What Shall I Draw?	Helen Dunmore	4
The Paint Box	E. V. Rieu	5
Childhood Painting Lesson	Henry Rago	6
My Teacher Taught Me How to See	John Kitching	6
Today, in Strong Colours	Sue Cowling	7
Modern Art	Peter Dixon	8
The Museum Says	Roger Stevens	9
The Art Gallery Says	Roger Stevens	10
I Asked the Little Boy Who Cannot See	Anon.	11
Jacob and the Angel	Joan Poulson	12
Matchstick King	John Kitching	13
Who's That on the Phone?	Pie Corbett	14
After Giacometti	Fred Sedgwick	16
The British Museum Print Room	Chrissie Gittins	17
Leonardo	Charles Causley	18
The Uncertainty of the Poet	Wendy Cope	20
The Boyhood of Raleigh	Roger McGough	21
The Artist's Model Daydreams	Pie Corbett	22
A Sort of Chinese Poem	Elizabeth Jennings	24
The Sand Artist	James Kirkup	25
Notes for an Autumn Painting	Adrian Henri	27

Contents

Jack Frost	Brenda Williams	29
Art Year Haikus	John Kitching	30
Notes		31

Music

Music . . .	Ann Bonner	35
We Got Rhythm	Mike Jubb	36
Everyday Music	James Berry	37
J is for Jazz-Man	Eleanor Farjeon	38
Embryonic Mega-Stars	Brian Patten	39
In the Bleak Mid-winter	Christina Rossetti	40
Seaside Sonata	Mary Green	42
Drum	Judith Nicholls	43
A Crack Band	Gina Douthwaite	44
Stereo Headphones	James Carter	45
Electric Guitars	James Carter	46
Heavy Metal, Stormy Weather	Ian Souter	47
The Music Lesson Rap	Clare Bevan	49
Song for a Banjo Dance	Langston Hughes	50
If I Were the Conductor	Richard Edwards	52
Song of the Animal World	Traditional	53
Making Music	Andrew Collett	55
The Rhythm of the Tom-tom	António Jacinto	
	trs Don Burness	56
The Group	Brian Moses	57
Lewis Has a Trumpet	Karla Kuskin	59

History

History	John Kitching	63
Historian	John Kitching	64

Contents

The Great Lizards   Dave Calder   65
Voice from the Pharaoh's Tomb   Patricia Leighton   67
A Liking for the Viking   Celia Warren   70
King Canute   Paul Bright   71
Roman Invasions   Celia Warren   72
Julius Caesar's Last Breakfast   Roger Stevens   73
Entering a Castle   Brian Moses   75
A Sense of History   Penny Kent   76
The Tudors   Clare Bevan   78
Guess Who?   Coral Rumble   80
Short Livers   John Kitching   81
Cutpurse Kit   David Harmer   82
Printer's Devil   Patricia Leighton   84
The Powder Monkey   Chrissie Gittins   85
From 'The Charge of the
   Light Brigade'   Alfred, Lord Tennyson   87
Cargoes   John Masefield   89
The Housemaid's Letter   Clare Bevan   90
Aunt Sue's Stories   Langston Hughes   92
My Mother Saw a Dancing Bear   Charles Causley   94
For the Fallen   Laurence Binyon   95
The Soldier   Rupert Brooke   97
Growing Up in the 1930s   Trevor Harvey   98
Post-war   Libby Houston   99
Remembrance Day – 11 November   Judith Nicholls   100
Notes   102

Geography

Geography   John Kitching   109
Island   Stanley Cook   110

Contents

Geography Lesson	Zulfikar Ghose	111
Walking to School	Stanley Cook	112
From My Window	Ian Souter	114
Houses	Sue Cowling	115
Building a Skyscraper	James S. Tippett	116
I Live in the City	Anon.	118
Early Last Sunday Morning	Ian Souter	119
Stream Story	Paul Bright	121
Day By Day I Float My Paper Boats	Rabindranath Tagore	122
The Hills	Rachel Field	123
Mountains	Ian Serraillier	124
The Train	Clive Sansom	125
Ocean Travel	Jennifer Tweedie	126
At the Seaside	Robert Louis Stevenson	127
Shell	Myra Cohn Livingston	128
Seashells	Anon. (Chinese child)	128
Points of View	Mina Johnson	129
Volcano	Mary Green	131
Rain	Anita Marie Sackett	132
Coral Reef	Clare Bevan	134
Geography Lesson	Brian Patten	136
Someday Someone Will Bet that You Can't Name All Fifty States	Judith Viorst	138
Haiku Calendar: Southern Version	Barrie Wade	140
Fearless Bushmen	Benjamin Zephaniah	142

Design, Technology and ICT

Technology Lesson	Clare Bevan	147
Excuses	Mary Green	149
The Oojamaflip	Paul Bright	151

Contents

Problem Solving	Peter Dixon	152
Inventions I'd Like to See	Douglas Florian	153
The Song of the Engine	H. Worsley-Benison	154
Scissors	Sue Dymoke	155
Go-cart	Una Leavy	156
Epitaph for a Blacksmith	William Hayley	157
Progress	Hilaire Belloc	158
Mowers	John Foster	159
First Television	Judith Nicholls	160
The Electronic House	Wes Magee	162
Space Shot	Gareth Owen	164
New Frontiers	Coral Rumble	165
Mega Star Rap	Valerie Bloom	166
Spellbound	Norman Vandal	167
Hickory Digital Clock	Steve Turner	168
Techno-Child	Adrian Mitchell	169
My Pet Mouse	David Whitehead	171
Printout, Wipe Out	Trevor Harvey	172
The Machine of the Three Big Ears	John Rice	173

Maths

One Pink Sari	Ann Marie Linden	179
Two Times Table	Anon.	180
Why Must it Be Minus Three?	Kali Dakos	182
Numberless!	Ian Souter	183
What Is a Million?	Wes Magee	184
Time	Valerie Bloom	185
Seven Fat Fishermen	Anon.	186
The Surprising Number 37	Anon.	187
Counting Horrors	Charles Thomson	188

Contents

A Bit of a Problem	John Kitching	189
Pyramid Pie	Mary Green	190
Teacher's Torture	Mary Green	191
Tall Story	Mike Johnson	192
Mathematically Telepathically Magical	Paul Cookson	193
Puzzler	Philip Waddell	194
Behind the Staffroom Door	Brian Moses	195
Three Frazzles in a Frimple	Brian Patten	197
Maths Person	Robert Hull	198
The Unit of Sleep	Jan Dean	200
If I Were a Shape	Brian Moses	201
Counting	Karla Kuskin	202

Science

Up in Smoke	Paul Bright	207
Earth's Clock	Pat Moon	208
Freddie Fox, Sally Sisson and Raymond Rix	John Kitching	209
Summer Storm	John Foster	210
Constant, Constant Little Light	John Rice	212
Information for Travellers	Dave Calder	214
Chalk	Roger Stevens	216
Science Lesson	Mike Johnson	216
experiment	Danielle Sensier	217
Star Turn	Frances Nagle	218
Breath	Trevor Harvey	220
The Shark	Lord Alfred Douglas	221
Gannet Diving	John Rice	223
Luck	Madeline Munro	224

Contents

Wonder Birds	Patricia Leighton	225
Snail	Patricia Leighton	226
Mouse Laughing	Mary Green	226
The Day's Eye	Pie Corbett	227
Winter Seeds	Penny Kent	229
Mushrooms	Kenneth C. Steven	230
The Hedgehog	Trevor Harvey	231
Dandelions	Gwen Dunn	232
The Wobbling Rainbow	Pie Corbett	233

Religious Education

I Thank You Lord	A Muslim prayer	237
Before the Paling of the Stars	Christina Rossetti	238
Innocent's Song	Charles Causley	239
Dedicating a Baby	Jan Dean	241
Disembarkation Chorus	Mervyn Peake	242
Psalm 150	King James Bible	243
Psalm 23	King James Bible	244
From 'The Sermon on the Mount'	King James Bible	245
In the Beginning	Steve Turner	246
Prayer for When I'm Cross	Jan Dean	247
Dipa (The Lamp)	Ann Bonner	248
Plague Frog	Judith Nicholls	249
Jonah and the Whale	Gareth Owen	250
Hindu Poem	Anon.	252
Hunting the Leaven	Tony Mitton	253
Ramadan	Stanley Cook	254
Mela	Jean Kenward	255
Light the Festive Candles	Aileen Fisher	256

Contents

Assemblies

It's a Wonderful World . . .	Judith Viorst	261
The World with its Countries	John Cotton	262
Thanksgiving	Ivy O. Eastwick	263
All in the Mind	Moira Andrew	264
Job Description	Daphne Kitching	265
Books for All Reasons	Nikki Giovanni	266
The Dawdling Dog	Roger Stevens	267
Mother to Son	Langston Hughes	269
The Most Important Rap	Roger Stevens	270
The News	David Harmer	272
Just One Wish	Janis Priestley	274
Finding Magic	Eric Finney	276
With My Hands	Steve Turner	277
All of Us	Kit Wright	279
A School Creed	Traditional	281
Listen	Clare Bevan	282
Carol of the Brown King	Langston Hughes	284
The Sky	Traditional (Ghana)	285
And My Heart Soars	Chief Dan George	286
An Alphabet for the Planet	Riad Nourallah	287
Thank You Letter	Eric Finney	289
Our Tree	David Harmer	291
Grown-ups	Peter Dixon	292
The Last Day of School	Jeff Moss	295

Personal, Social and Sensitive Issues

Extract from the Book of Ecclesiastes	King James Bible	299

Contents

Name-calling	Charles Thomson	300
Give Yourself a Hug	Grace Nichols	301
First Thing Today	Fred Sedgwick	302
Some Things Don't Make Any Sense at All	Judith Viorst	303
Staring	Lee Bennett Hopkins	304
It's Not the Same without Dad	Brian Moses	305
Divorce	Gina Douthwaite	306
Divorce	Jackie Kay	307
Bringing up a Single Parent	Brian Patten	309
Cousins	John Rice	311
Get Your Things Together, Hayley	Frances Nagle	312
The New House	Gareth Owen	313
This Is a Recorded Message	Philip Gross	315
Friends	Gareth Owen	316
Friendship	Véronique Tadjo	319
Friends	Elizabeth Jennings	321
Harvey	Judith Viorst	322
Dream Team	Frances Nagle	323
New Girl	Danielle Sensier	325
Shame	Tracey Blance	326
Bullied	Patricia Leighton	327
Sometimes	Coral Rumble	330
Dobbo's First Swimming Lesson	David Harmer	331
It Hurts	John Foster	332
Mr Mizen	John Rice	333
On the Streets	David Harmer	335
My Daddy Dances Tapstep	Peter Dixon	336
The World Is a Beautiful Place	Laurence Ferlinghetti	337
In the Garden	Philip Waddell	338

Contents

Citizen of the World	Dave Calder	339
The Soldiers Came	John Agard	341
Stranger	Les Baynton	342
Arturi's Story	Penny Kent	343
All that Space	Joan Poulson	347
Cowboy Games and the Good Death	John Coldwell	349
The Funeral	Lindsay MacRae	350
Mid-Term Break	Seamus Heaney	353
My First Dog	Patricia Leighton	355
Burying the Dog in the Garden	Brian Patten	357
Silver Moon	Frances Nagle	359
Death	Kuba (Africa)	360
Remember	Christina Rossetti	361

The Environment

Wilderness	Joan Poulson	365
Web of Life	Jane Clarke	366
Dolphin Dance	Judith Nicholls	367
Forest	Ann Bonner	368
Natural Numbers	Mike Johnson	369
Blake's Tyger – Revisited	Michaela Morgan	370
The Last Wolf Speaks from the Zoo	Pie Corbett	371
Important Notice	Philip Waddell	373
Names	Brian Moses	374
Dragonflies	Joan Poulson	376
Missing	Mike Johnson	377

Contents

Model Poems

Introduction		381
Poetry	Eleanor Farjeon	387
Alien Lullaby	Sue Cowling	388
Jabberwocky	Lewis Carroll	389
Jabbermockery	Trevor Millum	391
The Owl and the Pussy-cat	Edward Lear	393
The Cook and the Caretaker	Clare Bevan	395
Song Thrush Poster	Sue Cowling	396
Tom Thumb's Diary	Sue Cowling	397
There Was a Young Lady of Riga	Anon.	399
Low Owl	John Rice	400
Haiku of the Four Winds	Judith Nicholls	401
The Emperor and the Nightingale	Mike Jubb	402
Tanka: Red Leaves	Fred Sedgwick	403
December Cinquain	Fred Sedgwick	404
Kennings	Daphne Kitching	405
Two Witches Discuss Good Grooming	John Coldwell	406
In Marble Walls	Traditional	407
One Line Riddles	Pie Corbett	408
My First Is in Two	Sue Playdell	409
A Pin Has a Head	Christina Rossetti	410
What Am I?	Pie Corbett	411
The Tree Spell	John Rice	412
The Months	Christina Rossetti	413
Apple Pie	Anon.	414
Simple Seasons	Eric Finney	415

Contents

The Witch, the Prince and the Girl in the Tower	Sue Cowling	416
Litter Lout	Sue Cowling	417
My Dad's Amazing!	Ian Souter	418
Things to Do on the First Day of the Summer Holidays	Fred Sedgwick	419
Moses	Anon.	420
Childhood Tracks	James Berry	421
Mr Khan's Shop	Fred Sedgwick	423
What Do You Collect?	Wes Magee	425
Bonfire Night	Katherine Gallagher	426
Notes towards a Poem	Judith Nicholls	427
A Minute to Midnight	John Rice	428
Best Places	Eric Finney	429
The Dream Keeper	Langston Hughes	431
Dreams	Langston Hughes	432
All the world's a stage	William Shakespeare	433
Camilla Caterpillar	Mike Jubb	435
She Sells Seashells	Anon.	436
Barry and Beryl the Bubble Gum Blowers	Paul Cookson	437
Having My Ears Boxed	Roger McGough	438
Index of First Lines		441
Index of Poets		449
Acknowledgements		451

Introduction

This anthology is friend and travelling companion to the earlier anthology *The Works*. In that collection Paul Cookson gathered a vast compendium of poetic forms, techniques and subjects. It has become a standard reference work to be found in most primary schools.

In this collection we have gathered poems that relate to other areas of the curriculum – notably art, music, history, geography, technology, mathematics, science, religious education and the environment. Our search was a long haul, scanning many thousands of new poems as well as those already printed. Gradually we added more and more poems to the pile of possibilities. Our task was made harder because we did not want to revisit poems already to be found in *The Works*. Some subjects were obvious favourites with writers, while others received scant attention. Of course, school is about more than just subjects, so we also included poems that might be handy for assemblies.

While the pile of subject poems gradually became a ridge of hills and then a mountain, another cairn of poems began to grow around other themes – sensitive issues. Poems about those aspects of life that are not on the formal curriculum but have to be tackled – bullying,

sharing, death, friendship, divorce, memories, name-calling, wonder . . . So we dragged these together under a section titled 'Personal, Social and Sensitive Issues'.

The final section in the book is titled 'Model Poems'. These poems act as invitations to write. They lend themselves to children creating their own versions. They are the sort of poems that could be used in a poetry workshop to kick-start the children's own writing and would be a useful annexe to the original volume of *The Works*.

Poetry has the benefit of brevity – but at its best it introduces a new slant, creates an echo in the mind and prompts questioning, wonder and thought. It can forge links between the self and that which is not yet known. It is a special way of seeing things. Other subjects such as history present the facts. Stories can help facts live as if they were realities. And poetry digs under the skin, to preserve experience, to illuminate truth. It cannot be defined – only experienced, as it is language lit up by life and life lit up by language. It has a unique voice that speaks directly to children.

We imagined ourselves back in the classroom, tugging this book off the shelf, to enrich and throw light on other subject areas. For the poet is not so much interested in explaining reality, rather in recreating it, adding new dimensions and possibilities. We imagined ourselves using that five-minute slot at the end of a session. Or using a special poem to introduce a topic. We recalled the days when making links between subjects was an everyday occurrence, so that poetry,

art or drama might be used across the curriculum to deepen understanding.

You will find the direct and simple alongside the more demanding. Do not worry if a poem seems too hard – if it is well written, then the words will cast a spell anyway. The simpler poems may also hold a charm – do not be too dismissive of the simple. Let us not be too snobbish about what children like and value. Let us present a broad variety from the immediate to the puzzling, from the direct to those poems that demand a struggle – to help the whole curriculum sing.

Most of these poems are suitable for solo or group performances and will become part of a child's poetic repertoire. Poems cannot always be easily 'understood'. However, in great poems, the music and meaning of the words, rhythms and images resonate in the memory. Draw simple 'poetry maps' to help children remember the lines and use actions to support performance. Vary volume, pace and expression to emphasize meaning. Music, singing, dance, drama and art may also be used to make the poems memorable experiences rather then just words upon a page. Through rereading, savouring and performance, many of these poems will become favourites that children take to heart for the rest of their lives.

The poet Robert Greacen said that writing poetry is like trying to catch a black cat in a dark room. *The Works 2* is packed with black cats, mewling and miaowing for attention. Open the pages – let them purr awhile, their sharp green eyes illuminating all that they

see. Let them laze around sleepily and then suddenly surprise you, slipping through the dark parts of the mind, ready to spring, to pounce, to catch that bright spark – the imagination.

Pie Corbett

Art and
Design

First Art Lesson

My new paintbox's shining black lacquer lid
divided neatly into three oblong sections
reflects my funny face, the art room windows
white with autumn clouds and flecked with rain.

When I open it, the scented white enamel dazzles.
Inside, pure colours are displayed like blocks
of a bulb-grower's beds of flowers, toy spectrum
in china tubs and tin tubes, a cubist rainbow.

From my jam jar filled with fresh water at the sink
I pour a little liquid into each depression;
take the brush of silky camel hair; wet its plumpness
for the first time, and the last, between my lips.

Then dip its fine, dark tip into the water tanks,
and into the juicy wells of Crimson Lake, Gamboge, Sienna,
Peacock Blue, Burnt Ochre, Emerald, Olive, Terracotta,
Vermilion, Umber, Cadmium, Indigo, Intense Black.

Damp the paper. From the top edge, with sleek, loaded brush,
begin to release the first phantom of a pale-blue wash.

James Kirkup

What Shall I Draw?

Draw a house with four walls
a white fence with a gate in it
four windows, a smoking chimney –
and the path must be lined
with cockleshells and sunflowers

What shall I draw next?

An apple tree and a plum tree
a sheet of grass, pale green,
a tent made from a blanket,
washing on the washing-line.

What shall I put in the house?

A face at the window looking out,
four chairs, a table, a bowl of fruit
and in the room with the red curtains
you can draw yourself, sleeping.

You can draw yourself, sleeping.
Even when the doors are shut
you can draw your way home.

Helen Dunmore

The Paint Box

'Cobalt and umber and ultramarine,
Ivory black and emerald green—
What shall I paint to give pleasure to you?'
'Paint for me somebody utterly new.'

'I have painted you tigers in crimson and white,'
'The colours were good and you painted aright.'
'I have painted the cook and a camel in blue
And a panther in purple.' 'You painted them true.

Now mix me a colour that nobody knows,
And paint me a country where nobody goes,
And put in it people a little like you,
Watching a unicorn drinking the dew.'

E. V. Rieu

Childhood Painting Lesson

'Draw me,' the cypress said,
'I will hold quite still and bow my head.'

'Draw us,' the willows cried.
'We will lift our gentle skirts aside.'

The poppies called, 'We will give you red.'
'I will give you silver,' the river said.

I recall on this neglected lawn
How the world knelt sweetly to be drawn.

Henry Rago

My Teacher Taught Me How to See

My teacher taught me how to see
The lump within the daffodil's throat;
To look in clouds for the camel
And the bounding back of the stoat.

John Kitching

Today, in Strong Colours

Today, in strong colours,
I want you to welcome a visitor.
Give her
A purple wave
A bright-red smile
A round of green applause
A royal-blue handshake
And a yellow hello.
Place her firmly
On the palette of our friendship.

Sue Cowling

Anon.

Modern Art

It's easy – modern art is.
Anyone can do it.
Monkeys can do modern art
toads in holes
and cows with paintbrushes
        tied to their tails.
A dog could do modern art.
        Rats,
        cats,
        rabbits,
        and dead dinosaurs.
Even storks with chalks
and hens with pens
could do modern art.

It's almost as easy as writing poetry
that does not
        scan
        span
        or even rhyme properly
Or is't spelt rite.
Know what I meen?

Peter Dixon

The Museum Says

Be awed as you climb my heavy
stone steps. Built to last.
I am old by your standards.
Two hundred years have rolled past.
But young by the measure
of all of the treasure I hold.
Great books tell of kingdoms long gone
in vast rooms of old gold.
My pillars of marble reach up
to the cold, winter sky.
And my heart is of granite.
A dinosaur sleeping am I.

Roger Stevens

The Art Gallery Says

Hey. I'm cool.
My lines sweep. Zoom.
Catch the eye.
They turn beneath
a fresh spring sky.
Groovy textiles.
Razzamatazz.
This year's black.
I'm now.
Hip.
Jazz.
My wood is polished.
I have awkward seats.
Ergonomic.
White walls with crazy
coloured paintings.
Manic.
I am a bird about to rise
into the clouds.
I am organic.

Roger Stevens

I Asked the Little Boy Who Cannot See

I asked the little boy who cannot see,
'And what is colour like?'
'Why, green,' said he,
'Is like the rustle when the wind blows through
The forest; running water, that is blue;
And red is like a trumpet sound; and pink
Is like the smell of roses; and I think
That purple must be like a thunderstorm;
And yellow is like something soft and warm;
And white is a pleasant stillness when you lie
And dream.'

Anon

Jacob and the Angel

I went to an art gallery with Dad
saw a dead lobster
flame-red
lying on a telephone

some strange paintings
one of hands holding a knife and fork
eating their own insides

a man riding a rhinoceros
across the sky

then I saw these two massive men
a sculpture

one of them had wings

his hands were holding Jacob
as if he cared
that Jacob was very sad and scared

later we sat on the grass outside
had our picnic

and everywhere

that man's hands.

Joan Poulson

Matchstick King

Matchstick girls and matchstick boys
Matchstick houses, matchstick toys
Matchstick dogs and matchstick cats
Matchstick men in matchstick hats
Matchstick women in matchstick coats
Matchstick rivers, matchstick boats
Matchstick hands, matchstick heads
Matchstick dolls in matchstick beds
Matchstick houses, matchstick prams
Matchstick factories, matchstick trams

Everything is matchstick thin
But fat with life
Within
Within.

John Kitching

Who's That on the Phone?

(after Lobster Telephone *by Salvador Dali.)*

There's a lobster on the phone!

Not a crayfish
Or a seal,
Not a spider crab
Or an eel –
But a lobster!

Not a mobster
Full of threats,
Nor debt collector
seeking debts –
But a lobster!

Not a salesgirl,
Double-glazing,
Nor astrologer,
future-grazing –
But a lobster!

Not an emu
On the loose,
Nor a zebra,
Nor a moose,
Not a hangman
With a noose . . .

No, there's a lobster on the phone
And he wants to speak to you!

Pie Corbett

After Giacometti
(1901–1966)

Look –
this
man
is
very
very
thin
but
still
standing
up –
and
I
for
one
believe
that
is
some
sort of
achievement.

Fred Sedgwick

The British Museum Print Room

Van Gogh thought to be a preacher.
At twenty-one he came here and saw
the Rembrandt brown ink drawing over there,
then he did his own.

It lies in this glass case –
a splutter of rocks in the foreground,
a scruff of grass.
He drew every tree one behind the other
pulling right back to the horizon.

Dots became finer,
fields became thinner,
a track ripples to the right
while a train drags smoke to the left.

Stooks measure fields,
cypresses billow,
nothing is still.

Chrissie Gittins

Leonardo

Leonardo, painter, taking
　　Morning air
　　　　On Market Street
Saw the wild birds in their cages
　　Silent in
　　　　The dust, the heat.

Took his purse from out his pocket
　　Never questioning
　　　　The fee,
Bore the cages to the green shade
　　Of a hill-top
　　　　Cypress tree.

'What you lost,' said Leonardo,
　　'I now give to you
　　　　Again,
Free as noon and night and morning,
　　As the sunshine,
　　　　As the rain.'

And he took them from their prisons,
Held them to
The air, the sky;
Pointed them to the bright heaven.
'Fly!' said Leonardo.
'Fly!'

Charles Causley

The story is told of the Italian painter Leonardo da Vinci (1452–1519)

The Uncertainty of the Poet

I am a poet.
I am very fond of bananas.

I am bananas.
I am very fond of a poet.

I am a poet of bananas.
I am very fond.

A fond poet of 'I am, I am' –
Very bananas.

Fond of 'Am I bananas?
Am I?' – a very poet.

Bananas of a poet!
Am I fond? Am I very?

Poet bananas! I am.
I am fond of a 'very'.

I am of very fond bananas.
Am I a poet?

Wendy Cope

The Boyhood of Raleigh

Entranced, he listens to salty tales
Of derring-do and giant whales,

Uncharted seas and Spanish gold,
Tempests raging, pirates bold.

And his friend? 'God I'm bored.
As for Jolly Jack, I don't believe a word.

What a way to spend the afternoons,
The stink of fish, and those ghastly pantaloons!'

Roger McGough

The Artist's Model Daydreams

It's cold in here –
I wish he'd hurry up.

He keeps pausing to stare
First at the painting
And then at my bare shoulder –

It's embarrassing enough,
Sat here,
Cute in my birthday suit;
Not a stitch on –

And he gets so cross
If I move.
Even the slightest itch
Has to be ignored.

Bored?

Look – he's not like
That nice Mr Picasso –
A few quick dabs,
The odd line –
And it's done.
Of course,
He can't paint –
Poor chap.
His faces are a crooked mess –

And he couldn't care less
What colours he uses.

But no one loses.
The painting is slick.
Over quick –
And why should I worry
As long as he pays.

Pie Corbett

A Sort of Chinese Poem

The Chinese write poems
That don't look like poems.
They are more like paintings.

A cherry-tree, a snowstorm,
An old man in a boat –
These might be their subjects.

It all looks so easy –
But it isn't.
You have to be very simple,
Very straightforward,
To see so clearly.
Also, you have to have thousands of years of skill.

When I was a child, I once wrote a Chinese poem.
Now I'm too complicated.

Elizabeth Jennings

The Sand Artist

On the damp seashore
above dark rainbows of shells, seaweed, seacoal,
the sandman wanders, seeking for a pitch.

Ebb tide is his time. The sands are lonely,
but a few lost families
camp for the day on its Easter emptiness.

He seeks the firm dark sand of the retreating waves.
– With their sandwiches and flasks of tea, they
lay their towels on the dry slopes of dunes.

From the sea's edge he draws his pail
of bitter brine, and bears it carefully
towards the place of first creation.

There he begins his labours. Silent,
not looking up at passing shadows
of curious children, he moulds his dreams.

Not simple sandcastles, melting as they dry,
but galleons, anchors, dolphins, cornucopias of fish,
mermaids. Neptunes, dragons of the deep.

With a piece of stick, a playing card
and the blunt fingers of a working man
the artist resurrects existence from the sea.

And as the returning tide takes back its gifts,
he waits in silence by his pitman's cap
for pennies from the sky.

James Kirkup

Notes for an Autumn Painting

mist.

crisp leaves against grass.

pale sunrise.

michaelmas daisies by the railway line.

dead willowherb –
tops grey almost to indigo
– leaves burnt to sienna.

dying bracken.

saturated grasslands.

pale orange grass on hillsides, red purple
amid pale brown fallen leaves.

sky washed by the wind.

green and yellow
confetti
round silver birch trees.

mysterious rich viridian patches
across the valley.

in the foreground
grass yellowed almost to whiteness

and
a space where

the person who will no longer be in the picture
should be.

Adrian Henri

Jack Frost

He's been again
In the night
Painting windows
Sparkling white

Silver trees
And frosty paths
Crystal footprints
Spiky grass

Spiders' webs
Of wintry lace
Jack Frost's touch
In every place

Brenda Williams

Art Year Haikus

Spring morning sun bathes
Pink blossom and brave, bright birds.
I take out my paints.

Summer sun has come.
Fields of corn are gay with gold.
I paint before rain.

One bold rose remains
Despite night's slight bite of frost.
I'll save it in paint.

All is dressed in snow.
A fox pads across tight ice,
His brush caught by mine.

John Kitching

Notes

Leonardo da Vinci – a great Italian artist and thinker.

Van Gogh – a Dutch painter. His paintings were full of colour and movement. He painted people and rural scenes – sunflowers, wild skies, swirling cornfields.

Salvador Dali – Dali was an eccentric, surrealist painter from the south of Spain. He painted strange scenes that look like dreams. The *Lobster Telephone* is an old-fashioned phone that has a red lobster instead of the handset.

Alberto Giacometti – a famous Italian sculptor who created thin sculptures.

L. S. Lowry – Lowry was a painter from Manchester. You can always tell a Lowry painting because he painted people looking very thin – often described as 'looking like matchsticks'.

The Boyhood of Raleigh – this famous painting by Sir John Everett Millais shows two young boys listening to a sailor – who looks as if he is telling them stories.

Adrian Henri – Adrian Henri was one of the Liverpool poets. He was also a well-known painter and often made references to painting in his poems.

Music

Music . . .

is everywhere.
In the birds of the air.
In the hum of the honeybee.
In the song of the breeze
as it shivers the trees.
In the river that murmurs
over the stones.
In the snow wind that moans.

In the surge of the sea
lapping the shore.
In the roar of the storm
rattling the door.
In the drum of the rain
on the windowpane.
Music is here.
Filling your ear.

Ann Bonner

We Got Rhythm

Rhythm in your breathing, rhythm in your heartbeat,
Rhythm in your clapping and the tapping of your feet;
Rhythm when you swim, rhythm when you run;
Rhythm in the rising and the setting of the Sun;
Rhythm in the rain, and the chattering of teeth,
Rhythm in a caterpillar measuring a leaf;
Rhythm in a clock, and a telephone ringing;
Rhythm in a waterfall, and songbirds singing;
Rhythm in the wavelets lapping on a beach,
Rhythm in writing, rhythm in speech.

A rhythm may be noisy, or it may not make a sound,

Like the Rhythm of the Stars as they slowly dance around.

Mike Jubb

Everyday Music

All a mix together
village sounds make my music
   with horses' hooves clop-clopping
   flock of hens cackling
   wood-chopping echoing
   a donkey hehawing
   cocks all around crowing.

All a mix together
village sounds make my music
   with wind and rain rushing
   our flooded gulley babbling
   birds all around singing
   a lonely cow mooing
   rolling sea land-drumming.

All a mix together
village sounds make my music
   with fighting dogs yelping
   birds in trees twittering
   a lonely goat bleating
   hidden ground-doves cooing
   hidden mongoose shrieking.

James Berry

J is for Jazz-Man

Crash and
        CLANG!
Bash and
        BANG!
And up in the word the Jazz-Man sprang!
The One-Man-Jazz-Band playing in the street,
Drums with his Elbows, Cymbals with his Feet,
Pipes with his Mouth. Accordion with his Hand,
Playing all his Instruments to Beat the Band!
     TOOT and
        Tingle!
     HOOT and
        Jingle!
Oh, what a Clatter! How the tunes all mingle!
Twenty Children couldn't make as much Noise *as*
The Howling Pandemonium of the One-Man-Jazz!

Eleanor Farjeon

Embryonic Mega-Stars

We can play reggae music, funk and skiffle too,
We prefer heavy metal but the classics sometimes do.
We're keen on Tamla-Motown, folk and soul,
But most of all, what we like
Is basic rock and roll.
We can play the monochord, the heptachord and flute,
We're OK on the saxophone and think the glockenspiel is
    cute,
We really love the tuba, the balalaika and guitar
And our duets on the clavichord are bound to take us far.
We think castanets are smashing, harmonicas are fun,
And with the ocarina have only just begun.
We've mastered synthesizers, bassoons and violins
As well as hurdy-gurdies, pan pipes and mandolins.
The tom-tom and the tabor, the trumpet and the drum
        We learnt to play in between the tintinnabulum.
        We want to form a pop group
        And will when we're eleven,
        But at the moment Tracey's eight
        And I am only seven.

Brian Patten

In the Bleak Mid-winter

In the bleak mid-winter
  Frosty wind made moan,
Earth stood hard as iron,
  Water like a stone;
Snow had fallen, snow on snow,
  Snow on snow,
In the bleak mid-winter
  Long ago.

Our God, Heaven cannot hold Him
  Nor earth sustain;
Heaven and earth shall flee away
  When He comes to reign;
In the bleak mid-winter
  A stable-place sufficed
The Lord God Almighty
  Jesus Christ.

Enough for Him, whom cherubim
  Worship night and day,
A breastful of milk
  And a mangerful of hay;
Enough for Him, whom angels
  Fall down before,
The ox and ass and camel
  Which adore.

Angels and archangels
   May have gathered there,
Cherubim and seraphim
   Thronged the air;
But only His mother
   In her maiden bliss
Worshipped the Beloved
   With a kiss.

What can I give Him,
   Poor as I am?
If I were a shepherd
   I would bring a lamb,
If I were a Wise Man
   I would do my part,
Yet what I can I give Him,
   Give my heart.

Christina Rossetti

Seaside Sonata

(To be sung on the way home.)

a caravan · a travelling man · a razor shell · kiss and tell

a ferry quay · a ruffled sea · knotted wrack · a chalk stack

fish bone · wish bone · high tide · slip'n'slide

kittiwake · waterscape · shore line · strandline

a brittle star · a limpet jar · a muffled bell · a sudden swell

a falling sea · anemone

a melody · a memory

Mary Green

Drum

Played softly:
a badger's heartbeat,
mountain river,
tumbling.

Played louder:
soldiers marching,
giant's tummy,
rumbling.

Played loudest:
roll of thunder,
black volcano
grumbling.

Judith Nicholls

A Crack Band

Early morning boiler gives a bagpipe bellow,
starts to heat the water, makes it chuckle like a cello

radiators wake up with a tinging and a ping –
pizzicato plucking of a violin,

metal's making music on a xylophone,
pipes are groaning notes like an old trombone,

castanets are clacking, there's a clanging from a gong
as the house warms up and the band plays on.

Gina Douthwaite

Stereo Headphones

I'm sitting
on a train
and I'm
wearing my

Ste   reo
Head   phones

I'm putting
on my favourite
tape and pressing
'PLAY'

SSSSSSSS   SSSSSSSS
boom   boom
thumpity   thump
twang   kerrang
bippity   boom
kerbop   kerboom
kerrang   kerrtwang
asciddlybop   asciddlydoo
bbbbbbbb-   bbbbbbbb-
BOOOOM   *BOOOOM*

WOW!!!!
Why's everyone staring at me?!?

James Carter

45

Electric Guitars

I like electric guitars:
played mellow or moody
frantic or fast – on CDs
or tapes, at home or in
cars – live in the streets,
at gigs or in bars.
I like
electric
guitars:
played
choppy
l i k e
reggae
or angry
l i k e
rock or
chirpy
l i k e
jazz or
strummy
l i k e
pop or
h e a v y
l i k e
metal – it
bothers
me not.

I like electric guitars:
their strings and their straps
and their wild wammy bars – their
jangling and twanging and funky
wah-wahs – their fuzz boxes,
frets and multi-effects –
pick-ups, machine
heads, mahogany necks
– their plectrums, their wires
and big amplifiers. I like electric
guitars: played loudly, politely – dully
or brightly – daily or nightly – badly
or nicely. I like electric guitars:
bass, lead and rhythm –
I basically dig 'em –

I like electric guitars

James Carter

Heavy Metal, Stormy Weather

Flash, crash, rock and roll,
This week's weather's been out of control,
For storming up the charts together
Have been heavy metal and stormy weather!

For drip-dropping in on Monday we had:

'Wet Playtime and the Raincoats'.
Drip-drop de bop-hop, drip-drop de bop-hop,
Drip-drop de bop-hop, drip-dee-drop!

Freeze-breezing upon us on Tuesday we had:

'Strong Gale and the Hailstones'.
Freeze-breeze de sneeze, Freeze-breeze de sneeze
Freeze-breeze de sneeze – aatchoo!

Clog-fogging around us on Wednesday we had:

'Overcast and the Mistmakers'.
Thump-bump de bump-thump, thump-bump de bump-thump,
Thump-bump de bump-thump, thump-dee-bump!

Snow-blowing down on us on Thursday we had:

'Sludge-Budge and the Wet Wellies'.
Snow-blow de blow-go, snow-blow de blow-go,
Snow-blow de blow-go, snow-dee-blow!

And boom-banging above us on Friday we had:

'Rumble-Grumble and the Thunderbolts'.
Boom-bang de bang-boom, boom-bang de bang-boom,
Boom-bang de bang-boom, boom-dee-bang!

But next week we're hoping for a new number one.
Yes, 'Blue Skies and the HOT, HOT SUN'!

Ian Souter

The Music Lesson Rap

I'm the bongo kid,
I'm the big-drum-beater,
I'm the click-your-sticks,
I'm the tap-your-feeter.
When the lesson starts,
When we clap our hands,
Then it's me who dreams
Of the boom-boom bands,
And it's me who stamps,
And it's me who yells
For the biff-bang gong,
Or the ding-dong bells,
Or the cymbals (large),
Or the cymbals (small),
Or the tubes that chime
Round the bash-crash hall,
Or the tambourine,
Or the thunder-maker –
But all you give me
Is the sssh-sssh shaker!

Clare Bevan

Song for a Banjo Dance

Shake your brown feet, honey,
Shake your brown feet, chile,
Shake your brown feet, honey,
Shake 'em swift and wil' –
 Get way back, honey,
 Do that rockin' step.
 Slide on over, darling,
  Now! Come out
  With your left.
Shake your brown feet, honey,
Shake 'em, honey chile.

Sun's going down this evening –
Might never rise no mo'.
The sun's going down this very night –
Might never rise no mo'
So dance with swift feet, honey,
 (The banjo's sobbing low)
Dance with swift feet, honey –
 Might never dance no mo'.

Shake your brown feet, Liza,
Shake 'em, Liza, chile,
Shake your brown feet, Liza,
  (The music's soft and wil')
Shake your brown feet, Liza,
  (The banjo's sobbing low)
The sun's going down this very night –
Might never rise no mo'.

Langston Hughes

If I Were the Conductor

If I were the conductor
Of an orchestra I'd choose
Piano-playing monkeys
And, as cellists, kangaroos,
A hippo on the piccolo,
A sloth on xylophone
And one giant, eight-legged octopus
Who'd play four flutes alone.

Richard Edwards

Song of the Animal World

The fish goes . . .   Hip
The bird goes . . .   Viss!
The monkey goes . . .   Gnan!

I start to the left,
I twist to the right,
I am the fish
That slips through the water,
That slides,
That twists,
That leaps!

Everything lives,
Everything dances,
Everything sings:
The fish goes . . .   Hip!
The bird goes . . .   Viss!
The monkey goes . . .   Gnan!

The bird flies away,
Flies, flies, flies,
Goes, returns, passes,
Climbs, floats, swoops.
I am the bird!

Everything lives,
Everything dances,
Everything sings:
The fish goes . . .   Hip!
The bird goes . . .   Viss!
The monkey goes . . .   Gnan!

The monkey! From branch to branch
Runs, hops, jumps,
With his wife and baby,
Mouth stuffed full, tail in air,
Here's the monkey! Here's the
Monkey!

Everything lives,
Everything dances,
Everything sings:
The fish goes . . .   Hip!
The bird goes . . .   Viss!
The monkey goes . . .   Gnan!

Traditional (Zaire/Democratic Republic of Congo)

Making Music

I'm a BIG BASS drum
booming down the street,
tapping with my fingers
to the booming bass beat.

I'm a fiddle playing music
shooting notes up high,
watching as they fall
from a music-making sky.

I'm an old double bass
grumbling in my boots,
shaking every tree top
down to its roots.

I'm a small brass horn
singing to the stars,
swimming in their moonshine
and diving down to Mars.

I'm a cymbal sitting still
making not a sound,
waiting for the moment
when I CRASH to the ground.

Andrew Collett

The Rhythm of the Tom-tom

The rhythm of the tom-tom does not beat in my blood
Nor in my skin
Nor in my skin
The rhythm of the tom-tom beats in my heart
In my heart
In my heart
The rhythm of the tom-tom does not beat in my blood
Nor in my skin
Nor in my skin
The rhythm of the tom-tom beats especially
In the way that I think
In the way that I think
I think Africa, I feel Africa, I proclaim Africa
I hate in Africa
    I love in Africa
    And I am Africa
    The rhythm of the tom-tom beats especially
    In the way that I think
    In the way that I think
    I think Africa, I feel Africa, I proclaim Africa
    And I become silent
    Within you, for you, Africa
    Within you, for you, Africa
    A fri ca
        A fri ca
            A fri ca

António Jacinto (Angola) translated by Don Burness

The Group

There wasn't much to do today
so Malcolm and me and Ian Gray
planned how we might form a group
with me on keyboards, Malcolm on drums
and Ian who knew how to strum a C
or a G on his brother's guitar.

Then Ian's sister came waltzing in
with her friend Sharon and wanted to know
why they couldn't be in the group as well
and when we said no, they threatened to tell
some dreadful secret and Ian turned white,
said they could stay if they kept really quiet.

Then we argued a bit about the name:
'The Werewolves,' I said or 'The Sewer Rats'
or 'The Anti Everything Parents Say'
but Malc said no, it ought to be simple
and Ian said maybe 'The group with no name'
while his sister and Sharon said something silly
and Malcolm and I ignored them completely.

And I thought we ought to write some songs,
'Easy,' we said, 'it wouldn't take long
to knock off another *Hold on to your love,*
but don't let her go, oh no, no, no!
And Malc kept the beat with slaps on his knee
while I played kazoo or a paper and comb
till Sharon yawned, then got up and went home.

Then Ian's sister and Ian sat down
while we stood around and said what to write,
and it sounded all right till we tried it out
and discovered how awful it was
'Let's knock it on the head,' I said,
we'll need another year or two
before we get it right.

And later that night on the short walk home
I said to Malc that I thought we ought
to dump the others and go it alone.
We should have seen it all along,
two good looking dudes like us,
we'd be famous in no time.

But Malc said we were overlooking
one small but very important thing:
Neither of us could sing!

Brian Moses

Lewis Has a Trumpet

A trumpet
A trumpet
Lewis has a trumpet
A bright one that's yellow
A loud proud horn.
He blows it in the evening
When the moon is newly rising
He blows it when it's raining
In the cold and misty morn
It honks and it whistles
It roars like a lion
It rumbles like a lion
With a wheezy huffing hum
His parents say it's awful
Oh really simply awful
But
Lewis says he loves it
It's such a handsome trumpet
And when he's through with trumpets
He's going to buy a drum.

Karla Kuskin

History

History

History
Is more than dusty, rusty pages
About crooked princes, queens and kings,
Or victims chained in cold and cruel prison cages.

History
Is more than the mystery
Of wars, other mighty causes
And painful pauses
For great black plagues and fires.

History
Is also your small yesterday and mine.
It is our own comic and our curious.
It is what made us small folk
Fearful, fierce or furious.

History
Is the blended thread
That binds the living to the dead.

John Kitching

Historian

(A kenning)

Time-detective
Bone-collector
Stone-saver
Rune-reader
Parchment-keeper
Villain-hounder
Hero-maker
Grave-digger
Fact-hunter
Story-searcher
Truth-seeker
Year-counter
Age-teller
Past-banker

John Kitching

The Great Lizards

The great lizards are gone,
their bones are inlaid in land, or stand
in the high halls of museums,
gaunt and picked clean, pieced together
for the cold winds to blow through.

They're quiet, these bones.
No rippling scales, no huge eyes swivelling,
no rank hot stench of heavy flesh.
Apart from these bones, we must invent them ourselves,
monsters, dragons, creatures of our imagination.

Yet the bones do not show how they lived,
but how they died; and these great skeletons,
so carefully rebuilt, do not make me think of them
striding terribly across sprawling plains
or browsing enormous mouthfuls in steamy swamps
in a world so long before us that it seems wholly alien

but of them running out of time,
fleeing across a desert where earth melts
through clouds of driven sand and ash
under a sky of smoke and fire,
closing in, burning and choking;
of them howling as their feet stick
and stumble in scorching lava
or catch in cracks as the ground quakes and splits
and they fall into the history
of two-legged soft-skinned small creatures.

And the great gape of empty mouth
asks me to imagine what
will dig us up after another million years
and raise our bones to stare at
in bewildered curiosity.

Dave Calder

Voice from the Pharaoh's Tomb

Chill winds across the desert probe
the night-dark entrance to a tomb
and metres deep within stone walls,
beyond the ears of gods or men,
a spirit voice cries out.

'How many years have I lain here?
I cannot tell, I cannot tell.
Have only known the pain of theft
from my first journey here till now,
abandoned and bereft.

Even the gods deserted me.
They, too, were thieves; they, too, took all.
They took my sun, my life, my joys,
laughter of children still to come,
dream upon dream snuffed out.

Within four coffins shut me tight,
each tomb a treasure trove of jewels:
cornelian, quartz, cool ivory,
bright blue of
lapis lazuli.

Collars of gold to shackle me,
silks of deceit to clothe my corpse,
great masks pressed close against my face,
darkness to dull the memory
of all that life had been –

> the sun's warm touch upon my skin,
> the Nile's soft breezes on my cheek;
> my favourite hunting dog unleashed,
> flurry of birds flushed from the reeds,
> the boatman's echoing cry –

Chattels were all they left to me,
room upon room in crazy piles:
gold thrones and chariots, walking sticks,
sceptres and stools, rare amulets,
sad bunches of dried flowers.

And these, my cats, which long ago
wrapped sinuous bodies round my feet,
and purred and preened and licked my hand,
are brittle skeletons worn thin
within grey rotting bands.

Even these dusty memories
men have removed, men have erased.
Cold walls close in on empty space,
my soul can find no place to rest,
my spirit no release.'

Weak curses from dark shadows seep,
they wither on the desert air.
And deep within a barren tomb
a boy – a king – weeps golden tears.
Tutankhamen.

* Tutankhamen: say Toot-AN-ka-MOON

Patricia Leighton

A Liking for the Viking

I've always had a liking for the Viking;
His handsome horns; his rough and ready ways;
His rugged russet hair beneath his helmet
In those metal-rattle, battle-happy days.

I've always had a longing for a longboat;
To fly like a dragon through the sea
To peaceful evenings round a real fire,
Alive with legend; rich with poetry.

I've always had a yearning for the burning
Of brave flames irradiating valour;
For the fiery longboat carrying its Chieftain
To his final feast in glorious Valhalla.

Celia Warren

King Canute

The noble King Canute, they said
Could waves and tide abash
Canute said, 'All this flattery
Is really rather rash.
Let's make a little wager.
Do you have a little cash?'
Then he sat upon the beach, and waited. Splash! Splash!
   Splash!
Now the winds began to whistle
And the waves began to crash.
'Command it to recede,' they said
'Do try it. Have a bash!'
Canute said sternly, 'Turn! Begone!'
And twiddled his moustache
But all the time the waves kept coming. Splash! Splash!
   Splash!
'The tide is on the turn,' they said
With confident panache.
'Just give it time. One minute more!'
Canute said, 'Balderdash!
It's way above my ankles
And I think it's time to dash
'Cause I'm getting soaking wet with all this Splash! Splash!
   Splash!'

Paul Bright

Roman Invasions

BC55

Julius Caesar,
Roman geezer,
Came to Britain,
Wasn't smitten,
Back to Gaul
After all.

AD43

Emperor Claudius,
More maraudius,
Had his reasons,
Sent more legions.
They were stronger,
Stayed much longer,
Long enough
For roads and stuff,
Built some baths,
Had some laughs,
England greener
Greater, Cleaner!

Celia Warren

Julius Caesar's Last Breakfast

I'm tired this morning
Off my food
Hardly touched the olives, lark or dormouse
We stayed out late last night
With Lepidus
And talked of death
Drank too much wine
And now Calpurnia, my wife,
Is in a mood
She dreamed a death
And it was mine.

I'm tired this morning
The winds of March
Are blowing like a hurricane
Through Rome
At the Pontifical Palace
The God of Mars crashed to the floor
And what that means, I'm not quite sure.

I'm tired this morning
Upon the Ides of March
The Senate can convene without me
Yes, I think I'll stay at home.

(On the morning of Julius Caesar's assassination, the chamber at the Senate was full. But Caesar's chair was empty. He was nowhere to be found. The conspirators sent Marcus Brutus to Caesar's house to persuade him to attend.)

Roger Stevens

Entering a Castle

Don't enter a castle quietly
  or timidly.
don't enter it anxiously,
  ready to bolt
  at the slightest sound.
Don't enter it stealthily
  taking slow and thoughtful steps,
  considering with each footfall
  the mystery of history.
Don't be meek
  or frightened to speak.
For when you enter a castle
  you should *charge* through the gate
  and signal your arrival with a SHOUT!
  You should play the invading army
  and *barge* a way through.
You should *swagger* up to the door
    then *shove* it aside and announce,
    'Here I am! This is mine!'

This castle is here, it is waiting for you,
    and today,
        it is yours for the taking!

Brian Moses

A Sense of History

Dry were the words,
dry as the rustling page,
flatly describing extraordinary historical events;
the repeated rebellions of three princes, and
the king their father's dying rage.
The imprisoned queen was a dull figure,
silent actress on a paper stage.

But visiting the real royal castle
on a day trip from school,
metre-thick walls of cold grey stone
jarred imagination. Their senses were stimulated
by a sudden raw grasp of the reality of such rule.
Brutal spiked maces and double-edged swords
brought the youngest prince's cruel
actions frighteningly alive.
They smelled the stench of the midden,
heard squealing pigs and cackling fowl
among hovels hard by the grim defensive walls.
They saw guttering candles in draughty hidden
tower rooms, gloomy and bare, and shuddered
at the thought of being forbidden
ever to leave this damp, unhealthy place.
Ten years a captive guarded here?

Gladly they boarded the coach
for home and modern comforts,
history having momentarily come too near.

Penny Kent

The Tudors

Henry the Seventh,
A battling man,
Captured the crown
And the Tudors began.

Henry the Eighth
Was next in the line –
Married six wives,
Loved banquets and wine.

Edward the Sixth
Came after his dad –
King for six years
And a sickly young lad.

Mary the First,
A woman of pride,
Lit lots of bonfires
But very soon died.

Elizabeth R,
(Who was known as Queen Bess)
Reigned many years –
Forty-five, more or less.

With Shakespeare and Drake
She won fortune and fame,
But gave us no children
To carry her name.

So that was the end –
All the Tudors were dead . . .
Then along came the Stuarts
To rule us instead.

Clare Bevan

Guess Who?

(A kenning poem)

Horse rider
Joust glider
Music maker
Floor shaker
Tennis prancer
Heavy dancer
Diet hater
Serial dater
Dandy dresser
Wife stresser
Church leader
Poor breeder
Nifty speaker
Divorce seeker
Armour filler
Wife killer
Monk basher
Law smasher
Banquet boozer
Bad loser.

Coral Rumble

Short Livers

Some Tudor folk
Were rich and haughty.
Quite a few
Were cruel and naughty.

Most of them
Were dead by forty!

John Kitching

Cutpurse Kit

I go out hunting rabbits
large, fat, expensively dressed rabbits
with fine furs and velvet cloaks
golden clothing and leather belts.
They walk on two legs through St Paul's
or parade around the theatre.
combing their long, sleek whiskers
head in the air, eyes in the sky
my fat rabbits.

Watch me as I sidle and sneak
right up beside them
I point to the moon or the sun
through a cloud
of course they look up, twitch their noses
I take their purse
in my long, silent fingers
each knobble and bobble
a round gold coin.
Quick cut the purse strings
and it falls in my palm
like ripening fruit dropped from the tree.

I slip away
sly as a knife cut
sharp as a blade
I hear the rabbits start to squeal
mew like kittens
cry out loud for their gold
stuck in the blinding light of their panic.

David Harmer

Printer's Devil

I am the newest devil
Down at Caxton's printing shop.
I sweep the floor, I fetch the beer
And polish up the blocks.

Last week I practised inking,
A black catastrophe!
Half of it reached the letter dies –
The rest of it inked me!

Then yesterday when work was slack
Will Caxton let me set
A title page – all by myself –
And print it on the press.

The lettering was perfect,
The paper clean and white,
Except it said
   THE
   BIᗺEL
Well, I *nearly* got it right.

*Printer's Devil – a printer's apprentice, called a 'devil' because he was always covered in black ink.

Patricia Leighton

The Powder Monkey

This is the moment I dread,
my eyes sting with smoke,
my ears sing with cannon fire.
I see the terror rise inside me,
coil a rope in my belly to keep it down.
I chant inside my head to freeze my nerve.

Main mast, mizzen mast, foremast,
belfry, capstan, waist.

We must keep the fire coming.
If I dodge the sparks
my cartridge will be safe,
if I learn my lessons
I can be a seaman,
if I close my eyes to eat my biscuit
I won't see the weevils.

Main mast, mizzen mast, foremast,
shock lockers, bowsprit, gripe.

Don't stop to put out that fire,
run to the hold,
we must fire at them
or they will fire at us.

Main mast, mizzen mast, foremast,
belfry, capstan, waist.

My mother never knew me,
but she would want to know this –
I can keep a cannon going,
I do not need her kiss.

Before 1794 children aged six upwards went to sea. After 1794
the minimum age was thirteen.

Chrissie Gittins

From 'The Charge of the Light Brigade'

Half a league, half a league,
Half a league onward,
All in the valley of Death
Rode the six hundred.
'Forward, the Light Brigade!
Charge for the guns!' he said:
Into the valley of Death
Rode the six hundred.

'Forward, the Light Brigade!'
Was there a man dismay'd?
Not tho' the soldiers knew
Someone had blunder'd:
Theirs no to make reply,
Theirs not to reason why,
Theirs but to do and die:
Into the valley of Death
Rode the six hundred.

Cannon to the right of them,
Cannon to the left of them,
Cannon in front of them
Volley'd and thunder'd;
Storm'd at with shot and shell,
Boldly they rode and well,
Into the jaws of Death,
Into the mouth of Hell
Rode the six hundred.

Alfred, Lord Tennyson

Cargoes

Quinquireme of Nineveh from distant Ophir
Rowing home to haven in sunny Palestine,
With a cargo of ivory,
And apes and peacocks,
Sandalwood, cedarwood, and sweet white wine.

Stately Spanish galleon coming from the Isthmus,
Dipping through the Tropics by the palm-green shores,
With a cargo of diamonds,
Emeralds, amethysts,
Topazes, and cinnamon, and gold moidores.

Dirty British coaster with a salt-caked smoke stack
Butting through the Channel in the mad March days,
With a cargo of Tyne coal,
Road-rail, pig-lead,
Firewood, iron-ware, and cheap tin trays.

John Masefield

The Housemaid's Letter

Dear Mum,
>My life is very fine here
>Far from the village
>And the smells of home.

>I have a room in the roof
>Painted blue as a blackbird's egg,
>And a whole bed to myself,
>Which is lonely
>But so clean
>The sheets crackle like morning frost.

And I have tried
Truly
To make you proud of me, Mum.
I work hard all day,
Cleaning and polishing this great house
Till it sparkles as brightly
As a butterfly's wing.
Then I disappear down the Servants' Stair
Like a small, sweaty,
Fairy Godmother,
Unseen and unknown
By the golden ones above.

And I am happy enough, Mum.
The food is good
Though swallowed in silence.

The other girls smile
At my clumsy ways
And Cook can be kind
If the milk is sweet
And the butter cool.

But sometimes,
When the Sunday bells are ringing,
I still miss the warmth of the little ones
Curled beside me in the tumbled darkness,
And I hunger to hear
The homely peal
Of your lost laughter,
Mum.

Clare Bevan

Aunt Sue's Stories

Aunt Sue has a head full of stories.
Aunt Sue has a whole heart full of stories.
Summer nights on the front porch
Aunt Sue cuddles a brown-faced child to her bosom
And tells him stories.

Black slaves
Working in the hot sun,
And black slaves
Walking in the dewy night,
And black slaves
Singing sorrow songs on the banks of a mighty river
Mingle themselves softly
In the flow of old Aunt Sue's voice,
Mingle themselves softly
In the dark shadows that cross and recross
Aunt Sue's stories.

And the dark-faced child, listening,
Knows that Aunt Sue's stories are real stories.
He knows that Aunt Sue
Never got her stories out of any book at all,
But that they came
Right out of her own life.

And the dark-faced child is quiet
Of a summer night
Listening to Aunt Sue's stories.

Langston Hughes

My Mother Saw a Dancing Bear

My mother saw a dancing bear
By the schoolyard, a day in June.
The keeper stood with chain and bar
And whistle-pipe, and played a tune.

And bruin lifted up its head
And lifted up its dusty feet,
And all the children laughed to see
It caper in the summer heat.

They watched as for the Queen it died.
They watched it march. They watched it halt.
They heard the keeper as he cried,
'Now, roly-poly!' 'Somersault!'

And then, my mother said, there came
The keeper with a begging-cup,
The bear with burning coat of fur,
Shaming the laughter to a stop.

They paid a penny for the dance,
But what they saw was not the show;
Only, in bruin's aching eyes,
Far-distant forests, and the snow.

Charles Causley

For the Fallen

(September 1914)

With proud thanksgiving, a mother for her children,
England mourns for her dead across the sea.
Flesh of her flesh they were, spirit of her spirit,
Fallen in the cause of the free.

Solemn the drums thrill: Death august and royal
Sings sorrow up into immortal spheres.
There is music in the midst of desolation
And a glory that shines upon our tears.

They went with songs to the battle, they were young,
Straight of limb, true of eye, steady and aglow.
They were staunch to the end against odds uncounted,
They fell with their faces to the foe.

They shall grow not old, as we that are left grow old:
Age shall not weary them, nor the years condemn.
At the going down of the sun and in the morning
We will remember them.

They mingle not with their laughing comrades again;
They sit no more at familiar tables of home;
They have no lot in our labour of the day-time;
They sleep beyond England's foam.

But where our desires are and our hopes profound,
Felt as a well-spring that is hidden from sight,
To the innermost heart of their own land they are known
As the stars are known to the Night;

As the stars that shall be bright when we are dust,
Moving in marches upon the heavenly plain,
As the stars that are starry in the time of our darkness,
To the end, to the end, they remain.

Laurence Binyon

The Soldier

If I should die, think only this of me:
 That there's some corner of a foreign field
That is for ever England. There shall be
 In that rich earth a richer dust concealed;
A dust whom England bore, shaped, made aware,
 Gave, once, her flowers to love, her ways to roam,
A body of England's, breathing English air,
 Washed by the rivers, blest by suns of home.

And think, this heart, all evil shed away,
 A pulse in the eternal mind, no less
 Gives somewhere back the thoughts by
 England given;
Her sights and sounds; dreams happy as her day;
 And laughter, learnt of friends; and gentleness,
 In hearts at peace, under an English heaven.

Rupert Brooke

Growing Up in the 1930s

Liquorice plaits
And white sherbet dabs –
Gobstoppers, too –
Cost just pennies!
Picture card sets!
Coal from a cart!
Milk from a churn!
Cold custard tart!
'Bubble and Squeak' –
And black wellies!

Trousers (home made!)
And 'seventy-eights';
Thick flannel vests;
Gas-lit lights!
Skittles and hoops;
Jellies and jams;
Hopscotch and dolls;
Trolleys and trams!
'Wirelesses';
Mangles – and kites!

Trevor Harvey

Post-war

In 1943
my father
dropped bombs on the continent

I remember
my mother
talking about bananas
in 1944

when it rained,
creeping alone to the window sill,
I stared up the hill,
watching, watching,
watching without a blink
for the Mighty Bananas
to stride through the Blitz

they came in paper bags
in neighbour's hands
when they came
and took their time
over the coming

and still I don't know
where my father
flying home
took a wrong turning

Libby Houston

Remembrance Day – 11 November

Poppies? Oh, miss,
can I take round the tray?
It's only history next.
We're into '45 –
I KNOW who won the war,
no need to say.

> *Old man wears his flower*
> *with pride, his numbers dying now –*
> *but that's no news.*

Why buy? –
because I'm asked
because a flower looks good
to match my mate
not to seem too mean –
(what's ten pence anyway
to those of us who grew
with oranges, December lettuce
and square fish?)
Yes, I'll wear it –
for a while.
Until it's lost
or maybe picked apart
during some boring television news
and then, some idle moment,
tossed.

Poppies? Who cares
as long as there's
some corner of a foreign field
to bring me pineapple, papaya
and my two weeks' patch of sun? –
But I'll still have one
if you really want.
It isn't quite my scene but then
at least the colour's fun.

Old man stumbles
through November mud,
still keeps his silence
at the eleventh hour.

Judith Nicholls

Notes

Great Lizards – dinosaurs are a group of extinct reptiles that lived on the earth about 230–65 million years ago. The word 'dinosaur' means 'terrible lizard' – but dinosaurs were not all meat-eating monsters. Some were quite small and others ate vegetation. They died out 65 million years ago and no one knows exactly why. It may have been due to sudden volcanic activity, a cooling of the climate or the earth being hit by a massive asteroid.

Tutankhamen – was a pharaoh of Egypt (c. 1361–1352 BC). His tomb is in the Valley of the Kings and lay undiscovered until 1922 when an archaeologist called Howard Carter found it. The Pharaoh's body was mummified and kept inside a solid gold coffin. On his face was a golden death mask. In the tomb they found jewellery, weapons and provisions for the afterlife.

Valhalla – in Scandinavian mythology, Valhalla was a great hall for dead heroes who fell in battle. There they feasted with the god Odin.

King Canute – Canute was the king of Denmark and England (994–1035). He was very powerful and managed to bring peace to England. The story is told that to silence those in his court who flattered him, he showed them that even he could not stop the tide from coming in.

Julius Caesar – poor Caesar (100–44 BC) only ruled for one year before being assassinated by Brutus and Cassius. He invaded Britain in 55–54 BC, and was killed on 15 March.

Emperor Claudius – invaded Britain in 43 BC. His fourth wife is said to have poisoned him with mushrooms so that her son could take his place!

William Caxton – was a cloth merchant (1422–1491) who built the first printing press in England in 1476 by Westminster Abbey.

The Tudors – are a royal family (or royal house) who reigned from 1485–1603. The most famous was King Henry the Eighth who is known for having six wives. Sir Francis **Drake** (1540–1596) was the first Englishman to sail round the world. William **Shakespeare** (1564–1616) was the world's most famous playwright.

The Charge of the Light Brigade – this was a famous event in the Crimean War. It happened on 25 October 1854, and Tennyson, who was the Poet Laureate, wrote this poem to commemorate what happened. At the Battle of Balaclava, due to a misunderstanding, Lord Cardigan led 673 cavalry to charge towards the Russian lines with cannons on either side of them. 113 were killed and 134 wounded before they reached the Russian line.

Galleons – these were three-masted, square-rigged ships used in between the 15th and 18th centuries both for war and to carry cargo, such as gold and silver. **Nineveh** was an ancient city.

The Blitz – was the name given to the aerial bombardment of the cities of Britain, especially London, in 1940.

Remembrance Day – this day, usually known as Remembrance Sunday, is the Sunday nearest to 11 November, when those who were killed in the wars of 1914–18 and 1939–45 are commemorated. It is common for people to wear poppies in remembrance of the soldiers who died.

Geography

Geography

I love Geography.

Other people, other places,
Different customs, different faces,
Drought and desert, field and plain,
Snow and ice and monsoon rain,
Volcanoes, glaciers,
Bubbling springs,
Clouds and rainbows,
Countless things.
Stars and planets, distant space,
Whatever's ugly, full of grace.
Seas and rivers,
Cliffs and caves,
The wondrous ways this world behaves.
So much to learn; so much to know;
And so much farther still to go.

John Kitching

Island

Firing molten rock at the sky
And shrugging water off, the island-to-be
Rises steaming from the sea
Whose waters quench its volcanic sides.

Rising mountainous from the depths,
It takes its place with continents,
Though only a speck by comparison,
Above the tides and on the maps.

A part of the world has been rebuilt,
A staging post for birds to visit
And simple plants to inhabit
Once the years weather and cool it.

The forging from the earth's hot core
Settles into its final shape:
People will find it a name;
Someone one day will put ashore.

Stanley Cook

Geography Lesson

When the jet sprang into the sky,
it was clear why the city
had developed the way it had,
seeing it scaled six inches to the mile.
There seemed an inevitability
about what on ground had looked haphazard,
unplanned and without style
when the jet sprang into the sky.

When the jet reached ten thousand feet,
it was clear why the country
had cities where rivers ran
and why the valleys were populated.
The logic of geography –
that land and water attracted man –
was clearly delineated
when the jet reached ten thousand feet.

When the jet rose six miles high,
it was clear that the earth was round
and that it had more sea than land.
But it was difficult to understand
that the men on the earth found
causes to hate each other, to build
walls across cities and to kill.
From that height, it was not clear why.

Zulfikar Ghose

Walking to School

This is the road down which I go
Early to school every day
And these are the houses on the way
Parading in a long straight row.

This is the house of the motoring man
And the car he is mending sits
Without its wheels on piles of bricks
And he's taken the engine out of his van.

This is the house with a big wide drive
With a friendly retriever
Who wags his tail to greet you
And comes to the road to watch you arrive.

This is the house you can hardly see
Among so many lofty trees
That rise in the air like fountains of leaves
And who lives there's a mystery to me.

This is the house my friend lives in:
If he sees me coming he'll wait
Hiding behind his garden gate
And try to frighten me out of my skin.

This is the wooden bungalow
Where a seagull far from the sea
Calls from his perch on top of the chimney
And scolds the people down below.

This is the house with the rocky pool,
A little windmill, a wooden bridge
And a gnome who fishes at the water's edge
And here next to it is the gate to school.

Stanley Cook

From My Window

From my window I see
the lonely tree at the bottom of our garden
waving to catch my attention.
'Come and look, come and look,'
its long fingers seem to be saying.

But I am drawn upwards,
off towards black lumps of cloud
that swagger into view
as if they are chasing trouble.
'Move over sun, your time's up,'
they appear to announce
as daylight suffers a short power loss.

Down on the streets cars are playing,
'Now you see me, now you don't'
behind the neighbouring houses
while on the distant skyline
a train rushes along chattering,
'Mustn't be late, Mustn't be late!'

Ian Souter

Houses

Where would you live if you were me?
A lonely lighthouse in the sea
With a garden of waves and rocks?
A narrowboat nosing through locks?
A windmill with a winding stair
And round rooms stacked like building blocks –
Would you live there?

Where would I live if I were you?
A wooden ark, a floating zoo.
A swaying eyrie in a tree
Would do for me.
An igloo with an icy dome,
A painted gypsy caravan,
A paper palace in Japan
Could be my home.

Sue Cowling

Building a Skyscraper

They're building a skyscraper
Near our street,
Its height will be nearly
One thousand feet.

It covers completely
A city block.
They drilled its foundation
Through solid rock.

They made its framework
Of great steel beams
With riveted joints
And welded seams.

A swarm of workmen
Strain and strive,
Like busy bees
In a honeyed hive.

Building the skyscraper
Into the air
While crowds of people
Stand and stare.

Geography

Higher and higher
The tall tower rises
Like Jacob's ladder
Into the skies.

James S. Tippett

I Live in the City

I live in the city, yes I do,
I live in the city, yes I do,
I live in the city, yes I do,
Made by human hands.

Black hands, white hands, yellow and brown
All together built this town,
Black hands, white hands, yellow and brown
All together make the wheels go round.

Black hands, brown hands, yellow and white
Built the buildings tall and bright,
Black hands, brown hands, yellow and white
Filled them all with shining light.

Black hands, white hands, brown and tan
Milled the flour and cleaned the pan,
Black hands, white hands, brown and tan –
The working woman and the working man.

I live in the city, yes I do,
I live in the city, yes I do,
I live in the city, yes I do,
Made by human hands.

Anon.

Early Last Sunday Morning

Early last Sunday morning
Dad announced we needed a glass of fresh air
and a mouthful of greenness.
So off we slipped to the nearby park
where we crept in as soundless as snails.
Around us the day breathed air
that was as sharp as vinegar
reminding us that winter was well on its way.

Inside we watched the trees stretch and wake
while the grass stood up and shivered.
Soon I was pointing towards a spider
that was strung on a necklace web
while far behind it
the sun rolled out like a golden ball.

Suddenly Dad smiled
as a squirrel scampered from a bush
then turned to grey stone
until with a flick of its tail
it waved goodbye and was gone.

Later as we passed the children's playground
I looked at the lonely, red slide
and briefly remembered the summer days
when I flew its slippery, red tongue.
But a tug of wind pushed me past
until I just let the warmth in Dad's hand
finally lead me on towards home.

Ian Souter

Stream Story

Stream in the hillside,
Burbling, trickling,
Splashing through my fingers,
Tugging and tickling.

Tumbling to the valley,
Gurgling, growing,
Pooh-stick highway,
Filling and flowing.

Bustling with water life,
Flourishing, thriving
On water, underwater,
Swimming and diving.

Now a mighty waterway,
Ships in motion,
Taking all the traffic
To the great, grey ocean.

Paul Bright

Day By Day I Float My Paper Boats

Day by day I float my paper boats one by one
down the running stream.
In big black letters I write my name on them and
the name of the village where I live.
I hope that someone in some strange land will find
them and know who I am.
I load my little boats with shiuli flowers from our
garden, and hope that these blooms of the dawn
will be carried safely to land in the night.
I launch my paper boats and look into the sky and
see the little clouds setting their white
bulging sails.
I know not what playmate of mine in the sky
sends them down the air to race with my boats!
When night comes I bury my face in my arms
and dream that my paper boats float on and on
under the midnight stars.
The fairies of sleep are sailing in them, and the
lading is their baskets full of dreams . . .

Rabindranath Tagore

The Hills

Sometimes I think the hills
That loom across the harbour
Lie there like sleeping dragons,
Crouched one above another,
With trees for tufts of fur
Growing all up and down
The ridges and humps of their backs,
And orange cliffs for claws
Dipped in the sea below.
Sometimes a wisp of smoke
Rises out of the hollows,
As if in their dragon sleep
They dreamed of strange old battles.

What if the hills should stir
Some day and stretch themselves,
Shake off the clinging trees
And all the clustered houses?

Rachel Field

Mountains

Mountains are today, yesterday, and for ever,
They have no likes or dislikes, no opinions –
But moods, yes. Their moods change like the weather.
They argue and quarrel, loud
With angry thunder. They rain
Rivers of stinging tears.
They hide their sulky heads in cloud
For days and days. Then suddenly, all smiles again,
One by one
Their magic cliffs stand clear
And brave, above a sea of white wave,
Under the lighthouse of the sun.

Ian Serraillier

The Train

The train goes running along the line
Jicketty-can, jicketty-can.
I wish it were mine, I wish it were mine.
Jicketty-can, jicketty-can.
The engine driver stands in front,
He makes it run, he makes it shunt;

Out of the town,
Out of the town,
Over the hill,
Over the down,
Under the bridge,
Across the lea,
Over the ridge
And down by the sea,
With a jicketty-can, jicketty-can,
Jicketty-jicketty-jicketty can,
Jicketty-can, jicketty-can.

Clive Sansom

Ocean Travel

If I could travel
the oceans blue,
these are the things
that I would do:

Fly with puffins
under the sea.
Dive with seagulls.
Fish for my tea.

Cling to the tail
of a rolling whale.
Leap with dolphins
in a buffeting gale.

Soar with an eagle.
Hunt with a shark.
Frolic with seals.
Fly home before dark.

Jennifer Tweedie

At the Seaside

When I was down beside the sea
A wooden spade they gave to me
    To dig the sandy shore.
My holes were empty like a cup,
In every hole the sea came up
    Till it could come no more.

Robert Louis Stevenson

Shell

When it was time
for Show and Tell,
Adam brought a big pink shell.

He told about
the ocean roar
and walking on the sandy shore.

And then he passed
the shell around.
We listened to the water sound.

And that's the first time
I could hear
the wild waves calling to my ear.

Myra Cohn Livingston

Seashells

Seashells on the beach
Are like many empty rooms.
No one lives in them,
And they're not rented out.
Where are the ones who lived here?
Whatever could have happened to them?

Anon. (Chinese child)

Points of View

More black than white, Gran's photo –
all mills and chimneys
belching smoke.
Taken from this spot, Gran says,
before her house was built.

We look across the valley
from her window –
not one mill in sight.
A colourful skyline brushed by trees.

'That's where I used to work.'
Gran points to a busy car park
far below,
then shows me on the photo:
a mill among many.
'Our work was long and hard –
deafening, too, those looms.'

Back at the window,
she picks out a bypass
skirting the sunlit town.
'Bulldozed our terrace
to build that thing.'
We examine the photo –
it's kept her blackened terrace.
'Looks dark and rather gloomy.'
'The air was full of soot –

it clogged your lungs
and specked your washing with smuts.
And as for dusting –
what a joke!'

'I'm glad I didn't live then.'
'We had our good times, too.
Went on seaside outings
during wakes* –
and people spoke more –
helped you out.
There's nothing like
good neighbouring.'

I stare across the built-up valley
and see two different worlds.
The familiar view has changed.

*Wakes were annual holidays

Mina Johnson

Volcano

```
                        smoke
            heat        gas        flame
      flame                rocks          heat
            fire
                    eee  E  eee                    fi
     i   gas
   f re            xxx X xxx  X xxx X xxx
        PPPPPPPPPPPPP      P   PPPPPPPPPPPPP
   he   IIIIIIIIIIIIIIIIIII  L   IIIIIIIIIIIIIIIIIII
     l    a    oooooooooo     O    oooooooooo       rocks
          sssssssssssssss   S   sssssssssssssss
      t   iiiiiiiiiiiiiiiiiiiiiiii  I   iiiiiiiiiiiiiiiiiiiiiiiii   m
      k      ooooooo       O      ooooooo            l
   s          nnnn        N   nnnn                g
       m           E!     press    V            r
              RE!     pressure   VO
   la        IRE!     pressure   VOL           la
   va       FIRE!     pressure   VOLC           va
          C FIRE!     pressure   VOLCA
          IC FIRE!    pressure   VOLCAN
         NIC FIRE!    pressure   VOLCANI
        ANIC FIRE!    pressure   VOLCANIC
       CANIC FIRE!    pressure   VOLCANIC F
      LCANIC FIRE!    pressure   VOLCANIC FI
     OLCANIC FIRE!    pressure   VOLCANIC FIR
    VOLCANIC FIRE!    pressure   VOLCANIC FIRE!
```

Mary Green

Rain

She licked the film of dust
From her top lip.
Moved her arm across the gritty desk.
Children, listlessly worked,
Slatted shutters filtered the intense light.
Outside, the wind swirled
On the parched playing field,
A dust bowl, flanked by dry grass.
The bell rang,
Sweaty bodies ambled from the stifling room.

Exhausted,
She longed for a cool drink and shower.
As she left school,
The storm clouds clustered,
Unyielding their tantalizing promise.
Once home, Millie greeted her,
'De water lock off, Ma'am,
Must wait till six o'clock.'

A pool of clothes
Lay in the silent washing machine.
She slaked an iced Cola,
Then sank on to the bed and slept restlessly.
She awoke to strange sounds
Like falling tamarind pods,
Hitting the galvanized roof.
At first slow and intermittent,
Then with deafening staccato.

Through the shutters
She saw gigantic drops
Soaking into the dusty earth,
Watched globules of water
Form small pools on the marbled veranda.
Thunder followed lightning
And the rain ricocheted from the ground.
She and Millie ran into the torrent
Looked up and laughed,
'De rain a come, Ma'am,
De rain a come!'

Anita Marie Sackett

Coral Reef

I am a teeming city;
An underwater garden
Where fishes fly;
A lost forest
of skeleton trees;
A home for starry anemones;
A hiding place for frightened fishes;
A skulking place for prowling predators;
An alien world
Whose unseen monsters
Watch with luminous eyes;
An ancient palace topped by
Improbable towers;
A mermaid's maze;
A living barrier built on
Uncountable small deaths;
An endlessly growing sculpture;
A brittle mystery;
A vanishing trick;
A dazzling wonder
More magical than all
Your earthbound dreams;
I am a priceless treasure;
A precious heirloom,

Geography

And I am yours

To love
Or to lose
As you choose.

Clare Bevan

Geography Lesson

Our teacher told us one day he would leave
And sail across a warm blue sea
To places he had only known from maps,
And all his life had longed to be.

The house he lived in was narrow and grey
But in his mind's eye he could see
Sweet-scented jasmine clinging to the walls,
And green leaves burning on an orange tree.

He spoke of the lands he longed to visit,
Where it was never drab or cold.
I couldn't understand why he never left,
And shook off the school's stranglehold.

Then halfway through his final term
He took ill and never returned.
He never got to that place on the map
Where the green leaves of the orange trees burned.

The maps were redrawn on the classroom wall;
His name forgotten, he faded away.
But a lesson he never knew he taught
Is with me to this day.

I travel to where the green leaves burn,
To where the ocean's glass-clear and blue,
To places our teacher taught me to love –
And which he never knew.

Brian Patten

Someday Someone Will Bet that You Can't Name All Fifty States

California, Mississippi,
North and South Dakota.
New York, Jersey, Mexico, and
Hampshire, Minnesota.
Vermont, Wisconsin, Oregon,
Connecticut, and Maine.
Hawaii, Georgia, Maryland.
Virginia (West and plain).
Tennessee, Kentucky, Texas,
Illinois, Alaska.
Colorado, Utah, Florida,
Delaware, Nebraska.
The Carolinas (North and South).
Missouri. Idaho.
Plus Alabama, Washington,

And Indiana. O-
Klahoma. Also Iowa,
Arkansas, Montana,
Pennsylvania, Arizona,
And Louisiana.
Ohio, Massachusetts, and
Nevada. Michigan,
Rhode Island, and Wyoming. That
Makes forty-nine. You win
As soon as you say ——

Judith Viorst

[Answer: Kansas]

Haiku Calendar: Southern Version

In the sun's oven
New Year bakes to perfection
iced by the ocean.

February nights
with softness you can touch
like possums in gumtrees.

March dries orange leaves
on gnarled, blackened trunks after
the bushfire summer.

Like a kangaroo
this April afternoon lies
stretched in the cool dust.

From cold May mornings
the warmth of autumn soars in
canopies of blue.

Like an owl's feather
the year's first snowflake settles
into dusky June.

July holds its breath
in silent valleys muffled
by the drifted snow.

Cloud-splitting August
flashes silver rivers down
the sky's thunder mountains.

After winter rain
September like an emu
treads so warily.

October sunset:
a wedge of black cockatoos
calls wheel-oo wheel-oo.

November sunrise
feathers greying sky with pink:
galahs on the move.

Flaming December:
sulphur-crested cockatoos
dip the year in gold.

Barrie Wade

Fearless Bushmen

The bushmen of the Kalahari desert
Painted themselves on rocks
With wildebeests and giraffes
Thousands of years ago.
And still today they say
To boast is sinful
Arrogance is evil.
And although some say today that they
Are the earliest hunter-gatherers known
They never hunt for sport
They think that's rude,
They hunt for food.
They earn respect by sharing
Being true to their word
And caring.
They refuse to own land but
They can build a house in two days
And take it down in four hours.

Three generations will live together.
A girl will grow up to feed her mother
Who feeds the mother
That once fed her.
To get that food a girl will walk
Upon the hot desert sands
An average of a thousand miles a year.

Their footprints are uniquely small
For people who travel so much
To find melons or mongongo trees,
And those small dark and nimble feet
May spend two days chasing a deer.
Charity, respect and tolerance
Are watchwords for these ancient folk
Who spend their evenings singing songs
Around their campfires.

These hunter-gatherers are fearless
But peaceful,
They will never argue with a mamba snake,
When one is seen heading towards the village
They kiss the Earth
And move the village.

Benjamin Zephaniah

Design,
Technology
and ICT

Technology Lesson

We had to invent a toy
With gears and handles
And parts that swivelled
Or went up and down,
Or trundled and ran.

So I spent ages on
My best EVER design
For a shaking, quaking,
Wiggling, jiggling,
Twirling, whirling,
Astonishing, pull-along
Robot thing
With eyes that woggled
And boggled and span.

'Oh dear,' said our teacher.
'Only one idea?
Only one plan?'

So I covered a whole page
With toys that looked wonky,
Or not particularly strong,
Or useless
Or boring,
Or impossible to work,
Or just hopelessly wrong.

'Well done, dear,' said our teacher.
'That's fine.
But if I were you, I'd stick with
Your first design.'

Technology teachers really know
How to wind you up.

Clare Bevan

Excuses

Homework – to design and produce a flip-book
Materials – thin card
Fixers – glue
Specifications – 8 cms x 6 cms   20 pages
To be handed in no later than Thursday.

Dear Teacher,
Just to say,

I cut the card out carefully,
I drew the pictures too,

And I joined the little bits,
With a little bit of glue.

But my flip-book wouldn't flip,
It only flopped and flapped,

Then it fluttered to the floor,
To lie flat upon its back.

My brother in a bossy voice, said,
'Fling it over there!'

Then he took my little flip-book,
And flung it down the stair!

But it floated through the hallway,
And out the kitchen door,

And it floated up the path,
Of number twenty-four,

It found the open highway,
Without a flurry or a fuss,

When round the corner came –
A number ninety bus.

Mary Green

The Oojamaflip

Come and see! I've been building an oojamaflip.
It's easy, just follow the plan.
The widget screws into the thingummajig,
With a whatsit to hold on the fan.
The left flummadiddle clips on, just like this,
To connect with a gizmo up here.
And the whaddyacallit goes round and around
With a doofry to help you change gear.
My oojamaflip will be done in a jiff
In a mo, in a tick, never fear.
It's the biggest. The fastest. The mostest there's been.
The best oojamaflip of the year.
It's finished! It's ready! Who'll give it a try?
Don't shout all at once. Join the queue.
Just one little question. This oojamaflip.
What is it? I do wish I knew.

Paul Bright

Problem Solving

Our teacher likes us to
solve problems.
But I don't like
solving problems.
That's my problem.
I would like to invent
a way to make my teacher
disappear.
I try hard
but can not find the right solution.

Peter Dixon

Inventions I'd Like to See

A bully-pulley
A diaper-wiper
A teacher-screecher
A cold-feet-heater
A homework-shirker
An annoyer-destroyer
A sister-twister
A whiner-entwiner
A pester-ingester
A bragger-dragger
A blabber-grabber
A weekend-extender
A go-to-bed-shredder

Douglas Florian

The Song of the Engine

(Slowly)
With snort and pant the engine dragged
Its heavy train uphill,
And puffed these words the while she puffed
and laboured with a will:

(Very slowly)
'I think – I can – I think – I can,
I've got – to reach – the top,
I'm sure – I can – I will – get there,
I sim – ply must – not stop!'

(More quickly)
At last the top was reached and passed,
And then – how changed the song!
The wheels all joined in the engine's joy,
As quickly she tore along!

(Very fast)
'I knew I could do it, I knew I could win,
Oh, rickety rackety rack!
And now for a roaring rushing race
On my smooth and shining track!'

H. Worsley-Benison

Scissors

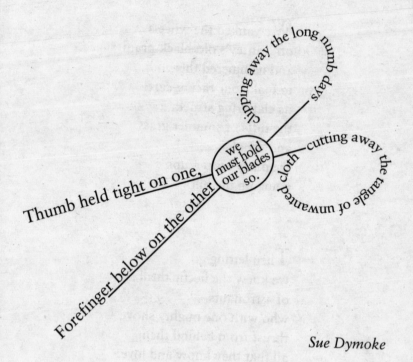

clipping away the long numb days

we must hold our blades so.

cutting away the tangle of unwanted cloth

Thumb held tight on one,

Forefinger below on the other,

Sue Dymoke

Go-cart

We yanked the wheels
off Tansey's old black pram
and hammered them
to make our racing-cart:
its clattering struck
the tufts of summer grass
and shook
the dusty buttercups
going up the hill.

Then letting go
we knew the hectic thrill
of astronauts
who with one mighty shove
thrust from behind them
all that they know and love.

Una Leavy

Epitaph for a Blacksmith

My sledge and hammer lie reclined,
My bellows, too, have lost their wind;
My fire's extinct, my forge decayed,
And in the dust my vice is laid.
My coal is spent, my iron's gone,
My nails are drove, my work is done;
My fire-dried corpse lies here at rest,
And, smoke-like, soars up to be bless'd.

Attributed to William Hayley

'Progress'

I am a sundial, and I make a botch
Of what is done far better by a watch.

Hilaire Belloc

Mowers

Jim's dad has a motor mower.
He says it has a mind of its own.
It charges up and down their lawn
Snorting like an angry bull,
Flinging grass cuttings everywhere.

Mrs Spencer next door has an electric mower.
She bustles up and down her lawn,
Ironing it into neat, straight lines
Until there's not a blade of grass out of place.
Her lawn is as flat as a cricket pitch.

Grandad's got a hand-mower.
It rattles and clanks as he pushes it along.
It tears at the grass, chewing it up.
Grandad's lawn looks as if it's had a haircut
With a blunt pair of scissors.

John Foster

First Television

It was 1953.
My dad had won the pools:
some pounds and shillings spare!
He'd buy our first TV.

Coronation coming up,
chance of a lifetime!
he cried excitedly.
I never thought we'd see!

And he,
abandoning his much-loved wireless,
settled down to dream in black and white
of London pomp.

On Coronation Day
I did begin to watch,
to please my dad . . .

But back in school,
to celebrate, they'd handed out
free tickets for the fair.
It wasn't long before
I grew impatient,
tired of moving images,
seen from a lolling chair.
And drawn instead by dodgems,
ghost trains, candy floss,
I walked out on those early pictures
snatched from air.

Judith Nicholls

The Electronic House

cooker. blanket.
toothbrush. fire.
iron. lightbulb.
TV. drier.
fridge. radio.
robot. drill.
crimper. speaker.
kettle. grill.
slicer. grinder.
meters. fan.
slide-projector.
deep-fry pan.
vacuum-cleaner.
fuses. shocks.
freezer. shaver.
junction box.

water heater.
Christmas lamps.
knife. recorder.
cables. amps.
door chimes. organ.
infra red.
guitar. video.
sunlamp bed.
synthesizer.
night light glow.
cultivator.
stereo.
calculator.
metronome.
toaster. teasmade!
ohm, sweet, ohm.

Wes Magee

Space Shot

Out of the furnace
The great fish rose
Its silver tail on fire
But with a slowness
Like something sorry
To be rid of earth.
The boiling mountains
Of snow white cloud
Searched for a space to go into
And the ground thundered
With a roar
That set teacups
Rattling in a kitchen
Twenty miles away.
Across the blue it arched
Milk bottle white
But shimmering in the haze.
And the watchers by the fence
Held tinted glass against their eyes
And wondered at what man could do
To make so large a thing
To fly so far and free.
While the unknown Universe waited;
For waiting
Was what it had always been good at.

Gareth Owen

New Frontiers

I am a techno traveller,
I have the gear you need
To travel all around the world
With supersonic speed.

Inside my office block you'll find
A very special room
Where all the latest gadgets are
To help me quickly zoom

Across the globe and back again,
(Though my passport is at home)
Without a plane or car or train
I'm completely free to roam,

Because I am a techno traveller,
Though I never move a metre,
With computer, fax and telephone
I'm the land speed record beater!

Coral Rumble

Mega Star Rap

I'm the king of the keyboard, star of the screen,
They call me Gamesmaster, you know what I mean,
'Cause I am just ace on the Nintendo action,
When I get in my stride, you know, I don't give a fraction,
With Super Mario I'm a real daredevil,
I'm cool, I'm wicked, on a different level!
I'll take on anyone who wants to challenge me,
No matter what the problem is, I hold the key.
I can tell you every shortcut on the Megadrive,
I can put the Sonic Hedgehog into overdrive,
And I would, I really would like to accept your dare,
But I've just run out of batteries for my Sega Game Gear.

Valerie Bloom

Spellbound

I have a spelling chequer
It came with my PC
It plainly marks four my revue
Miss takes I cannot sea.
I've run this poem threw it
I'm shore your pleased too no;
It's letter perfect in it's weigh
My chequer tolled me sew.

Norman Vandal

Hickory Digital Clock

Hickory digital dock
The mouse clicks on the clock
The clock comes on
A CD-ROM
Hickory digital dock.

Steve Turner

Techno-Child

My dad was a kung fu fighter in a video game called
  Death Cult Army
He lurked around on the seventh level waiting for smug
  contestants so he could chop them up like salami
He was good for nothing but kick jab punch gouge headbutt
  kick in the bum
And all his friends were stuperollificated when he fell in love
  and married my mum

My mum was a thirty-two colour hologram at a Medical
  Convention in Beverly Hills
She represented the Statue of Liberty and she advertised
  Anti-Indigestion Pills
She was half the size of the statue itself and the tourists
  she attracted were fewer
And if you ever reached out to touch her robes, well
  your hand just went straight through her

They met in the Robocop Theme Park on a hullabaloo
  of a night
When my dad saw off some Gremlins on Camels who
  had challenged mum to a fight
They sat together and watched the moon from
  a swing-chair on Popeye's porch
Then my father proposed in Japanese and my mother
  she dropped her torch

They were married and put on a floppy disc by
   the Bishop of IBM
Pac-Man, Count Duckula and all the Power Rangers
   came and celebrated with them
The fun was going ballistic but it nearly ended
   in tears
For those old Space Invaders started a ruck with
   the Mortal Kombateers

Since my mum's a mirage of electrons and my dad
   is strictly 2-D
You may wonder how I was born at all in this
   Virtual Reality
Well they're close as a Mouse and its Mouse-mat
   and they taught me just what I should do –
I fight video-gamesters and indigestion with
   pills and a torch and kung fu.

Adrian Mitchell

My Pet Mouse

I have a friendly little mouse,
He is my special pet.
I keep him safely on a lead.
I haven't lost him yet.

I never need to feed him,
Not even bits of cheese.
He's never chased by any cat
And he does just as I please.

He likes it when I stroke him
For he's smooth and grey and fat.
He helps me sometimes with my games,
When he runs around my mat.

I've never ever known a mouse
That could really be much cuter.
He's my extra special electric mouse
That works my home computer.

David Whitehead

Printout, Wipe Out

Our school's word processor
Can process more words
Than there are peas
In a can of processed peas.
A perfect procession
Parades across the screen.

If we're keen,
We add new words
Subtract old ones
Rearrange the order
Add a zigzag border –
Or wipe out the lot
(By accident . . .)

We've perfected
Our technique
To make ONE sentence
Last a week.

Our teacher
Thinks we're still
Learning.

We already have.

Trevor Harvey

The Machine of the Three Big Ears

*(LISA, the Laser Interferometer Space Antenna,
will be launched in 2008 and is intended to prove
the existence of 'sounds in space')*

Only part of me is metal,
only part of me is fibreglass,
for I am nothing but
a triangle of ears.

And high in the heavens,
motionless and steady,
my Three Big Ears will listen
for the waterless waves that rise and fall
across the oceans of space.

By star, by day, throughout the years
of your childhood, your adulthood,
I shall be listening for those waves
with my Three Big Ears,
my no head, my no body, my no legs,
millions of miles apart,
connected by laser beam.
My nothing but Three Big Ears connected
as you grow in body and brain.

What shall I listen for
with my Three Big Ears?

For the singing of the supernova,
for the ringing of runaway stars,
for the plug-hole suck of black holes,
for the chirrup of galaxies colliding.

And reader, in your old age,
you will think of my Three Big Ears
catching the tiny tinkling sounds of space
and catapulting them to Earth,
to the Two Small Ears
on your curious body machine.

John Rice

Maths

One Pink Sari

One pink sari for a pretty girl,
Two dancing women all in a whirl,
Three charmed cobras rising from a basket,
Four fat rubies, in the Rajah's casket,
Five water carriers straight and tall,
Six wicked vultures sitting on the wall,
Seven fierce tigers hiding in the grass,
Eight elephants rolling in a warm mud bath,
Nine green parrots in the coconut tree,
Ten twinkling stars, a-twinkling at me!

Ann Marie Linden

Two Times Table

Twice one are two,
Violets white and blue.

Twice two are four,
Sunflowers at the door.

Twice three are six,
Sweet peas on their sticks.

Twice four are eight,
Poppies at the gate.

Twice five are ten,
Pansies bloom again.

Twice six are twelve,
Pinks for those who delve.

Twice seven are fourteen,
Flowers of the runner bean.

Twice eight are sixteen,
Clinging ivy ever green.

Twice nine are eighteen,
Purple thistles to be seen.

Twice ten are twenty,
Hollyhocks in plenty.

Twice eleven are twenty-two,
Daisies wet with morning dew.

Twice twelve are twenty-four,
Roses . . . who could ask for more.

Anon.

Why Must it Be Minus Three?

When I had
Three wrong
Out of twenty,
My teacher wrote
– 3

But that's like crying
When a few weeks
Of the summer holidays are over,
Instead of rejoicing
Because there are so many left,

Or fretting
About the cupcakes
With rainbow sprinkles
That have been eaten,
Instead of admiring

The luscious ones
Still waiting on the plate.

I think my teacher
Should have written

+ 17

Kali Dakos (USA)

Numberless!

If all the numbers in the world were
rubbed out,
removed,
taken away:
I wouldn't know how old I was,
I wouldn't know the time of day,
I wouldn't know which bus to catch,
I wouldn't know the number of goals I had scored,
I wouldn't know how many scoops of ice cream I had,
I wouldn't know my phone number,
I wouldn't know the page on my reading book,
I wouldn't know how tall I was,
I wouldn't know how much I weighed,
I wouldn't know how many sides there are in a hexagon,
I wouldn't know how many days in the month,
I wouldn't be able to work my calculator.
And I wouldn't be able to play hide-and-seek!
But I would know,
as far as my mum was concerned,
I was still her NUMBER ONE!

Ian Souter

What Is a Million?

The blades of grass growing
　　on your back lawn.
The people you've met
　　since the day you were born.

The age of a fossil
　　you found by the sea.
The years it would take you
　　to reach Octran Three.

The water drops needed
　　to fill the fish pool.
The words you have read
　　since you started school.

Wes Magee

Time

Time's a bird, which leaves its footprints
At the corners of your eyes,
Time's a jockey, racing horses,
The sun and moon across the skies.
Time's a thief, stealing your beauty,
Leaving you with tears and sighs,
But you waste time trying to catch him,
Time's a bird and Time just flies.

Valerie Bloom

Seven Fat Fishermen

Seven fat fishermen,
Sitting side by side,
Fished from a bridge,
By the banks of the Clyde.

The first caught a tiddler,
The second caught a crab,
The third caught a winkle,
The fourth caught a dab.

The fifth caught a tadpole,
The sixth caught an eel,
But the seventh, he caught
An old cartwheel.

Anon.

The Surprising Number 37

The number 37 has a special magic to it.
If you multiply 37 × 3, you get   111.
If you multiply 37 × 6, you get   222.
If you multiply 37 × 9, you get   333.
If you multiply 37 × 12, you get   444.
If you multiply 37 × 15, you get   555.
If you multiply 37 × 18, you get   666.
If you multiply 37 × 21, you get   777.
If you multiply 37 × 24, you get   888.
If you multiply 37 × 27, you get   999.

Anon.

Counting Horrors

1 witch with 1 broomstick,
1 tooth and 1 cat,
1 cauldron, 1 spider:
how many is that?   [   ]

2 fangs and 1 dracula,
speared by 1 stake,
8 victims around him:
now what does that make?   [   ]

9 ghosts scare 12 people
in dark stormy weather,
then hide in 3 castles:
what's that altogether?   [   ]

1 monster with 10 legs,
8 toes (not a lot),
20 eyes and 9 heads:
add them up – it makes what?   [   ]

When you've found the four numbers,
write them down and then see
what you think the next number
in line ought to be.   [   ]

Charles Thomson

[Answers: 6, 12, 24, 48, 96]

A Bit of a Problem

I love my teacher
I'm going to marry her one day.
But, as I'm only half her age,
'That's quite absurd,' you'll say.

It's not as silly as you think.
Reflect upon my words:
If she can wait eleven years,
The fraction is two thirds.

If Miss can be quite patient,
Like any good man's daughters,
And wait eleven short years more,
I'm catching up: three quarters.

If life is only long enough,
Before we leave the stage
I will have married lovely Miss,
And we'll both be the same age!

How old am I?

John Kitching

[Answer: 11]

Pyramid Pie

To
make a
pyramid
take thirty-six
syllables, eight lines,
some spaces in between,
a dash of logic and mix
with a few grains of desert sand.

Mary Green

Teacher's Torture

Add two times twenty-two,
To twelve and twenty more,
Take forty-five from fifty-five,
Add four by forty-four.

Add six and six to sixteen,
To eighteen by eleven,
To nine and nine and ninety-nine,
Add nine from ninety-seven.

Add thirty-three and thirteen,
Take seven from twenty-four,
Add seventy-seven to sixty-six,
And total up your score.

You can count them on your fingers,
You can count them on your toes,
You can count them out with counters,
You can count them out in rows.

And when you've got the answer,
When you're sure, and only then –
You can add another hundred
And count them all again!

Mary Green

[Answer: 999]

Tall Story

                                                    graph

my

on

it

fit

not

could

but

giraffe,

a

measure

to

went

I went to measure a giraffe, but could not fit it on my

Mike Johnson

Mathematically Telepathically Magical

Think of a number from one to ten.
Any one will do.
Are you ready with your number then . . .
multiply it by two.

Once you have the answer
add another six.
Have you got this total?
Here's what you do next . . .

Halve the total you have got
(and this is the magical mystery)
Subtract the number you first thought of
and your answer must be . . . three!

It's mathematically telepathically magical you see.
It works with any number from one right up to ten.
Carefully follow each of the steps, your answer's always three.
Think of another number and try it again and again.

Paul Cookson

Puzzler

I am ten and you are two –
I am five times older than you.
So, my little sister, Jessy,
How come you're ten times as messy?

Philip Waddell

Behind the Staffroom Door

Ten tired teachers slumped in the staffroom at playtime,
one collapsed when the coffee ran out, then there were nine.

Nine tired teachers making lists of things they hate,
one remembered playground duty, then there were eight.

Eight tired teachers thinking of holidays in Devon,
one slipped off to pack his case, then there were seven.

Seven tired teachers, weary of children's tricks,
one hid in the stock cupboard, then there were six.

Six tired teachers, under the weather, barely alive,
one gave an enormous sneeze, then there were five.

Five tired teachers, gazing at the open door,
one made a quick getaway, then there were four.

Four tired teachers, faces lined with misery,
one locked herself in the ladies, then there were three.

Three tired teachers, wondering what to do,
one started screaming when the bell rang, then there were two.

Two tired teachers, thinking life really ought to be fun,
one was summoned to see the Head, then there was one.

One tired teacher caught napping in the afternoon sun,
fled quickly from the staffroom, then there were none.

Brian Moses

Three Frazzles in a Frimple

1 snunk in a snuncle
2 gripes in a grimp,
3 frazzles in a frimple
4 blips in a blimp.
5 nips in a nimple
6 nerps in a neep,
7 gloops in a gloople
8 flurps in a fleap.
9 snozzles in a snoozle,
10 leaps in a bunny,
some sums are ridiculous
and some sums are funny.

Brian Patten

Maths Person

'Maths gets everywhere,'
he used to say.
'Observe things.'

'Look at me for instance,
notice the spheroidal
bald bonce, the nose
fit for a hypotenuse,
the parabolas
of the bushy eyebrows.
And the clothes.
Which bit of gear's
a rectangle
with a trapezium
on each end? Clue – yellow
with blue spots. Like it? No?
Well bow ties
are worn daft this year.

Note the symmetrical
glasses, the a-
symmetrical
face. Observe
the trousers' nearly parallel
creases and behind as I rotate
through 180 degrees,
the intersecting
cool braces in red
with nattily adjacent
and also opposite
angles. *Spot*
the elliptical
hole in the right sock.'

Lesson over. Spheroidal
head gleaming, he walks a straight
shortest-distance-between-two-points
down the corridor, the elliptical
hole in the right sock
winking at us.
We notice this year
shoe-heels are worn
nearly triangular.

                              Robert Hull

The Unit of Sleep

I measure fun in grandads –
The best slide in the park is three whole grandads long.

I measure ponds in duckfuls –
This is a lake. Tons of ducks. Swans. Green mud, good pong.

Picnics are weighed in chocolate biscuits –
Don't care if they do melt, so long as there's a lot.

Holidays stretch in miles of sunshine –
Sand, seaslap, shingle. Donkey smell and leather. Hot.

Journeys are times in songs and stories –
From here to Aunt Em's house the wicked witch schemes
And as we arrive there, the Princess rescues Snow White.

The unit of sleep is dreams.

Jan Dean

If I Were a Shape

If I were a shape
I'd be a rectangle,
I'd be a snooker table with Steve Davies potting the black,
I'd be a football pitch where Spurs would always be winning,
I'd be a chocolate bar that you could never finish,
If I were a rectangle.

If I were a circle,
I'd be a hoop rolling down a mountainside,
I'd be a wheel on a fast Ferrari,
I'd be a porthole in Captain Nemo's submarine,
If I were a circle.

If I were a cone,
I'd be a black hat on a wicked witch's head,
I'd be a warning to motorists, one of thousands,
I'd be a tooth in a T Rex's jaw,
If I were a cone.

But if I were a star . . .
I'd be Robbie Williams!

Brian Moses

Counting

To count myself
Is quickly done.
There's never more of me
Than one.

Counting bears
Is fun by ones
But funnier in pairs.

Counting the birds
On the branches of trees
Is hard on the neck
But it's easy on the knees.

It's even harder
Counting leaves
Than counting tiny birds.
They shift their shadows
With the breeze
Among the branches
Of the trees
More numerous
Than whispered words.

Counting fingers
And counting toes is
A harder kind of counting
Than counting noses.

Counting rabbits running
Rabbit races on the lawn
Must be done while one is sunning
And before a rabbit's gone.

Counting the stars
As they glitter bright white
Is lovely indeed
And a marvellous sight
When the air is as fresh
As the first night in fall.
But I always have a feeling
That comes very softly stealing
When my head with stars is reeling
That I didn't count them all.

Karla Kuskin

Science

Up in Smoke

Cornelius loved Chemistry
It had a strange attraction
The final words he spoke were 'Sir?
Is this a chain reaction?'

Paul Bright

Earth's Clock

Imagine that the earth was shaped
Twenty-four hours ago,
Then at 6 a.m. rains fell from the skies
To form the seas below.
At 8 a.m. in these soupy seas
The first signs of life appeared.
The dinosaurs called seventy minutes ago
But at twenty to twelve disappeared.
Man arrived just one minute ago
Then at thirty seconds to midnight,
Raised himself from his stooping stance
And started walking upright.
In the thirty seconds man's walked the earth
See what he's managed to do.

Earth's clock continues ticking;
The rest is up to you.

Pat Moon

Freddie Fox, Sally Sisson and Raymond Rix

Here lies the body
Of Sally Sisson.
Big explosion:
Didn't listen.

Here lies the body
Of Raymond Rix:
Was sure those chemicals
Would mix.

Here lies the body
Of Freddie Fox.
Water plus cable?
Nasty shocks!

John Kitching

Summer Storm

Light travels, said Miss,
Faster than sound.
Next time there's a storm,
When you see the lightning,
Start counting slowly in seconds.
If you divide
The number of seconds by three,
It will tell you
How many kilometres you are
From the centre of the storm.

Two nights later
I was woken
By the lashing rain,
The lightning
And the thunder's crash.

I lay,
Huddled beneath the sheet,
As the rain poured down
And lightning lit up the bedroom,
Slowly counting the seconds,
Listening for the thunder
And calculating the distance
As the storm closed in –

Until,
With a blinding flash
And a simultaneous ear-splitting crash,
The storm passed
Directly overhead.

And I shook with fright
As the storm passed on,
Leaving the branches shuddering
And the leaves weeping.

John Foster

Constant, Constant Little Light

Constant, constant, little light,
catch my eye in darkest night.
What can speed so fast, so high,
laser like across the sky?

When the sleepy sun has set
and the night has cast her net.
It's then your orbit forms a ring,
round the earth a song to sing.

Constant, constant little light,
I know you're a satellite.

Cruising, spinning, seldom seen,
beaming pictures to our screens.
Weather-watching, tracking storms,
plotting maps and all life forms.

Scanning, spying from above,
are you hawk or are you dove?
Silent, stealthy space age Thor,
armed with weapons for a real star war.

From your tiny, silver glow,
who can tell what wrongs may flow.
But for now I hold you bright,
constant, constant little light.

Constant, constant, little light,
I know you're a satellite.

John Rice

Information for Travellers

As you read this poem you are on a spacecraft
travelling at sixty-six thousand miles an hour.
It spins as it flies: since you began to read
it has already turned nine miles to the east.
Be honest, you didn't feel a thing.
You are orbiting a star, not a very big one
compared to many of the ten thousand million others
that go round on the same galactic wheel,
and are flying at a height above its surface
of some ninety-three million miles.
We hope to cruise at this distance for another
eight thousand million years. What happens then
is anybody's guess. Despite its speed and size
this craft is a space station, a satellite, not designed
for interstellar flight. Its passengers
rely on the comfort of a pressurized cabin

to enjoy the voyage. We must advise you that,
in the event of collision, loss of atmosphere,
or any alteration in course which may result
in overheating or extreme cold, this craft is not
equipped with parachutes or emergency exits.
On a brighter note, the spaceship contains
an enormous variety of in-flight magazines,
meals to suit every taste, and enough
games, puzzles and adventures
to last a lifetime.
We hope you enjoy your voyage.
Thank you for flying Planet Earth.

Dave Calder

Chalk

As we walk across this hill of chalk
It's hard to imagine
That once these hills
Were below the sea
That chalk is the sediment
Left by a million tiny creatures
On the sea bed
It's hard to imagine
As we walk upon this thin skin
Of earth and grass
Beneath a blue sky
And a burning sun.

Roger Stevens

Science Lesson

We've done 'Water' and 'Metals' and 'Plastic',
today it's the turn of 'Elastic':
Sir sets up a test . . .
Wow, that was the best –
he whizzed through the window. Fantastic!

Mike Johnson

experiment

at school we're doing growing things
   with cress.
sprinkly seeds in plastic pots
   of cotton wool.

Kate's cress sits up on the sill
   she gives it water.
mine is shut inside the cupboard
   dark and dry.

now her pot has great big clumps
   of green
mine hasn't.
Mrs Martin calls it Science
   I call it mean.

Danielle Sensier

Star Turn

Ladies *and* Gentlemen
We are proud to present
On this auspicious occasion
The one, the only,
The amazing,
The tremendous,
The sensational,
The eighth wonder of the world,
In all its phenomenal glory . . .
MY BODY
(Plus, of course, its clothes).

Marvel with me, if you will,
At the chambers of my heart
(With their cunning one-way doors)
Pumping my blood around
100,000 times
Every single day.

And don't you have to admire
My more than 200 bones,
600 muscles,
25,000, yes *25,000*,
Cells in my brilliant brain.

And for our grand finale
I request
Silence.
Lower the house lights, please
For a live demonstration
Of something *beyond belief*.
Prepare yourselves for the sight,
Wondrous to behold,
Of this stretchy waterproof bag
That I've come to know as
My Skin.

Isn't it fantastic how something so thin
Can hold so much in?

Frances Nagle

Breath

I breathe in –
And an ocean flows through my body.
I breathe out –
And it drains away, unseen;
Leaving me
To wait
Until the next breath
Floods me with life again.

Trevor Harvey

The Shark

A treacherous monster is the Shark,
He never makes the least remark.

And when he sees you on the sand,
He doesn't seem to want to land.

He watches you take off your clothes,
And not the least excitement shows.

His eyes do not grow bright or roll,
He has astounding self-control.

He waits till you are quite undressed,
And seems to take no interest.

And when towards the sea you leap,
He looks as if he were asleep.

But when you once get in his range,
His whole demeanour seems to change.

He throws his body right about
And his true character comes out.

It's no use crying or appealing,
He seems to lose all decent feeling.

After his warning you will wish
To keep clear of this treacherous fish.

His back is black, his stomach white,
He has a very dangerous bite.

Lord Alfred Douglas

Gannet Diving

Beak,
harpoon, or cocktail stick.

Neck,
brushed yellowy snowbridge.

Wings,
a flash of glassy light,
tipped black as school socks.

Tail,
a trailing shirt tail,
freshly ironed.

Dives,
a white arrowhead
speeding from silk blue sky
to ice blue water.

Rises,
from white frothy broth
with wriggling silver prize.

Gulps,
goes for gold.

John Rice

Luck

Bedraggled feathers are uneasy
on the eye. Yet here was this little hen
being washed in a bowl, the woman
cupping her hands, spilling
the water over the bird, gently
as with a newborn child. There was no struggle.
The towel wrap, the soft blow-dry
were beauty salon pleasures. And the finished,
fluffed-up, white creation
stayed content in the holding hands. She was
keeping close to love. close to luck.

Madeline Munro

Wonder Birds

In the forest's shadows
jewelled hummingbirds
wordsearch vibrant flowers;
up, down, across, diagonally,
backwards and forwards they fly.

Their tiny, rotor blade wings
make music on air.
They hover and sip,
hover and sip,
knitting patterns of words
across sheets of leaves:

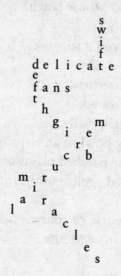

Patricia Leighton

Snail

Steady explorer
you crawl on your stomach foot
    along silver trails;
stretch your soft neck, grasp a leaf
rasp it with sandpaper tongue.

Patricia Leighton

Mouse Laughing

Have you ever heard Mouse laugh?
You'd be surprised.
It doesn't sound as you'd suppose.
No it doesn't.
No squeaks, no twitterings,
No pussy-footing around.
More of a belly laugh, really.
Like the trumpeting howl of an elephant
Thudding across the parched plains of Africa,
Or the deep-throated rumble of the earth
At its centre.
You needn't believe me, of course.
But, next time you meet Mouse,
Don't tickle him.

Mary Greeen

The Day's Eye

The sun rises,
surprises the weary night,
like a sudden joke.
Daylight.

The sun gleams,
beams kindly heat
like an oven's plate.
Streets sweat.

The sun sneaks,
peeks through misty cloud,
like a sly thief,
alone in a crowd.

The sun sleeps,
creeps into cool shade,
like a honey cat.
Shadows fade.

The sun slips,
dips into night,
like a closing mouth,
swallowing light.

Pie Corbett

Winter Seeds

All among the leaf litter
lie the winter seeds,
acorns, beech nuts, conkers, berries;
seeds from garden weeds.

All the long, cold winter
through frost, hail, sleet and snow,
seeds wait, nestling near the earth,
for the time when they can grow.

Penny Kent

Mushrooms

The night before a great moon full of honey
Had flowed up behind the hills and poured across the fields.

The leaves were rusting, the wheat whispered
Dry and gold in the wind's hands.

Andrew and I went to Foss. We drove over the hills
That were blustery with huge gusts of sunlight.

We stopped and walked to the loch, left two trails
Through the grass, came on the mushrooms by accident,

A village of strewn white hats,
The folds of their gills underneath as soft as skin.

We almost did not want to take them, as if
It would be theft – wronging the hills, the trees, the grass.

But in the end we did, we picked them with reverence;
And they broke like bread between our hands, we carried
whole armfuls home,

Pieces of field, smelling of earth and autumn;
A thanksgiving, a blessing.

Kenneth C. Steven

The Hedgehog

Far too cold
For things to grow –
Too much frost
And too much snow;
Too much wind
And too much rain –
Time I went
To sleep again!
Curled up small
(Quite snug and warm),
I'll be safe
From wind and storm.

See you next spring!

Trevor Harvey

Dandelions

Dandelions shout
Barmaid fashion,
'We're out!'
And suddenly winter's gone.
They display together
Sunshine bright,
In bitter weather,
Flaunting their generous gold
Until they're old.
Ghosts in summer
They set their silken seeds
And grow with joy
To be another gallant flowering hoi polloi.
Even the leaves are edible.
Dandelions are incredible.

Gwen Dunn

The Wobbling Rainbow

Why don't rainbows
  wobble in the wind?
How can tuna
  end up tinned?
Why do airwaves
  not make a sound?
How can a mole
  make a hole
    underground?
Why don't we drop
  off the face
    of the earth?
Why does difference
  cause such mirth?
Why do magnets
  stick together?
Why do snails like
  rainy weather?
Why would an eel
  give a nasty shock?
Why does water
  turn hard as rock?
Why does my mind
  keep wondering why?
Where do we begin,
  and what happens when we die?

Pie Corbett

Religious
Education

I Thank You Lord

I thank you Lord, for knowing me
   better than I know myself,
And for letting me know myself
   better than others know me.
Make me, I ask you then,
   better than others know me.
Make me, I ask you then,
   better than they suppose,
And forgive me for what they do not know.

A Muslim prayer

Before the Paling of the Stars

Before the paling of the stars,
  Before the winter morn,
  Before the earliest cock-crow,
  Jesus Christ was born:
    Born in a stable,
    Cradles in a manger,
In the world His hands had made
    Born a stranger.

Priest and King lay fast asleep
  In Jerusalem;
Young and old lay fast asleep
  In crowded Bethlehem;
Saint and Angel, ox and ass,
  Kept a watch together,
  Before the Christmas daybreak
  In the winter weather.

Jesus on His Mother's breast
  In the stable cold,
Spotless Lamb of God was He,
  Shepherd of the fold:
Let us kneel with Mary Maid,
  With Joseph bent and hoary,
With Saint and Angel, ox and ass,
  To hail the King of Glory.

Christina Rossetti

Innocent's Song

Who's that knocking on the window,
Who's that standing at the door,
What are all those presents
Lying on the kitchen floor?

Who is the smiling stranger
With hair as white as gin,
What is he doing with the children
And who could have let him in?

Why has he rubies on his fingers,
A cold, cold crown on his head,
Why, when he caws his carol,
Does the salty snow run red?

Why does he ferry my fireside
As a spider on a thread,
His fingers made of fuses
And his tongue of gingerbread?

Why does the world before him
Melt in a million suns,
Why do his yellow, yearning eyes
Burn like saffron buns?

Watch where he comes walking
Out of the Christmas flame,
Dancing, double-talking:

Herod is his name.

Charles Causley

Dedicating a Baby
(from the pygmy tradition)

Life is a tree – rooted in the earth,
An old tree – our family tree.

God planted the tree –
He makes it grow
Strong roots,
Wide branches.

And now we bring this baby,
A bud on the great tree

All life is God's life
And the life in this baby is God's life.

We – the roots and branches of the ancient tree
Offer this new bud baby to our Creator God.

Together we will grow.

Jan Dean

Disembarkation Chorus

So disembark! The storm has found its ending,
The rains have poured their very selves away,
The rocks are all a-gleaming and a-blending,
And we shall step ashore this very day

On Ararat,
On Ararat,
Sweet Ararat, the golden.

Ashore! Ashore! All birds! All flies! All fishes!
And every kind of animal, give way
To Captain Noah, and obey his wishes,
For he has found safe anchorage today

On Ararat,
On Ararat,
Sweet Ararat, the golden.

Praise be to all the Angels and the Voices,
Praise be to this great sun that burns the rain,
Praise be to Rainbows when the heart rejoices
To see the colours of the world again

On Ararat,
On Ararat,
Sweet Ararat, the golden.

Mervyn Peake

Psalm 150

O praise God in his holiness: praise him
in the firmament of his power.
Praise him in his noble acts: praise him
according to his excellent greatness.
Praise him in the sound of the trumpet:
praise him upon the lute and harp.
Praise him in the cymbals and dances:
praise him upon the strings and pipe.
Praise him upon the well-tuned cymbals:
praise him upon the loud cymbals.
Let every thing that hath breath:
praise the Lord

King James Bible

Psalm 23
A Psalm of David

The Lord *is* my shepherd; I shall not want.
He maketh me to lie down in green pastures: he leadeth
me beside the still waters.
He restoreth my soul: he leadeth me in the paths of
righteousness for his name's sake.
Yea, though I walk through the valley of the shadow of
death, I will fear no evil: for thou *art* with me; thy rod
and thy staff they comfort me.
Thou preparest a table before me in the presence of mine
enemies: thou anointest my head with oil; my cup runneth
over.
Surely goodness and mercy shall follow me all the days of
my life: and I will dwell in the house of the LORD for
ever.

Psalm 23:1–6
King James Bible

From 'The Sermon on the Mount'

Blessed are the poor in spirit:
For theirs is the kingdom of heaven.

Blessed are they that mourn:
For they shall be comforted.

Blessed are the meek:
For they shall inherit the earth.

Blessed are they which do hunger and thirst after righteousness:
For they shall be filled.

Blessed are the merciful:
For they shall obtain mercy.

Blessed are the pure in heart:
For they shall see God.

Blessed are the peacemakers:
For they shall be called the children of God.

Blessed are they which are persecuted for righteousness' sake:
For theirs is the kingdom of heaven.

King James Bible

In the Beginning

God said WORLD
and the world spun round,
God said LIGHT
and the light beamed down,
God said LAND
and the sea rolled back,
God said NIGHT
and the sky went black.

God said LEAF
and the shoot pushed through,
God said FIN
and the first fish grew,
God said BEAK
and the big bird soared,
God said FUR
and the jungle roared.

God said SKIN
and the man breathed air,
God said BONE
and the girl stood there,
God said GOOD
and the world was great,
God said REST
and they all slept late.

Steve Turner

Prayer for When I'm Cross

Dear Jesus, when I feel my black bad temper
Bristle in me like a porcupine
Lay your gentle hand upon my anger
And soften every spiteful prickly spine.

Jan Dean

Dipa (The Lamp)

(A song for Divali)

Light the lamp now.
Make bright
the falling night
wrapped in the leaves
of autumn.

Gone is the day.
Kindle the flame
to burn
in the dark.
Let it show
the way.

Lit is the lamp
of the moon.
Brilliant the stars.
Make them shine.
Let them unite.
Let there be light.

Ann Bonner

Plague Frog

I am
   the frog
      that leapt
         from the Nile
            that hopped
               to the palace
                  that flipped
                     to the bedroom
                        that slipped
                           in the sheet
                              that flopped
                                 with a smile
                                    then nipped
                                       at the feet
                                          of the king who
                                             kept Moses in Egypt.

Judith Nicholls

Jonah and the Whale

Well, to start with
It was dark
So dark
You couldn't see
Your hand in front of your face;
And huge
Huge as an acre of farmland.
How do I know?
Well, I paced it out
Length and breadth
That's how.
And if you was to shout
You'd hear your own voice resound,
Bouncing along the ridges of its stomach,
Like when you call out
Under a bridge
Or in an empty hall.
Hear anything?
No not much,
Only the normal

Kind of sounds
You'd expect to hear
Inside a whale's stomach;
The sea swishing far away,
Food gurgling, the wind
And suchlike sounds;
Then there was me screaming for help,
But who'd be likely to hear,
Us being miles from
Any shipping lines
And anyway
Supposing someone did hear,
Who'd think of looking inside a whale?
That's not the sort of thing
That people do.
Smell? I'll say there was a smell.
And cold. The wind blew in
Something terrible from the South
Each time he opened his mouth
Or took a swallow of some tit bit.
The only way I found
To keep alive at all
Was to wrap my arms
Tight around myself
And race from wall to wall.
Damp? You can say that again;
When the ocean came sluicing in
I had to climb his ribs
To save myself from drowning.
Fibs? You think I'm telling you fibs,

I haven't told the half of it brother.
I'm only giving a modest account
Of what these two eyes have seen
And that's the truth on it.
Here, one thing I'll say
Before I'm done –
Catch me eating fish
From now on.

Gareth Owen

Hindu Poem

Sky so bright
Blue and light
Stars – how many have you?
Countless stars
Countless times
Shall our God be praised now.
Forest green
Cool, serene,
Leaves – how many have you?
Countless leaves
Countless times
Shall our God be praised now.

Anon.

Hunting the Leaven

Passover

Take a candle, take a feather,
hunt in every crack.
Find each piece of leavened food
and quickly bring it back.

We'll clean our home from top to bottom,
clear out all the yeast.
And then we'll lay the table
for our special Seder feast.

Tony Mitton

Ramadan

The moon that once was full, ripe and golden,
Wasted away, thin as the rind of a melon,
Like those poor whom sudden ill fortune
Has wasted away like a waning moon.

Like the generous who leave behind
All that was selfish and unkind,
The moon comes out of the tent of the night
And finds its way with a lamp of light.

The lamp of the moon is relit
And the hungry and thirsty
In the desert or the city
Make a feast to welcome it.

Stanley Cook

Mela

Listen to the reading,
   listen to the hymn.
Today it is a holy day.
   Let us think of him
who guided us
   and brought us
from darkness
   into light –
into sudden morning
   out of thick night.

Let us eat together.
   Let us take our ease.
Let us throw our weapons down.

   Here, is peace.

Jean Kenward

Light the Festive Candles

(For Hanukkah)

Light the first of eight tonight –
the farthest candle to the right.

Light the first and second, too,
when tomorrow's day is through.

Then light three, and then light four –
every dusk one candle more

Till all eight burn bright and high,
honouring a day gone by

When the Temple was restored,
rescued from the Syrian lord,

And an eight-day feast proclaimed –
The Festival of Lights – well named

To celebrate the joyous day
when we regained the right to pray
to our one God in our own way.

Aileen Fisher

Assemblies

It's a Wonderful World, but They Made a Few Mistakes

It's a wonderful world, but they made a few mistakes.
Like leaving out unicorns and putting in snakes.
Like no magic carpets, no wishing wells, no genies.
Like good guys getting picked on by the meanies.
Like arithmetic, especially multiplication.
Like expecting a person to stay at home for one whole week
    with a sitter while that person's mother and father take a
    vacation.
Like needing to finish the green beans to get the dessert.
Like everyone caring *way too much* about dirt.
Like letting there by a cavity in a tooth.
Like calling it a lie when all that this person has done is not
    mention part of the truth.
Like raining on soccer games, and liver for supper.
Like bunk beds where the younger person always gets stuck
    with the lower and the older person always gets the upper.
Like leaving out mermaids and putting in splinters and bee
    stings and wars and tornadoes and stomach aches.

It's a wonderful world, but they made a few mistakes.

Judith Viorst

The World with its Countries

The world with its countries,
Mountains and seas,
People and creatures,
Flowers and trees,
The fish in the waters,
The birds in the air
Are calling to ask us
All to take care.

These are our treasures,
A gift from above,
We should say thank you
With a care that shows love
For the blue of the ocean,
The clearness of air,
The wonder of forests
And the valleys so fair.

The song of the skylark,
The warmth of the sun,
The rushing of clear streams
And new life begun
Are gifts we should cherish,
So join in the call
To strive to preserve them
For the future of all.

John Cotton

Thanksgiving

Thank You
   for all my hands can hold –
    apples red,
     and melons gold,
      yellow corn
       both ripe and sweet,
      peas and beans
        so good to eat!

Thank You
   for all my eyes can see –
    lovely sunlight,
    field and tree,
     white cloud-boats
      in sea-deep sky,
     soaring bird
      and butterfly.

Thank You
   for all my ears can hear –
    birds' song echoing
    far and near,
     songs of little
      stream, big sea,
       cricket, bullfrog,
       duck and bee!

Ivy O. Eastwick

All in the Mind

Peace is a bird,
white-feathered
as a winter tree
frothed in snow.

It is silence
leaking from cupped
hands like ice-cold
mountain water.

Peace is a petal
on the summer wind,
fine-spun as a
dragonfly's wing.

It is a promise
straddling the skies
like a rainbow
after the storm.

Moira Andrew

Job Description

A very special person
For a very special post.
Someone who knows how to cook,
(Especially beans on toast.)
Someone who can clean the house
And drive children to school,
And buy the food and clothes and shoes
And use most household tools.
A teacher of all subjects,
A referee of fights,
Who, as relief from boredom,
Is an 'on call' nurse at night.
A hairdresser and swimming coach,
At ease with dogs and cats,
(And hamsters, rabbits, fish and snakes,
Stick insects, birds and rats!)
Has laundry skills, a taxi cab,
Makes costumes for school plays.
Who *never* goes off duty
And whom no one *ever* pays.

Daphne Kitching

Books for All Reasons

the reason i like chocolate
is i can lick my fingers
and nobody tells me i'm not polite

i especially like scarey movies
cause i can snuggle with mommy
or my big sister and they don't laugh

i like to cry sometimes cause
everybody says 'what's the matter
don't cry'

and i like books
for all those reasons
but mostly cause they just make me happy

and i really like
to be happy

                              Nikki Giovanni

The Dawdling Dog

From the West African Myth of Creation

Said Chuku, Creator of the world
And everything in it,
My children will live forever
And thrive
But when they appear to die
They must lie on the ground
To be covered in ashes
And then they will revive.

Said Chuku to his new creation – Dog
Tell my children what to do
So that they will never die.
Go do as I bid.

But, dear child, the Dog dawdled
Dog dawdled
He did.

Said Chuku to his new creation – Sheep
Tell my children what to do
So that they will never die.
Go do as I ask.
But, quite frankly, Sheep wasn't up to the task
And, his thinking being rather woolly,
He said to the children of Chuku –
When you die, dig a hole
A hole for the dead.
And when the children asked why
Sheep said, It's good for the soul.

When Dog arrived late
And said to Chuku's children, No!
You must lay the dead on the ground
And cover them in ashes
And they will revive –
The children laughed and said,
Who are you trying to kid?
Sheep told us the truth.

And that is why
The children of Chuku
Grow old and die.
For Dog dawdled,
He dawdled
He did.

Roger Stevens

Mother to Son

Well, son, I'll tell you:
Life for me ain't been no crystal stair.
It's had tacks in it,
And splinters,
And boards torn up,
And places with no carpet on the floor –
Bare.
But all the time
I'se been a-climbin' on,
And reachin' landin's,
And turnin' corners,
And sometimes goin' in the dark
Where there ain't been no light.
So, boy, don't you turn back.
Don't you set down on the steps
'Cause you find it's kinder hard.
Don't you fall now –
For I'se still goin', honey,
I'se still climbin',
And life for me ain't been no crystal stair.

Langston Hughes

The Most Important Rap

I am an astronaut
I circle the stars
I walk on the moon
I travel to Mars
I'm brave and tall
There is nothing I fear
And I am the most important person here.

I am a teacher
I taught you it all
I taught you why your
spaceship doesn't fall
If you couldn't read or write
Where would you be?
The most important person here is me.

Who are you kidding?
Are you taking the mick?
Who makes you better
when you're feeling sick?
I am a doctor
and I'm always on call
and I am more important than you all.

But I'm your mother
Don't forget me
If it wasn't for your mother
where would you be?
I washed your nappies
and changed your vest
I'm the most important
and mummy knows best.

I am a child
and the future I see
and there'd be no future
if it wasn't for me
I hold the safety
of the planet in my hand
I'm the most important
and you'd better understand.

Now just hold on
I've a message for you all
Together we stand
and divided we fall
So let's make a circle
And all remember this
Who's the most important?
Everybody is.
Who's the most important?
EVERYBODY IS!

Roger Stevens

The News

I don't like news
that explodes
leaves refugees
crying, homeless

that orders tanks
into cities
blasting down
schools and houses.

News that blows up
hospitals
news that kills
and fills deep graves.

I don't like news
that screams abuse
kicks the legs
from under wingers.

taps their ankles
argues back
news that won't learn
how to lose.

I like news
that's just been born
news that puts
food in stomachs.

news that rescues
news that cures
that celebrates
its hundredth birthday

news that will make today
happier than the day before.

David Harmer

Just One Wish (feeling full of joy)

If I had only one wish
I would drop it in a rippling pool
and watch the concentric circles
it would make as it plunged downwards
fragmenting the surface of the water.

If I had only one wish
I'd throw it high into the blue heaven
and watch it as it arched over
and tumbled down, creating
a rainbow of joy in the roof of the world.

If I had only one wish
I'd plant it deep in brown earth
and watch as it pierced the loam
with a pointed spear
and grew into a magnificent tree.

If I had only one wish
I'd burn it like incense
and savour the aroma as it wafted
far away on the winds of perfume
and dissipated on the thermals of life.

If I had only one wish
I should wish that everyone
could once again be filled with childlike joy
So that the magic and beauty of the world
would once again be a daily miracle.

Janis Priestley

Finding Magic

Are you looking for magic?
It's everywhere.
See how a kestrel
Hovers in air;
Watch a cat move:
What elegant grace!
See how a conker
Fits its case.
Watch a butterfly come
From a chrysalis,
Or a chick from an egg –
There's magic in this;
Then think of the
Marvellous mystery
Of an acorn becoming
A huge oak tree.
There's magic in sunsets
And patterned skies:
There's magic in moonlight –
Just use your eyes!
If you're looking for magic
It's easily found:
It's everywhere,
It's all around.

Eric Finney

With My Hands

Flap them in the air
(wave)
Shove the ball away
(save)
Smooth a doggie's fur
(stroke)
Dig into a rib
(poke).

Grasp another hand
(shake)
Stick two bits of wood
(make)
Squeeze an empty can
(crunch)
Fingers in a fist
(punch).

Slip a silver coin
(pay)
Push them palm to palm
(pray)
Test the water's heat
(dip)
Hang on for your life
(grip)

Push or pull a chair
　(shift)
Raise a weight up high
　(lift)
Press the button down
　(click)
Finger up your nose
　(pick)

Grab an arm or leg
　(catch)
Give an itch a bash
　(scratch)
Knock on someone's door
　(rap)
Thank you very much
　(clap)

Steve Turner

All of Us

All of us are afraid
More often than we tell.

There are times we cling like mussels to the sea wall,
And pray that the pounding waves
Won't smash our shell.

Times we hear nothing but the sound
Of our loneliness, like a cracked bell
From fields far away where the trees are in icy shade.

O many a time in the night-time and in the day,
More often than we say,
We are afraid.

If people say they are never frightened,
I don't believe them
If people say they are frightened,
I want to retrieve them.

From that dark shivering haunt
Where they don't want to be,
Nor I.

Let's make of ourselves, therefore, an enormous sky
Over whatever
We hold most dear.

And we'll comfort each other,
Comfort each other's
Fear.

Kit Wright

A School Creed

This is our school.
Let peace dwell here,
Let the room(s) be full of contentment,
Let love abide here,
Love of one another,
Love of mankind,
Love of life itself,
And love of God.
Let us remember
That, as many hands build a house,
So many hearts make a school.

Traditional (used by a school in Canada)

Listen

Listen.
Far away, the snort of a camel,
The swish of boots in the endless sand,
The whisper of silk and the clatter of ceremonial swords,
Far away.

Listen.
Not so far, the slam of a castle door,
A cry of rage on the midnight air,
A jangle of spurs and the cold thrust of a soldier's
    command,
Not so far.

Listen.
Closer now, the homely bleat of a ewe among the grasses,
The answering call of her lamb, fresh born,
The rattle of stones on a hillside path,
Closer now.

Listen.
Closer still, the murmur of women in the dark,
The kindly creak of a stable door,
The steady breathing of the sleepy beasts,
Closer still.

Listen.
So close you are almost there,
The singing of the stars,
The soundless flurry of wings,
The soft whimper of a child amongst the straw,
So close you are almost there.

Clare Bevan

Carol of the Brown King

Of the three Wise Men
Who came to the King,
One was a brown man,
So they sing.

Of the three Wise Men
Who followed the Star,
One was a brown king
From afar.

They brought fine gifts
Of spices and gold
In jewelled boxes
Of beauty untold.

Unto His humble
Manger they came
And bowed their heads
In Jesus' name.

Three Wise Men,
One dark like me –
Part of His
Nativity.

Langston Hughes

The Sky

The sky at night is like a big city
Where beast and men abound.
But never once has anyone
Killed a fowl or a goat,
And no bear has ever killed a prey.
There are no accidents: there are no losses.
Everything knows its way.

Traditional, Ewe (Ghana)

And My Heart Soars

The beauty of the trees,
the softness of the air,
the fragrance of the grass,
　　speaks to me.

The summit of the mountain,
the thunder of the sky,
the rhythm of the sea,
　　speaks to me.

The faintness of the stars,
the freshness of the morning,
the dew drop on the flower,
　　speaks to me.

The strength of fire,
the taste of salmon,
the trail of the sun,
and the life that never goes away,
　　they speak to me.

And my heart soars.

Chief Dan George

An Alphabet for the Planet

A for air.
The gentle breeze by which we live.
B for bread.
A food to bake, and take – and *give*.
C for climate.
It can be warm, it can be cold . . .
D for dolphin.
A smiling friend no net should hold.
E for Earth.
Our ship through space, and home to share.
F for family.
Which also means people *everywhere*.
G for green.
Colour of life we'll help to spread.
H for healthy.
Happy and strong, no fumes with lead.
I for ivory.
The elephant's tusks, his *own* to keep.
J for jungle.
A rainforest. No axe should creep.
K for kindly.
To everyone, gentle and good.
L for life.
It fills the sea and town and wood.

M for mother.
She may feel hurt, but loves us all.
N for nest.
A tiny home for chicks so small.
O for Ozone.
It shields our Earth from harmful rays.
P for peace.
'My happy dream,' the Planet says.
Q for quiet.
Where no loud noise can get at you.
R for recycled.
Old cans and cards as good as new.
S for Sun.
The nearest star. It gives us light.
T for tree.
A grander plant, a green delight.
U for united.
Working as one to put things right.
V for victory.
Winning over disease and war.
W for water.
The whole earth drinks when rainclouds pour.
X for Xylophone.
Music from wood – the high notes soar!
Y for yummy.
Those tasty fruits 'organically grown'.
Z for zoo.
A cage, a condor – sad, alone.

Riad Nourallah

Thank You Letter

Dear Sun,
Just a line to say:
Thanks for this
And every day.
Your dawns and sunsets
Are just great –
Bang on time,
Never late.
On dismal days,
As grey as slate,
Behind a cloud
You calmly wait,
Till out you sail
With cheerful grace
To put a smile
On the whole world's face.
Thanks for those

Blazing days on beaches.
For ripening apples,
Pears and peaches;
For sharing out
Your noble glow;
For sunsets – the
Loveliest things I know.
Please carry on:
We know your worth.

Love from
A Friend on Planet Earth

Eric Finney

Our Tree

It takes so long for a tree to grow
So many years of pushing the sky.

Long branches stretch their arms
Reach out with their wooden fingers.

Years drift by, fall like leaves
From green to yellow then back to green.

Since my grandad was a boy
And then before his father's father

There's been an elm outside our school
Its shadow long across our playground.

Today three men ripped it down.
Chopped it up. It took ten minutes.

David Harmer

Grown-ups

Where are your trainers and where is your coat
Where is your pen and where are your books
Where is the paper and where is the key
Where is the sugar and where is the tea
Where are your socks
Your bag and your hat?
Tidy your room!
Look after the cat!

You're hopeless
Untidy
You lose everything.

Where is your bracelet and where is your ring
Where is your ruler
Hymn book and shoes
Where is your scarf?
You lose and you lose.

You're hopeless
Untidy
You lose everything.

Careless and casual
You drop and you fling
You're destructive and thoughtless
You don't seem to care
Your coat's on the floor
Your boots on the chair

Why don't you think
Why don't you try
Learn to be helpful; like your father and I.

Mum . . . Dad . . .

Where are the woodlands, the corncrake and the whales
Where are all the dolphins, the tigers and dales
Where are the Indians, the buffalo herds
Fishes and forests and great flying birds

Where are the rivers
Where are the seas
Where are the marshes
And where are the trees

Where is the pure air
Acid-free showers
Where are the moorlands
The meadows and flowers?

These were your treasures
Your keepsakes of time
You've lost them
You've sold them
And they could have been mine.

Peter Dixon

The Last Day of School

I'm so glad it's finally over!
I've waited all year for this day!
It's ended, concluded and finished!
The one word for that is *hooray*!
So why am I getting this feeling
That maybe I'll miss everyone?
And why is there always some sadness
When everything's over and done?

Jeff Moss

Personal, Social and Sensitive Issues

Extract from the Book of Ecclesiastes

To every thing there is a season,
   and a time to every purpose under heaven:
A time to be born, and a time to die;
   a time to plant, and a time to pluck up that which is planted;
A time to kill, and a time to heal;
   a time to break down, and a time to build up;
A time to weep, and a time to laugh;
   a time to mourn, and a time to dance;
A time to cast away stones, and a time to gather stones together;
   a time to embrace, and a time to refrain from embracing;
A time to get, and a time to lose;
   a time to keep, and a time to cast away;
A time to rend, and a time to sew;
   a time to keep silence, and a time to speak;
   A time to love, and a time to hate;
   a time of war, and a time of peace.

King James Bible

Name-calling

They called me frog-face with ears like a bat.
I said, 'I'm not – I'm worse than that.'

They called me rat-nose with a tongue like a shoe.
I said, 'Is that the best you can do?'

They called me mouse-eyes, skunk-breath, dog-head.
I said, 'I'm worse than all that you've said.'

They said, 'It's no fun calling you a name.'
I called, 'That's a pity – I'm enjoying this game.'

Charles Thomson

Give Yourself a Hug

Give yourself a hug
when you feel unloved

Give yourself a hug
when people put on airs
to make you feel a bug

Give yourself a hug
when everyone seems to give you
a cold-shoulder shrug

Give yourself a hug –
a big big hug

And keep on singing,
'Only one in a million like me
Only one in a million-billion-thrillion-zillion
like me.'

Grace Nichols

First Thing Today

(for Jimmy)

First thing today before
the cockerel crowed –
a baby's cry from
across the road.

Hi there, baby,
damp and furled,
hi there. Welcome
to our world.

Here's the little finger
of my right hand
and here's a teddy
you won't understand

yet

and

here's

flowers for your mummy
and what about this? –
Here's my first hug
and my first kiss.

Fred Sedgwick

Some Things Don't Make Any Sense at All

My mum says I'm her sugarplum.
My mum says I'm her lamb.
My mum says I'm completely perfect
Just the way I am.
My mum says I'm a super-special wonderful terrific little guy.
My mum just had another baby.
Why?

Judith Viorst

Staring

out
the window
on the long ride
to
South Eighth Street School
on the
bursting
crowded
city bus

I wonder
if Daddy
ever –

even for a
little while –

thinks
about me –

thinks
about
us.

Lee Bennett Hopkins

It's Not the Same without Dad

I always sat on his knee
for the scary bits when we watched TV,
my head tucked into his chest.
Mum always fidgets, Dad was best.

And it's not the same without Dad.

He piggy-backed me up the stairs,
pulled sticky bubblegum out of my hair,
didn't tell Mum when he should have done,
when Dad played around it was really fun.

And it's not the same without Dad.

We fed the ducks down at the park,
he held me when I was scared of the dark,
he didn't mind if I got things wrong,
when I felt weak, he was sure to be strong.

But everything's changed now he's gone.

Brian Moses

Divorce

Dad's left.   Is that right?

Yes.
It all
centred
on something
Mum said.

So   does   leave

where   that   you?

Gina Douthwaite

306

Divorce

I did not promise
to stay with you till death us do part, or
anything like that,
so part I must, and quickly. There are things
I cannot suffer
any longer: Mother, you have never, ever, said
a kind word
or a thank you for all the tedious chores I have done;
Father, your breath
smells like a camel's and gives me the hump;
all you ever say is:
'Are you off in the cream puff, Lady Muck?'
In this day and age?
I would be better off in an orphanage.

I want a divorce.
There are parents in the world whose faces turn
up to the light
who speak in the soft murmur of rivers
and never shout.
There are parents who stroke their children's cheeks
in the dead night
and sing in the colourful voices of rainbows,
red to blue.
These parents are not you. I never chose you.
You are rough and wild,
I don't want to be your child. All you do is shout
and that's not right.
I will file for divorce in the morning at first light.

Jackie Kay

Bringing up a Single Parent

It's tough bringing up a single parent.
They get really annoyed when they can't stay out late,
or when you complain about them acting soppy
over some nerdy new friend,
(even though you are doing it for their own good).
It's exhausting sometimes, the way you have to please them,
and do things you absolutely hate while pretending
it's exactly what you want.
Yep. Bringing up a single parent
is a real chore.
You don't get extra pocket money for them,
or special grants,
and you have to get up in the morning
and allow them to take you to school
so they can boast to their friends
about how clever you are.
And what's worse,
you have to allow them to fret over you,
otherwise they get terribly worried.
And if you're out doing something interesting after school
you have to keep popping home all the time
to check they're not getting up to any mischief
with a new friend, or smoking, or drinking too much.
You have to try and give single parents
that extra bit of attention.
But once you've got them trained,
with a bit of patience and fortitude
they're relatively easy to look after.

Still, it can be tough
bringing up a single parent.

Brian Patten

Cousins

Every evening
when the dark creeps in
like a smothering black cape,
our little family
– Mum, Dad, Brother, Sister, Gogo the Cat and me –
we get together to huddle and cuddle
and keep us each safe.

Every night
when the moon rises like a white saucer,
our little family
– Mum, Dad, Brother, Sister, Gogo the Cat and me –
go to bed in our warm rooms.
We tuck each other in
and sleep safe in green dreams.

But in another land,
when the same dark creeps in,
a broken family in a wild wind
looks to the same moon, red and angry,
and each makes a wish.
– Mum, Dad, Brother, Sister, Asmara the Stray Dog –
all ask for food, for medicine, for peace, for rain.
Just these, only these, do our beautiful cousins ask for.

John Rice

Get Your Things Together, Hayley

Mum said the dreaded words this morning:
Get your things together, Hayley,
We're moving.

I've at last made a friend, and Mrs Gray
Has just stopped calling me
The New Girl.

Why do we have to go now
When I'm just beginning
To belong?

It's OK for my sister,
She's good with people.
They like her.

But I can't face the thought
Of starting all over again
In the wrong uniform.

Knowing the wrong things,
In a class full of strangers
Who've palled up already.

And don't need me.
Mum says: *It's character-forming, Hayley.*
I say it's terribly lonely.

Frances Nagle

The New House

I don't much like this bedroom
The bedroom doesn't like me
It looks like a sort of policeman
Inspecting a refugee.

I don't like the look of the bathroom
It's just an empty space
And the mirror seems used to staring at
A completely different face.

I don't like the smell of the kitchen
And the garden wet with rain
It feels like an empty station
Where I'm waiting for a train.

I can't kick a ball against this wall,
I can't build a house in this tree
And the streets are as quiet and deserted
As the local cemetery.

I don't like the look of the kids next door
Playing in the beat-up car
Why do they stand and stare at me?
Who do they think they are?

The big boy's coming over
He's just about my height
Why has he got a brick in his hand?
Is he going to pick a fight?

But he asks me into their garden
Tells me his name is Ben
And Jane is the name of his sister
And will I help build their den.

We can't get it finished by dinner
We won't get it finished by tea
But there's plenty of time in the days ahead
For Ben and for Jane and for me.

Gareth Owen

This Is a Recorded Message

Ring home, ring home . . .
She's punched her last coin in.
There's a pinball flicker of connections, then
The ansafone –

a so-familiar voice, slow,
strained, strange, like a brain-
washed hostage. *Please leave your name
and address. Please speak after the tone.*

Meeeee . . . bleats the ghost
in the machine that's waiting
in an empty house a hundred miles away. What can she say?
'This is me. I've left home.'

Philip Gross

Friends

When first I went to school
I walked with Sally.
She carried my lunch pack,
Told me about a book she'd read
With a handsome hero
So I said,
'You be my best friend.'
After break I went right off her.
I can't say why
And anyway I met Joan
Who's pretty with dark curls
And we sat in a corner of the playground
And giggled about the boy who brought the milk.
Joan upset me at lunch,
I can't remember what she said actually,
But I was definitely upset
And took up with Hilary
Who's frightfully brilliant and everything
And showed me her history
Which I considered very decent.
The trouble with Hilary is
She has to let you know how clever she is
And I said,
'You're not the only one who's clever you know,'
And she went all quiet and funny

And hasn't spoken to me since.
Good riddance I say
And anyway Linda is much more my type of girl;
She does my hair in plaits
And says how pretty I look,
She really says what she thinks
And I appreciate that.
Nadine said she was common
When we saw her on the bus that time
Sitting with three boys from that other school,
And I had to agree
There was something in what she said.
There's a difference between friendliness
And being cheap
And I thought it my duty
To tell her what I thought.
Well she laughed right in my face
And then pretended I wasn't there
So I went right off her.
If there's one thing I can't stand
It's being ignored and laughed at.
Nadine understood what I meant,
Understood right away
And that's jolly nice in a friend.

I must tell you one thing about her,
She's rather a snob.
I get the feeling
She looks down on me
And she'll never come to my house
Though I've asked her thousands of times.
I thought it best to have it out with her
And she went off in a huff
Which rather proved my point
And I considered myself well rid.

At the moment
I walk home on my own
But I'm keeping my eyes open
And when I see somebody I consider suitable
I'll befriend her.

Gareth Owen

Friendship

Friendship
Is precious
Keep it
Protect it
You will need it
Don't throw it away
Don't break it
Don't neglect it
Keep it
Somewhere
In your heart
If you want to
Somewhere in your thoughts
If you want to
But keep it
For, friendship

Has no borders
And its boundary
Is that of the world
It is the colour
Of the rainbow
And it has the beauty
Of a dream
Never listen
To those who say
It doesn't exist any more
It is here
It is yours
When you want it
All you have to do is:
Open
Your eyes

Véronique Tadjo (Côte d'Ivoire)

Friends

I fear it's very wrong of me
And yet I must admit
When someone offers friendship
I want the *whole* of it.
I don't want everybody else
To share my friends with me.
At least, I want *one* special one,
Who, indisputably
   Likes me much more than all the rest,
Who's always on my side.
Who never cares what others say,
Who lets me come and hide
Within his shadow, in his house –
It doesn't matter where –
Who lets me simply be myself,
Who's always, *always* there.

Elizabeth Jennings

Harvey

Harvey doesn't laugh about how I stay short while
  everybody grows.
Harvey remembers I like jellybeans – except black.
Harvey lends me shirts I don't have to give back.
I'm scared of ghosts and only Harvey knows.

Harvey thinks I will when I say someday I will marry
  Margie Rose.
Harvey shares his lemonade – sip for sip.
He whispers 'zip' when I forget to zip.
He swears I don't have funny looking toes

Harvey calls me up when I'm in bed with a sore throat and
  runny nose.
Harvey says I'm nice – but not *too* nice.
And if there's a train to Paradise.
I won't get on it unless Harvey goes.

Judith Viorst

Dream Team

My team
Will have all the people in it
Who're normally picked last.

Such as me.

When it's my turn to be chooser
I'll overlook Nick Magic-Feet-Jones
And Supersonic Simon Hughes

And I'll point at my best friend Sean
Who'll faint with surprise
And delight.

And at Robin who's always the one
Left at the end that no one chose –
Unless he's away, in which case it's guess who?

And Tim who can't see a thing
Without his glasses.
I'll pick him.

And the rest of the guys that Mr Miller
Calls dead-legs but only need their chance
To show what they're made of.

We'll play in the cup final
In front of the class, the school, the town,
The world, the galaxy.

And due to the masterly leadership shown
By their captain, not forgetting
His three out-of-this-world goals,

We'll WIN.

Frances Nagle

New Girl

Have you seen the new girl?
first-day-at-our-school girl
not-sure-what-to-do girl
no-partner-in-the-queue girl
mouth-stuck-down-like-glue girl
looking-a-little-blue girl
needs-a-friend-or-two girl
So what are you going to *do* girl?

Danielle Sensier

Shame

There's a girl at school
we teased today;
made jokes, called her names.
My friends all laughed,
called it harmless fun,
said it was just a game.

Now I'm at home
feeling horrid inside,
long gone that thoughtless grin.
How will I face her
tomorrow at school?
I wish I hadn't joined in.

Tracey Blance

Bullied

Bullies get you.
I don't know how but they do.
They seem to have some
secret inborn radar
tuned in to loners,
quiet ones,
different ones.

You don't have to
do anything, say anything.
Seems you just have to be you.

Grown-ups think they know.
Bullies? Just cowards, they say,
unsure of themselves,
needing to act big.
But it's hard to believe
when jeering faces
zoom up to yours.

When they're hassling you,
calling you names,
leading the chanting,
the whispering,
urging the others on,
a relentless horde
of nagging, pecking birds.

Then there's the 'in-betweens',
the waiting, the not knowing,
just sure that
sooner or later
it's going to come.
The worst times;
the thinking times.

Don't ask me the answer.
I don't know but –
I'm getting there.

Keep my eyes skinned,
find a crowd to vanish into
before *they* see *me*.
Cornered, I know I can't look them
in the eye – but I've learned
not to look at the floor,
to try and walk tall.

Mostly I've learned
to talk in my head,
tell myself
it's not me, I'm all right –
they're the idiots, the misfits.
Eventually
it begins to sink in.

I'm getting tougher inside.
It's working.
Just don't give in.

Try anything, anything.
But don't *let* them win.

Patricia Leighton

Sometimes

(A cinquain)

Sometimes
They just stare hard
Nudge each other and smile,
And I pretend that I don't care –
Sometimes

Coral Rumble

Dobbo's First Swimming Lesson

Dobbo's fists
spiked me to the playground wall
nailed me to the railings.

The plastic ball
he kicked against my skinny legs
on winter playtimes

Bounced a stinging red-hot bruise
across the icy tarmac.

The day we started swimming
we all jumped in
laughed and splashed, sank beneath
the funny tasting water.

Shivering in a corner
Dobbo crouched, stuck to the side
sobbing like my baby brother
when all the lights go out.

David Harmer

It Hurts

It hurts when someone makes remarks
About the clothes I wear,
About the foods I refuse to eat
Or the way I cover my hair.

It hurts when someone laughs and jokes
About the way I speak.
'Ignore them,' says my dad, but it's hard
To turn the other cheek.

It hurts when someone calls me names
Because of the colour of my skin.
Everyone's different outside
But we're all the same within.

John Foster

Mr Mizen

Mr Mizen fell in the street.
Old and frail, his step was unsure on the ice.
No one saw him fall
but the cry of the concrete shook the town.

A passing runner stopped to help.
But strong as he was
he had no understanding of old age,
the slowness it brings, how the wind
tangles weak limbs, how hard it is
to heave tired legs over uneven pavement slabs.

After falling Mr Mizen had no idea
what had happened to him.
He asked if his pipe was broken,
he fumbled for his glasses
and asked if he could go home.

'Is there someone at home
who'll look after you?'
'No, I'm on my own.'

No wife, no son, no daughter
to wipe his bleeding chin,
to put him to bed,
to make him some soup,
to see that he recovered.

So when Mr Mizen fell in the street
the authorities decided he couldn't go home
but that he should go to hospital,
to be another number.

A week later the local newspaper
reported that he had 'died of natural causes'.

But, being as alone as he was,
is not what you'd call 'natural'.

John Rice

On the Streets

Welcome to Cardboard City
No windows, doors, or locks
All you need is a sleeping bag
All you need is a box.

It starts with a row at home
A rumble, a hassle, a fight
Your mum and dad chuck you out
And you've got no bed for the night.

You can beg for a bit of money
Spend it on beer and draw
Just watch out for the boots and knives
And the steady beat of the Law.

You've joined the homeless people
Dropped here until you rot
No one much cares if you live or die
You're the one everybody forgot.

David Harmer

My Daddy Dances Tapstep

Roger's daddy's clever
Daisy's flies a plane
Michael does computers
And has a house in Spain.
Lucy's goes to London
He stays there every week . . .
 But my daddy has an earring
 and lovely dancing feet.

He hasn't got a briefcase
He hasn't got a phone
He hasn't got a mortgage
And we haven't got a home.
He hasn't got a fax machine
We haven't got a car
 But he can dance and fiddle
 And my daddy is
 A Star.

Peter Dixon

The World Is a Beautiful Place

The world is a beautiful place
　　　　to be born into
if you don't mind happiness
　　　　not always being
　　　　　　　so very much fun
if you don't mind a touch of hell
　　　　now and then
just when everything is fine
　　　　　　　because even in heaven
　　　　they don't sing
　　　　　　all the time
　　The world is a beautiful place
　　　　　　to be born into
if you don't mind some people dying
　　　　　all the time
or maybe only starving
　　　　　　some of the time
　　which isn't half so bad
　　　　　　　　if it isn't you.

Laurence Ferlinghetti

In the Garden

There's a plant in the garden with white flowers
And a plant in the garden with blue,
Which of them is better?
Neither one said Sue.

There's a plant in the garden with cream flowers
And a plant in the garden with red,
Which of them is better?
Neither Simon said.

Those plants in the garden so tiny
And those trees in the garden so tall,
Which of them is better?
Neither answered Paul . . .
The garden needs them all.

Philip Waddell

Citizen of the World

when you are very small
maybe not quite born
your parents move
for some reason you may never understand they move
from their own town
from their own land
and you grow up in a place
that is never quite your home

and all your childhood people
with a smile or a fist say
you're not from here are you
and part of you says fiercely yes I am
and part of you feels no I'm not
I belong where my parents belonged

but when you go to their town, their country
people there also say
you're not from here are you
and part of you says no I'm not
and part of you feels fiercely yes I am

and so you grow up both and neither
and belong everywhere and nowhere much the same
both stronger and weaker for the lack of ground
able to fly but not to rest

339

and all over the world, though you feel alone
are millions like you, like a great flock of swallows
soaring or falling exhausted, wings beating the rhythm
of the wind that laughs at fences or frontiers,
whose home is itself, and the whole world it moves over.

Dave Calder

The Soldiers Came

The soldiers came
and dropped their bombs.
The soldiers didn't take long
to bring the forest down.

With the forest gone
the birds are gone.
With the birds gone
who will sing their song?

But the soldiers forgot
to take the forest
out of the people's hearts.
The soldiers forgot
to take the birds
out of the people's dreams.
And in the people's dreams
the birds still sing their song.

Now the children
are planting seedlings
to help the forest grow again.
they eat a simple meal of soft rice
wrapped in a banana leaf.
And the land welcomes their smiling
like a shower of rain.

John Agard

Stranger

You looked so sad when you came to us,
From a land so faraway.
You left your friends, your favourite foods,
The language that you spoke so well.
But you came to us with a lovely smile,
A beautiful dress, and a small soft voice,
Sometimes I know you felt so lost,
In the street of unfriendly noise.
And your mother smiled too,
She couldn't say much.
But I didn't need words to speak to you,
I knew from your smile
And the touch of your hand,
That we wouldn't be strangers
. . . for long.

Les Baynton

Arturi's Story

Arturi's skin is sort of grey,
grubby looking, know what I mean?
Miss Hampton says his country is at war
so he didn't get very good food before.
He's very quiet, doesn't talk much
about the things he saw
in his war.
I've never seen him laugh.
He hardly even smiles
but he often cries.
Our teacher tries to comfort him
with soothing words,
a warm hand on his shoulder,
a troubled look in her eyes.
Arturi's mother brought him here
to her sister's home.
His father is still there.
Arturi and his mum are not sure where.
Funny, I never took much notice
of the TV news until now.
Unreal, somehow.
These days in every scene
of buildings ripped apart
by banging shells,
seeing women duck and run,
a soldier at a corner
aiming a gun,
I think maybe Arturi's father is one
of the people caught up in that.

In the playground the other day
Tim and I were talking about the shops
on the way to school;
the green off-licence,
sweets in the post office
and how the smell
of fish and chips makes us drool.
Arturi was listening, hanging his head
the corners of his mouth turned down.
'My school was up in the mountains,'
he suddenly said.
That caught our attention right away.
We waited to hear what else
he might have to say.
'I had to get up
and eat breakfast in the night
because we had to be
at school in daytime,
there was no electric light.
My friend Thomas and I
we didn't like walking
up the mountain track in the dark
for two hours every day.
Spiders' webs hung on wet bushes.

The gloomy trees were spooky and grey.
Our voices echoed,
they startled us, sounding so loud.
We were frightened there might be
soldiers somewhere near
who would take us away.
The worst place on the way
was the rushing stream,
it was so fast and wide
with slippery wet stones
to balance and jump along
to reach the other side.
When our feet got wet
they were freezing cold all day.
Our school was just one big room
with a leaking roof,
no glass in the windows, no door,
a floor of muddy clay.
In the middle the old iron stove
stood, burning hot,
giving off fumes and smoke.
If you sat near enough
you warmed up a bit
but the fumes made you cough and choke.
Outside we'd piled rocks
halfway up the gaping window holes
to keep out the wind and cold.
We had a few wooden desks
with benches, all scored
with scratches, really old.'

Tim and I stand silent,
shuffle our feet.
'You must be glad to be here now,'
blurts Tim. I see he feels like me
as our eyes meet.
'Yes, but my best friend Tomas
is still doing that every day
up the mountain all alone,' Arturi groans.
We can see from the way
he swallows and rubs an eye
he's trying not to cry.
'What about . . . well,
why don't you write him a letter
asking, "Are you OK?"
Here Arturi. Have a sweet,' I awkwardly say.
And Tim and I resolve
Arturi deserves new friends
remembering Tomas
alone on the mountain
every day
that way.

Penny Kent

All that Space

Great-grandad
used to tell me stories,
tales about when he was a lad,

fled city streets,
flew on his bike
down lanes between cornfields,
past Kenyon's Brick Works
to the Moss,

sitting for hours
in all that space,

played his mouth organ,
and watched . . .
peewits   wild violets   silhouette
of chimneys against the sky,

his shabby jersey, battered clogs,
livened by new-moon-silver buds of willow,
baby-skin softness of dog-rose petal.

In the Home, people try to interest him
in television, don't understand
when he turns his chair to the wall
– the print of Constable's *Haywain*,
curves his fingers round
his smiling mouth,
and tilts his head, listening . . .

sitting for hours   in all that space.

Joan Poulson

Cowboy Games and the Good Death

In cowboy games we tumbled and cried in deaths so good
    that we got up and died all over again.
In those days death was often a matter for negotiation
    between killer and killed.
'You're dead.'
'Missed.'
'You aren't taking it.'
'It went under my arm.'
'You're out the game then.'
'OK. You got me. But I'm just knocked out.'
I dropped to the floor,
Held my arm
Shook my head
Staggered to my feet
Free to enjoy
A whole playtime of deaths.

Nan didn't fall down when she died
Because she was in hospital
Held down by blankets and tubes.
She didn't argue
She took it
And died just the once.

John Coldwell

The Funeral

Everyone is silent in the huge black car.
A cloud full of swallowed tears
gliding two feet above the ground
towards a storm.

We're trying to be brave.
Mum holds my hand tightly.
Her fingers are like clothes pegs
clinging to washing
in a force 9 gale.
'You're hurting me,' I say.
She lets me go –
a forgotten balloon
and smiles a smile from far away,
like a smile in a photograph
in a place you can't quite remember.

We wait in line.
People mumble past us
trying not to catch our eyes.
I look at the coffin
and try to imagine Granny inside.
Can she hear me singing?
I'm singing really loudly so she'll hear.

Is she in heaven yet?
Still old and in pain?
Or whirring swiftly backwards
like a rewound tape
which pauses
at your very favourite bit.

Are hosts of heavenly angels
even as we sing
loosening her tight grey perm
and itchy curls?
Making the hair flow
like a coppery stream
down her strong young back.

I wonder if she'll wear
her tartan slippers
to dance on the clouds.

Afterwards, outside,
we weave through furious rain
towards the car.
Inside and warm again,
Mum sighs
Like summer
drifting through an open window
A feather
     or a present
          from a sky-blue
              sky.

Lindsay MacRae

Mid-Term Break

I sat all morning in the college sick bay
Counting bells knelling classes to a close.
At two o'clock our neighbours drove me home.

In the porch I met my father crying –
He had always taken funerals in his stride –
And Big Jim Evans saying it was a hard blow.

The baby cooed and laughed and rocked the pram
When I came in, and I was embarrassed
By old men standing up to shake my hand

And tell me they were 'sorry for my trouble';
Whispers informed strangers I was the eldest,
Away at school, as my mother held my hand

In hers and coughed out angry tearless sighs.
At ten o'clock the ambulance arrived
With the corpse, stanched and bandaged by the nurses.

Next morning I went up into the room. Snowdrops
And candles soothed the bedside; I saw him
For the first time in six weeks. Paler now,

Wearing a poppy bruise on his left temple,
He lay in the four foot box as in his cot.
No gaudy scars, the bumper knocked him clear.

A four foot box, a foot for every year.

Seamus Heaney

My First Dog

Prince was my dog,
no one else's.
I couldn't remember a time
    when he wasn't there.

We grew up together,
roamed together,
got into trouble together,
winked at each other
and took our tellings-off
together.

He was my black-and-tan shadow,
sleeking along at my heels
tongue out,
chasing down the green hill
and the alleyway
to the corner shop.

He was my talisman;
with him I was safe.
He was my freedom,
his soft coat the cushion
of my dreams as I lay
tracing cloud
       patterns
           in
              the
            sky.

And when he gashed his leg
on a rusted railing,
when my mother quietly told me
he had been put down,
he was the first black hole
of my young life.

The loneliness
of empty arms
and no warm neck
to put them round.

Patricia Leighton

Burying the Dog in the Garden

When we buried
the dog in
the garden on
the grave we put
a cross and
the tall man
next door was
cross.
'Animals have no
souls,' he said.
'They must have animals'
souls,' we said. 'No,'
he said and
shook his head.
'Do you need a
soul to go
to Heaven?' we
asked. He nodded
his head. 'Yes,'
he said.

'That means my
hamster's not
in Heaven,' said
Kevin. 'Nor is
my dog,' I said.
'My cat could sneak
in anywhere,' said
Clare. And we thought
what a strange place Heaven
must be with
nothing to stroke
for eternity.
We were all
seven.
We decided we
did not want to
go to Heaven.
For that the
tall man next
door is to blame.

Brian Patten

Silver Moon

When Amelia looks on the silver moon
She remembers her mother's smile,
The warmth of her arms around her,
The breeze of her breath on her brow,
And she wants her here with her now.

When Amelia looks on the silver moon
She forgets the many times
Her rebel ways or cheekiness
Made her mother frown,
And she wants her here with her now.

From beyond the moon, beyond the stars,
Beyond the deep, deep sky,
Her mother calls to her each night
'Amelia, I am here.'
And she calls back 'So am I.'

Frances Nagle

Death

There is no needle without piercing point.
There is no razor without trenchant blade.
Death comes to us in many forms.

With our feet we walk the goat's earth.
With our hands we touch God's sky.
Some future day in the heat of noon,
I shall be carried shoulder high
Through the village of the dead.
When I die, don't bury me under forest trees,
I fear their thorns.
When I die, don't bury me under forest trees,
I fear the dripping water.
Bury me under the great shade trees in the market,
I want to hear the drums beating
I want to feel the dancers' feet.

Kuba (Africa)

Remember

Remember me when I am gone away,
   Gone far away into the silent land;
   When you can no more hold me by the hand,
Nor I half turn to go yet turning stay.
Remember me when no more day by day
   You tell me of our future that you plann'd:
   Only remember me; you understand
It will be late to counsel then or pray.
Yet if you should forget me for a while
   And afterwards remember, do not grieve:
   For if the darkness and corruption leave
   A vestige of the thoughts that once I had,
Better by far you should forget and smile
   Than that you should remember and be sad.

Christina Rossetti

The Environment

Wilderness

Miss says wilderness
is beautiful, natural, endless . . .
is space.

Mum's *Oxford English Dictionary* states:
'wild or uncultivated land'.

At the end of our garden
there's a lime tree.
I climb it, high as I can.

Sometimes
I sit up there for hours,
especially in the dark
staring at the stars,
touching wilderness,

out there
and inside me.

Joan Poulson

Web of Life

An invisible web,
as fragile as dreams,
links mountains to forests
and rivers to streams.

Through woodlands and forests;
where seas flow and ebb,
over ice caps and deserts,
life weaves a great web.

From plankton to whales,
all life great and small
depends on each other.
Life's web links us all.

And we must take care
of each gossamer thread,
for we are all part of
this great world wide web.

Jane Clarke

Dolphin Dance

We are darters and divers
from secret sea-caves.
We're dippers and gliders,
we dance through the waves.

We spiral and curl,
we weave as we fly,
stitch shimmering arches
from ocean to sky.

Judith Nicholls

Forest

The forest stretches for miles,
a place where labourers
poached rabbit for the pot,
where deer roamed free.
An ancient place, root and tree
firmly established,
majestic oaks spreading
into an eternity of time.

Still those oaks, now shedding
tough brown leaves, are here.
The forest floor rustles
with the sound of leaf
upon leaf of history.
Oak and birch set new seed,
regenerate themselves,
and slender saplings rise.

The forest is evolving, ever-
changing, yet the same.
Belonging to itself, never
planted, never tame.
Let this wish be granted:
that the forest will remain.

Ann Bonner

Natural Numbers

*Example: Divide 5,000 buffaloes
by fifty hunters = almost nothing left.*

1. Divide 200 elephants
by seventeen ivory poachers =

2. Divide two rainforests
by eight logging companies =

3. Divide one beautiful planet
by one greedy species =

Mike Johnson

Blake's Tyger – Revisited

*On hearing that tigers in captivity can gradually
lose their colour, losing their camouflaging stripes
and fading gradually to white.*

Tiger! Tiger! Turning white
In a cage just twice your height
Six paces left, six paces right,
A long slow day, a longer night.

Tiger! Tiger! Dreaming still
Of the scent? The chase? The kill?
And now? No need. No place. No scope.
No space. No point. No hope.

Tiger! Tiger! Paces. Paces.
Once he flashed through open spaces.
His world once echoed to his roars.
Now he's quiet. He stares. He snores.

An inch of sky glimpsed through the bars.
A puddle. Concrete. Smells of cars.
He sniffs the air. He slumps. He sighs.
And stares and stares through jaundiced eyes.

Michaela Morgan

The Last Wolf Speaks from the Zoo

By day

I hid in the ferns
pressed to the earth,
dressed in a coat
brown as turf.

Sunlight warmed
the patches where
my wolf pack once lay.

Day after day
childflesh spills past the wire;
they pause, point and stare –
I size them up –
glare back –
through thin red eyes.

Years back
my sister caught one –
cracked a finger –
left the childflesh
to scowl and howl.

The next day
they took my sister away.
But her smell stayed
trapped in the earth's spoor.
It took a full moon's span
for it to fade.

Now, alone,
I watch
and wait for her.

At night
the stars glisten.
I listen for the pack.
I sing to the moon.
I croon an ancient tune.
But she is muzzled
and cannot answer back.

                    Pie Corbett

Important Notice

World Wildlife Industries sadly announces
that we may soon have to close due to fierce
competition from Human Beings International.

Many of our famous products are already
unavailable including, to name but three, our dodo,
quagga and once healthy passenger pigeon lines.

Currently under threat are many of our
ancient stock of mammals and fishes as well as
birds, reptiles, amphibians *and* insects.

But even now we could be helped to survive.
Work together with your parents and teachers
to find out how you could all help before it is too late.

And remember – without us and the products
of our other branch, World Vegetation Industries,
our world too might soon be without *your* company.

Let's work together to stay in business.

Mother Nature

Managing Director

Philip Waddell

Names

My name is 'Couldn't care less',
just let the forests die.
My name is 'Can't be bothered',
who cares about holes in the sky?

My name is 'I'm too busy',
let someone else do the worrying,
there's nothing that I can do
if the ice caps are wearing thin.

My name is 'Leave me alone',
just don't go preaching to me.
Gossip is what I care about
not oil that's spilt in the sea.

My name is 'I'm all right Jack',
there's really no cause for alarm.
Hens are silly birds, who cares
if they suffer at the factory farm?

Who cares about global warming?
I like a spot of hot weather.
My name is 'Sit on the fence',
my name is 'All of a dither'.

So stop saying what I should think,
I don't want to believe what I'm told.
My name is 'Hope it will go away',
my name is 'Don't get involved'.

And who do you think you are,
telling us all we should worry?
WELL, MY NAME'S A WARNING FROM FUTURE YEARS,
IT'S 'LISTEN OR YOU'LL BE SORRY'.

Brian Moses

Dragonflies

They used to fly
over all the ponds
in summer, Granny says

like sparkling sapphire helicopters,
purple aeroplanes,
with eyes of bright topaz,
wings flashing emerald light,
brightening the countryside
in their jewelled flight.

Sun-glow brilliance winging
over every pond,
someday I hope to see one
– smallest last dragon.

Joan Poulson

Missing

Missing: our
one and only planet,
known to her friends as
'Earth'.

Yes, an old photograph
when she was clothed in
gorgeous greens,
wilderness white,
brilliant blues.

Somehow, got into
bad company:
blistered brown,
gaunt grey,
faded. Jaded,

left one morning;
no forwarding address.

We just didn't think . . .
We just didn't know . . .
what to do.

If you
have any information
that can help us trace
our beautiful planet,
please get in touch.

Please get in touch.

Mike Johnson

Model
Poems

Introduction

This section provides a broad range of poems that could be used as models for the children's own writing. Do not worry too much if the children find it difficult to adhere strictly to a form – concentrate on the quality of the language. Encourage them to use the poet's toolkit of techniques: precise nouns, powerful verbs, necessary adjectives, exact detail, contrasting and surprising combinations, alliteration, similes, metaphor, personification.

- 'Poetry' – make a list of rhyming couplets, using the same form, e.g. *Not the rain,/but the cool touch of rain;/Not the lion,/but the lion's mane*, etc.
- 'Alien Lullaby – either use the same structure (or base own poem on another well-known rhyme), e.g. *Hush little Hobbit, don't you cry!/Momma's gonna give you a plane to fly./and if that plane's wings should break/Momma's gonna take you to the lake . . .*
- 'Jabbermockery'/'Jabberwocky' and 'The Cook and the Caretaker'/'The Owl and the Pussy Cat' – further examples of poems based on the structure of an original.
- 'Song Thrush Poster' – poem in another form (other possibilities include diary, letters, for sale notices, phone conversations, etc.).
- 'Tom Thumb's Diary' – a good example of responding to a well-known rhyme or fairy tale, in another form – diary, letter, news item, for instance.
- 'There was a young lady . . .' – limericks are not an easy form. Rhyming dictionaries do help! When writing,

children should say the poem aloud to listen for the rhythm/beat.

- 'Low Owl' – this is a poem that only uses one of the five vowels (in this case the letter 'o'). Begin by trying to write sentences with only one vowel, e.g. *An ant can walk and talk*.

- 'Haiku of the Four Winds' – pupils could use the same format to write a similar haiku based on the sun, moon, rain, wind, thunder, etc. Note that the haiku do not have to stick strictly to 5/7/5 syllables but should aim to capture the essence of a scene in a few words. Begin by choosing a season to describe – list typical sights and sounds. Use this brainstorm as a basis for the poem. Short forms such as haiku lend themselves to writing a cycle of linked poems, such as a calendar of haiku.

- 'The Emperor and the Nightingale' – these three haiku keep to a strict pattern. They are connected and form a poem – called a rensaku.

- 'Tanka' – tease out the syllabic pattern (5/7/5/7/7). Note how like the haiku this is a verbal snapshot, related to one of the seasons.

- 'Cinquain' – again, let children work out the pattern (5 lines – 2/4/6/8/2 syllables). Imitate by selecting a month, listing sights and sounds and then using this list to construct a cinquain. Concentrate more on the quality of the words than fitting the pattern exactly.

- 'Kennings' – a Nordic form of poetry. Like a riddle the poem describes something in different ways. Choose something simple like a cat or dog and try a class example, e.g. *flea carrier/loud growler/ankle biter . . .*

Model Poems

- 'Two Witches Discuss . . .' – writing simple conversations between two characters can form the basis of a poem. Try well-known story characters, e.g. Jack meeting the giant.
- 'In Marble Walls' – see who can work out the riddle. Give this several days if need be. As a class choose a subject, e.g. a candle. List all that is known about the subject and turn these into clues – as in 'What am I?'
- 'One line riddles' – give these as homework – who can work out what they are? Select subjects and offer one clue only.
- 'My First Is in Two . . .' – tease out from the spelling the answer to this riddle. Use it as a basis for class riddles written in the same style.
- 'A Pin Has a Head' – list other words that have several meanings (*watch, wave, crane, rose, ring, club, bank, light, pop, tug, stand, book, leaves, flat, safe, jam, arms, bat*) and let children invent similar sentences, perhaps as one line 'word plays', e.g. *A watch has hands but no fingers.*
- 'What Am I?' – to make a simple riddle take a common subject (mirror, windows, lock, etc.). Brainstorm associations (*mirror – glass, reflections, thin, cannot lie, seven years' bad luck, 'mirror, mirror on the wall'*, etc.). Create a poem by listing clues, e.g. *I am made of glass/and reflect all that I see./I seem to hold the world/and yet I am empty./Drop me – and you'll/have seven years' bad luck . . . etc.*
- 'The Tree Spell' – what about using the same format for an animal such as a badger which hibernates?
- 'The Months' – write a simple poem in which you use one or two lines to describe what happens in each month, e.g. *January is snow bound./In February icicles hang from the roof . . .*

- 'Apple Pie' – choose a different subject and use the same pattern. For instance, a poem based on a pencil might start – *A altered it, B bit it, C cracked it in half, D dug it into a table top, E elongated it* . . .
- 'Simple Seasons' – these acrostics look easy but are difficult to write effectively. Try writing some based on months rather than seasons, e.g.

   Dull,
   Early nights.
   Christmas lights gleam.
   Empty streets, sirens scream.
   Misty windows.
   Baubles like tiny planets.
   Enticing shop displays.
   Rough winds and frosted days.

- 'The Witch, the Prince and the Girl in the Tower' – an interesting concrete poem. The shape adds to the meaning – it is twisted in a plait. Try writing another thin poem where two characters speak to each other in the same sort of format. What might Jack say and the Giant reply? Keep it to just one sentence each. Do not worry too much about rhyme as this so often gets in the way of the quality of the writing.
- 'Litter Lout' – another shape poem where the pattern visually represents the meaning. Make a list of similes for the snow – using 'like' and 'as' (as cold as . . .). List what else snow does – how does it fall, how does it lie, how does it feel, what does it remind you of, etc. Use these ideas to create a similar shape poem.
- 'My Dad's Amazing' – make a list of other idioms and try the same sort of idea.

- 'Things to Do' – other possibilities would include – things to do on holiday, at the beach, in the park, after school, at a party.
- 'Moses' – invent other tongue-twisters by using words that alliterate and rhyme.
- 'Childhood Tracks' – this poem uses the senses and a simple format. Copy it, brainstorming ideas and basing it firmly in the children's own lives and memories.
- 'Mr Khan's Shop' – write a list poem based on foods that we eat – the variety is surprising, e.g. *In my mum's kitchen cupboard/there are round potatoes, slim courgettes,/orange onions with peeling skin,/violet bulbs of garlic . . .*
- 'What Do You Collect?' – a straightforward imitation of this poem would be possible to write rhyming couplets. The rhyme may be hard and children should abandon words if sensible rhymes cannot be found. Writing in pairs can work well for this sort of task.
- 'Bonfire Night' – rather like a haiku, this simple, short poem makes a useful model. Select a special event, such as a visit to the seaside. Let pupils take one sense impression, and see if they can write a short poem concentrating on selecting powerful language, e.g. *Taste of ice cream/frozen crystals – the sun glares down/melting the crisp edges.*
- 'Notes towards a Poem' – use the phrase 'inside my head' to write a list poem of all the things that might be inside the mind – memories, fears, wishes, dreams, etc. Compare this poem to Miroslav Holub's poem 'A Boy's Head' and Katherine Gallagher's poem 'A Girl's Head', both found in *Ramshackle Rainbow, Poems for Year 5*, edited by Pie Corbett (Macmillan Children's Books).

- 'A Minute to Midnight' – imitate this contrasting list poem by listing all the things that are still or moving at a given time of day. Try adding in more description.

- 'Best Places' – list favourite places, objects, memories, events and use the same sort of pattern to create individual list poems.

- 'The Dream Keeper' – use the repeating phrase 'bring me all of your . . .' to write a similar poem. This could include memories, hopes, wishes, etc.

- 'Dreams' – use this poem as a basic pattern to create a list poem using metaphors, e.g. Hold fast to dreams/ for if dreams live/ Life would be a red racing car/ whispering the motorway.

- 'All the world's a stage . . .' – use this poem as a basis to trigger writing, listing all the things on the world's stage that we enjoy, e.g. *On the world's stage/ I see the sea rippling in the blue./ I see the football smack into the net./ I see . . . etc.*

- 'Camilla Caterpillar' etc – children love tongue-twisters and playing with alliteration. Write simple tongue-twisters about animals by seeing how many words can be used that share the same opening sound, e.g. cat – *the curious cat crept carefully, concealing a clammy cod!*

- 'Having My Ears Boxed' – look at how the poem is built around the possible different meanings of 'having my ears boxed' – a pun. Look at other words that might mean several different things, e.g. *bat, watch, wave.* 'A Pin Has No Head' is another poem that involves this sort of word play.

Poetry

What is Poetry? Who Knows?
Not a rose, but the scent of the rose;
Not the sky, but the light in the sky;
Not the fly, but the gleam of the fly;
Not the sea, but the sound of the sea;
Not myself, but what makes me
See, hear, and feel something that prose
Cannot: and what it is, who knows?

Eleanor Farjeon

Alien Lullaby

Hush, little alien, don't you cry!
Mamma's gonna bake you a moonbeam pie

And if that moonbeam pie goes stale
Mamma's gonna catch you a comet's tail

And if that comet's tail won't flip
Mamma's gonna make you a rocket ship

And if that rocket ship won't stay
Mamma's gonna buy you the Milky Way

And if the Milky Way's too far
Mamma's gonna bring you a shooting star

And if that shooting star falls down –
You're still the sweetest little alien in town!

Sue Cowling

Jabberwocky

'Twas brillig, and slithy toves
Did gyre and gimble in the wabe;
All mimsy were the borogoves,
And the mome raths outgrabe.

'Beware the Jabberwock, my son!
The jaws that bite, the claws that catch!
Beware the Jubjub bird, and shun
The frumious Bandersnatch!'

He took his vorpal sword in hand:
Long time the manxome foe he sought –
So rested he by the Tumtum tree,
And stood awhile in thought.

And as in uffish thought he stood,
The Jabberwock, with eyes of flame,
Came whiffling through the tulgey wood
And burbled as it came!

One, two! One, two! And through and through
The vorpal blade went snicker-snack!
He left it dead, and with its head
He went galumphing back.

'And hast thou slain the Jabberwock?
Come to my arms, my beamish boy!
O frabjous day! Callooh! Callay!'
He chortled in his joy.

'Twas brillig, and the slithy toves
Did gyre and gimble in the wabe;
All mimsy were the borogoves,
And the mome raths outgrabe.

Lewis Carroll

Jabbermockery

Twas Thursday and the bottom set
Did gyre and gimble in the gym.
All mimsy was Miss Borogrove
And the Head of Maths was grim.

'Beware the Mathematix, my friend!
His sums that snarl. His coordinates that catch!
Beware the Deputy Bird, and shun
The evil Earring-snatch!'

She took her ballpoint pen in hand:
Long time the problem's end she sought –
So rested she by the lavatory
And sat awhile in thought.

And as in toughish thought she sat,
The Mathematix with eyes of flame
Came calculating through the cloakroom doors
And subtracted as he came.

She thought real fast as he went past;
The well placed soap went slickersmack!
She left him stunned and with the sums
She went galumphing back.

'And hast thou got the answers, Jackie?
Come to our desk,' beamed idle boys.
'Oh, frabjous day, Quelle heure! Calais!'
They chortled in their joy.

Twas Thursday and the bottom set
Did gyre and gimble in the gym.
All mimsy was Miss Borogrove
And the Head of Maths was *grim*.

Trevor Millum

The Owl and the Pussy-cat

The Owl and the Pussy-cat went to sea
   In a beautiful pea-green boat,
They took some honey, and plenty of money,
   Wrapped up in a five-pound note.
The Owl looked up to the stars above,
   And sang to a small guitar,
'O lovely Pussy! O Pussy, my love,
   What a beautiful Pussy you are,
     You are,
     You are!
   What a beautiful Pussy you are!'

Pussy said to Owl, 'You elegant fowl!
   How charmingly sweet you sing!
O let us be married! too long we have tarried:
   But what shall we do for a ring?'
They sailed away, for a year and a day,
   To the land where the Bong-tree grows
And there in a wood a Piggy-wig stood
   With a ring at the end of his nose,
     His nose,
     His nose,
   With a ring at the end of his nose.

'Dear Pig, are you willing to sell for one shilling
    Your ring?' Said the Piggy, 'I will.'
So they took it away, and were married next day
    By the Turkey who lives on the hill.
They dined on mince, and slices of quince,
    Which they ate with a runcible spoon;
And hand in hand, on the edge of the sand,
    They danced by the light of the moon,
        The moon,
        The moon,
    They danced by the light of the moon.

Edward Lear

The Cook and the Caretaker

*(The Cook being rather Owlish,
and the caretaker a real Pussycat.)*

The Cook and the Caretaker stirred their tea
And grumbled about the school.
'The children are rude, they play with their food.'
'And the Head is a first-class fool.'
The Cook washed up the Caretaker's cup
And she sighed as she rinsed his spoon,
'How fondly I ache to bake you a cake –
Do you fancy a fresh macaroon,
Aroon,
Aroon,
Do you fancy a fresh macaroon?'

Clare Bevan

Song Thrush Poster

WORM SHORTAGE
due to hard ground.
There are
SNAIL-BASHING LESSONS
today at the rockery.
Learn how to spot
poisoned slugs
and snails!
6 a.m. prompt.
PLEASE WATCH OUT
FOR CATS!

Sue Cowling

Tom Thumb's Diary

Monday: Fell in Mother's pudding bowl! Kicked and struggled so she thought pudding was bewitched and gave it to passing tinker.

Tuesday: Called out 'Bless you!' when tinker sneezed – got thrown into bushes (still in pudding!) for my pains. Ran home – Mother glad to see me. Had bath in teacup to get rid of pudding mixture.

Wednesday: To fields to milk cows with Mother – was tied to a flower stalk for safety. Eaten by cow. Fought and scratched till cow spat me out.

Thursday: Fields again – ploughing with Father. Got lost in furrow. Picked up by eagle (scary!). Flown to seaside and dumped in sea. Swallowed by large fish, caught and presented to King. Everyone surprised to find *me* inside fish!

Friday: Was made official Little Knight of the Court. Fame at last!

Saturday: A bit homesick – asked permission to visit
Mother and Father for the day. Not sure how
I'll manage to carry purse full of gold, though.

Sunday: Mother and Father *very* pleased to see me. So
tired from carrying gold had to stop on way
back for nap in flowerpot. Luckily butterfly
passing when woke up so hitched a ride.
Nobles rushed about trying to catch crazy
butterfly but no luck. Fell off eventually –
landed in compost heap. King tickled pink at
safe return – feasting all next week!

Sue Cowling

There Was a Young Lady of Riga

There was a young lady of Riga
Who went for a ride on a tiger;
They returned from the ride
With the lady inside
And a smile on the face of the tiger.

Anon.

Low Owl

(a univocalic*)

Cold morn: on fork of two o'clock
owl's hoot flows from hood of wood.

Owl's song rolls from blood to brood,
owl's hoot loops on to top of town roofs,
owl's song swoops on strong doors.

Owl's slow whoop – long, forlorn –
soft flood of moon song.

John Rice

*a poem which uses only one of the five vowels: in this case the letter 'o'.

Haiku of the Four Winds

The wind of the north
hurls itself over lonely oceans,
breathing ice into earth's lungs.

The wind from the east
is a sharp-toothed beast, wilfully
biting into day.

The wind from the south
slithers through summer grasses,
made lazy by the sun.

The wind from the west
is a wind of rest, drifting,
whispering from the sunset . . .

Judith Nicholls

The Emperor and the Nightingale

Silent nightingale,
the cage that you occupy
is not the whole world.

Never-a-song songbird,
treated like a clockwork toy,
sing inside your head.

No consolation:
the Emperor too is trapped
with no song to sing.

Mike Jubb

Tanka: Red leaves

Tonight I saw the
caretaker sweeping dead red
    leaves. Whose school is this
Sir? I asked him. He stood up.
Mine . . . and the leaves', he replied.

Fred Sedgwick

December Cinquain

Rainbow
against lead in
the winter sky: a gull
floats on the wind. Starlings rest on
chimneys.

Fred Sedgwick

Kennings

Wild howler
Night prowler
Free mealer
Chicken stealer
Earth liver
Fright giver
Rusty splasher
Hunted dasher
Fox.

Daphne Kitching

Two Witches Discuss Good Grooming

'How do you keep your teeth so green
Whilst mine remain quite white?
Although I rub them vigorously
With cold slime every night.

Your eyes are such a lovely shade
Of bloodshot, streaked with puce.
I prod mine daily with a stick
But it isn't any use.

I envy so, the spots and boils
That brighten your complexion
Even rat spit on my face
Left no trace of infection.

I've even failed to have bad breath
After eating sewage raw,
Yet your halitosis
Can strip paint from a door.'

'My dear, there is no secret,
Now I don't mean to brag.
What you see is nature's work
I'm just a natural hag.'

John Coldwell

In Marble Walls

In marble walls as white as milk,
Lined with a skin as soft as silk;
Within a fountain crystal clear,
A golden apple doth appear.
No doors there are to this stronghold
Yet thieves break in and steal the gold.

Traditional

[Answer: an egg]

One Line Riddles

Golden coin in blue.

*

Many teeth but no bite.

*

Ballet dancer accomplishes the splits.

*

Visionary twins.

*

Muddying the sky.

*

One that holds a thousand.

Pie Corbett

[Answers: Sun, Comb, Scissors, Spectacles, Clouds, Seed.]

My First Is in Two

My first is in two but not in a pair,
My second's in round and also in square;
My third is in heat but never in cold,
My fourth is in new but not in old.
My fifth's not in silver but is in gold,
My sixth is in honest, if the truth be told.
My whole is one strand of the heavenly arc
Where sun and rain meet to leave their mark.

Sue Playdell

[Answer: orange]

A Pin Has a Head

A pin has a head, but has no hair;
A clock has a face, but no mouth there;
Needles have eyes, but they cannot see;
A fly has a trunk without lock or key;
A timepiece may lose, but cannot win;
A corn-field dimples without a chin;
A hill has no leg, but has a foot;
A wine-glass a stem, but not a root;
Rivers run, though they have no feet;
A saw has teeth, but it does not eat;
Ash-trees have keys, yet never a lock;
And a baby crows, without being a cock.

Christina Rossetti

What Am I?

I am a soft boomerang,
That will never spin round.
An unwrapped present,
Found far from the ground.
Don't monkey about –
I live in fear of that.

At a glance, I look
Like a giant's yellow fingers,
But the smell that lingers
Is oh, so much sweeter.

Leave me too long
And I'll turn rotten.
Forgotten – and I'll ooze.

Watch out for my skin –
Or you'll lose your step,
And slip flat
On your back
to crack
Your head wide open.

Pie Corbett

The Tree Spell

January, sleep tight.
February, wake up.

April, come into leaf.
May, open catkins.

June, salute the sun.

September, ripen acorns.
October, let leaves fall.

December, cast spell again.

John Rice

The Months

January cold desolate;
February all dripping wet;
March wind ranges;
April changes;
Birds sing in tune
  To flowers of May,
And sunny June
  Brings longest day;
In scorched July
The storm-clouds fly
Lightning-torn
August bears corn.
September fruit;
In rough October
Earth must disrobe her;
Stars fall and shoot
In keen November;
And night is long
And cold is strong
In bleak December.

Christina Rossetti

Apple Pie

A was an Apple pie
B bit it, C cut it, D dealt it,
E enjoyed it, F fought for it,
G got it, H hoped for it,
I inquired about it,
J jumped on it, K kept it,
L longed for it, M mourned for it,
N nodded at it, O opened it,
P peered in it, Q quartered it,
R ran for it, S sat on it, T took it,
U upset it, V viewed it, W wanted it,
X crossed it, Y yearned for it,
And Z put it in his pocket, and said,
'Well done!'

Anon.

Simple Seasons

Swallows
Primroses
Return.
It's
New,
Green!

Skylarks
Up,
Meadows
Motley,
Elms
Regal.

Apples
Untold,
Trees
Unruly;
Mists
Now.

Waters
Icebound,
Naked
Trees;
Earth
Rests.

Eric Finney

The Witch, the Prince and the Girl in the Tower

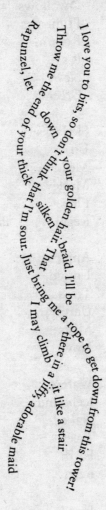

I love you to bits, so don't your golden hair. braid. I'll be there in a jiffy, adorable maid

Throw me the down think silken. That

Rapunzel, let end of your thick er I'm sour. Just bring me a rope to get down from this tower!

Sue Cowling

Litter Lout

Snow

      throws

confetti

        at

everyone

                  Empties

                     out

             litter

             bins

                  high

               in

             the

      Snow   air

        shreds

          its

   bus

   tickets

          scatters

             them

   Laughs

       as

        they

     flutter down

   Snow

doesn't

     care

Sue Cowling

My Dad's Amazing!

My dad's *amazing* for he can:

make mountains out of molehills,
teach Granny to suck eggs,
make Mum's blood boil
and then drive her up the wall.

My dad's *amazing* for he also:

walks around with his head in the clouds,
has my sister eating out of his hand,
says he's got eyes in the back of his head
and can read me like a book.

But,
the most *amazing* thing of all is:

when he's caught someone red-handed,
first he jumps down their throat
and then he bites their head off!

Ian Souter

Things to Do on the First Day
of the Summer Holidays

Lie in bed late   lounging and lolling about
Eat eggs and bacon   for breakfast at eleven

Sprawl on the lawn   with a long glass of lemonade
Eat salad and seafood   Travel the town T-shirted

Greeting mates   grinning with freedom   Bowl
Bash those bails down   Belt a leather ball

Bouncing to the boundary   bounce bounce   Bring
A take-away home   parathas and poppadums

Talk about treats   sunlight through trees and sand
Sleep in deep silence between sheets   Dream

Fred Sedgwick

Moses

Moses supposes his toeses are roses,
But Moses supposes erroneously;
For nobody's toeses are posies of roses
As Moses supposes his toeses to be.

Anon.

Childhood Tracks

Eating crisp fried fish with plain bread.
Eating sheared ice made into 'snowball'
with syrup in a glass.
Eating young jelly-coconut, mixed
with village-made wet sugar.
Drinking cool water from a calabash gourd
on worked land in the hills.

Smelling a patch of fermenting pineapples
in stillness of hot sunlight.
Smelling mixed whiffs of fish, mango, coffee,
mint, hanging in a market.
smelling sweaty padding lifted off a donkey's back.

Hearing a nightingale in song
in moonlight and sea-sound.
Hearing dawn-crowing of cocks, in answer
to others around the village.
Hearing the laughter
of barefeet children carrying water.
Hearing a distant braying of a donkey
in a silent hot afternoon.
Hearing palmtrees' leaves rattle
on and on at Christmas time.

Seeing a woman walking in loose floral frock.
Seeing a village workman with bag and machete
under a tree, resting, sweat-washed.
Seeing a tangled land-piece of banana trees
with goats in shades cud-chewing.
Seeing a coil of plaited tobacco
like rope, sold, going in bits.
Seeing children playing in schoolyard
between palm and almond trees.
Seeing children toy-making in a yard
while slants of evening sunlight slowly disappear.
Seeing an evening's dusk hour lit up
by dotted lamplight.
Seeing fishing nets repaired between canoes.

James Berry

Mr Khan's Shop

is dark and beautiful.
There are parathas,

garam masala,
nan breads full of fruit.

There are bhajees, samosas, dhal,
garlic, ground cumin seeds.

Shiny emerald chillies
lie like incendiary bombs.

There are bhindi in sacks,
aloo to eat with hot puris

and mango pickle. There's
rice, yogurt,

cucumber and mint –
raita to cool the tongue.

Sometimes you see
where the shop darkens

Mr Khan, his wife
and their children

round the table.
The smells have come alive.

He serves me
poppadums, smiles,

re-enters the dark.
Perhaps one day

he'll ask me to dine with them:
bhajees, samosas, pakoras,

coriander, dhall.
I'll give him this poem: *Sit down*

young man, he'll say
and eat your words.

Fred Sedgwick

What Do You Collect?

What do you collect?
Coins, dolls from other lands?
Or jokes that no one understands?

What do you collect?
Skulls, posters, badges, bells?
Or walking sticks, or seaside shells?

What do you collect?
Stamps, gemstones, model cars?
Or wrappers torn from chocolate bars?

What do you collect?
Leaves, photographs of cats?
Or horror masks and rubber bats?

What do you collect?
Books, fossils, records, rocks?
Or comics in a cardboard box?

Wes Magee

Bonfire Night

Smells of bonfires,
backyards burning –
all the leaves
have finished turning.

Katherine Gallagher

Notes towards a Poem

Sky, grey. Late frost
laces glass, distracts.
Trees, still. Paper, white.

Inside my head
red lava rumbles
in an unquiet earth;
black storm clouds gather,
tigers poise to spring,
a yellowed river
presses at its banks.
Ice binds nothing here
and over lightning flash
and ocean roar
the mountain bursts.
Tigers crash,
white ocean horses
gallop in flood-tide
and down the mountainside
the red-hot torrent pours.

Sky, grey. Late frost.
Trees, laced glass, lost.
Paper, black on white.

Judith Nicholls

A Minute to Midnight

A *minute to midnight*
and all is still.

For example, these are things that are still:
ornaments, coins, lamp-posts,
the cooker, Major Clark's home for old folk
(just opposite our house, which is also still),
the newsagent's, a hut, soap, tractors,
freshly ironed trousers draped over the chair.

A *minute to midnight*
and all is still
except for the things that are moving.

Like, for example,
rivers, clouds, leaves, flags,
creaky windmills, lungs, birds' feathers,
digital clocks, grass, the wind,
non-sleeping animals (especially wolves),
planet Earth, the moon, satellites in space,
toenails (well they grow, don't they),
videos that are set to record
programmes in the middle of the night,
washing lines,
mobiles above babies' cots –
and babies' eyelids, they always flicker.

John Rice

Best Places

Hill-tops: when getting there's been tough
And you've earned the view
With leg ache and puff;
Dungeons in castles:
Earth floors, mossy stones –
Stand still and listen
To the chink of chains, the groans!
Waterfalls;
Cool riversides with trees;
Docksides and quays
With the bustle of shipping;
Circuses:
Clowns casually backflipping;
Small, secret beaches
Tucked under a cliff face;
Cathedrals,
Mighty with silence and space;
My grandad's old shed:
I could poke about for hours;
Bridges, belfries, battlements, towers;
Fairgrounds and funfairs –
All thump and throb and glare;

Orchards, hedgerows, cornfields:
The quietness there;
Cities:
I love Edinburgh,
Mum's for Paris and Dad, Rome,
But when all said and done,
   The Best Place is Home.

Eric Finney

The Dream Keeper

Bring me all of your dreams,
You dreamers,
Bring me all of your
Heart melodies
That I may wrap them
In a blue cloud-cloth
Away from the too-rough fingers
Of the world.

Langston Hughes

Dreams

Hold fast to dreams
For if dreams die
Life is a broken-winged bird
That cannot fly

Hold fast to dreams
For when dreams go
Life is a barren field
Frozen with snow.

Langston Hughes

All the world's a stage

All the world's a stage,
And all the men and women merely players:
They have their exits and their entrances;
And one man in his time plays many parts,
His acts being seven ages. At first the infant,
Mewling and puking in the nurse's arms.
And then the whining schoolboy, with his satchel,
And shining morning face, creeping like snail
Unwillingly to school. And then the lover,
Sighing like furnace, with a woeful ballad
Made to his mistress' eyebrow. Then a soldier,
Full of strange oaths, and bearded like the pard,
Jealous in honour, sudden and quick in quarrel,
Seeking the bubble reputation
Even in the cannon's mouth. And then the justice,
In fair round belly with good capon lin'd,
With eyes severe, and beard of formal cut,
Full of wise saws and modern instances;

And so he plays his part. The sixth age shifts
Into the lean and slipper'd pantaloon,
With spectacles on nose and pouch on side,
His youthful hose well sav'd, a world too wide
For his shrunk shank; and his big manly voice,
Turning again toward childish treble, pipes
And whistles in his sound. Last scene of all,
That ends this strange eventful history,
Is second childishness and mere oblivion,
Sans teeth, sans eyes, sans taste, sans everything.

William Shakespeare

Camilla Caterpillar

Camilla Caterpillar kept a caterpillar killer-cat.
A caterpillar killer categorically she kept.
But alas the caterpillar killer-cat attacked Camilla
As Camilla caterpillar catastrophically slept.

Mike Jubb

She Sells Seashells

She sells seashells on the sea shore;
The shells that she sells are seashells I'm sure.
So if she sells seashells on the sea shore,
I'm sure that the shells are sea-shore shells.

Anon.

Barry and Beryl the Bubble Gum Blowers

Barry and Beryl the bubble gum blowers
blew bubble gum bubbles as big as balloons.
All shapes and sizes, zebras and zeppelins,
swordfish and sea lions, sharks and baboons,
babies and buckets, bottles and biplanes,
buffaloes, bees, trombones and bassoons
Barry and Beryl the bubble gum blowers
blew bubble gum bubbles as big as balloons.

Barry and Beryl the bubble gum blowers
blew bubble gum bubbles all over the place.
Big ones in bed, on backseats of buses,
blowing their bubbles in baths with bad taste,
they blew and they bubbled from breakfast till bedtime
the biggest gum bubble that history traced.
One last big breath . . . and the bubble exploded
bursting and blasting their heads into space.
Yes Barry and Beryl the bubble gum blowers
blew bubbles that blasted their heads into space.

Paul Cookson

Having My Ears Boxed

I am waiting in the corridor
To have my ears boxed.
I am nervous, for Mr O'Hanlon
Is a beast of his word.

For the last twenty minutes
I have let my imagination
Run away with itself.
But I am too scared to follow.

Will he use that Swiss Army knife
To slice through cleanly? Bite them off?
Tear carefully along perforated lines?
Tug sharply like loose Elastoplasts?

Acknowledging the crowd's roar
Will he hold my head aloft
As if it were the FA cup
And pull the handles? Aagghhrr . . .

And then the box. Cardboard?
Old cigar-box possibly? Or a pair?
Separate coffins of polished pine.
L and R. 'Gone to a better place.'

Impatient now, I want to get it
Over with. Roll on four o'clock.
When, hands over where-my-ears-used-to-be
I run the gauntlet of jeering kids.

At six, Mother arrives home weary
After a hard day at the breadcrumb factory.
I give her the box. She opens it
And screams something. I say:

'Pardon?'

Roger McGough

Index of First Lines

1 snunk in a snuncle   197
1 witch with 1 broomstick   188
1. Divide 200 elephants   369
A bully-pulley   153
A caravan a travelling man a razor shell kiss and tell   42
A for air   287
A minute to midnight   428
A pin has a head, but has no hair   410
A treacherous monster is the Shark   221
A trumpet   59
A very special person   265
A was an Apple pie   414
Add two times twenty-two   191
All a mix together   37
All among the leaf litter   229
All of us are afraid   279
All the world's a stage   433
An invisible web   366
Are you looking for magic?   276
Arturi's skin is sort of grey   344
As we walk across this hill of chalk   216
As you read this poem you are on a spacecraft   214
At school we're doing growing things   217
Aunt Sue has a head full of stories   92
Barry and Beryl the bubble gum blowers   437
BC   72
Beak   223
Be awed as you climb my heavy   9
Bedraggled feathers are uneasy   224
Before the paling of the stars   238
Blessed are the poor in spirit   245
Bring me all of your dreams   431
Bullies get you   327
By day   371
California, Mississippi   138
Camilla Caterpillar kept a caterpillar killer-cat   435
Chill winds across the desert probe   67
Cobalt and umber and ultramarine   5

Index of First Lines

Cold morn: on fork of two o'clock	400
Come and see! I've been building an oojamaflip	151
Constant, constant, little light	212
cooker. blanket	162
Cornelius loved Chemistry	207
Crash and	38
Dad's left. Is that right?	306
Dandelions shout	232
Day by day I float my paper boats one by one	122
Dear Jesus, when I feel my black bad temper	247
Dear Mum	90
Dear Sun	289
Dobbo's fists	331
Don't enter a castle quietly	75
Draw a house with four walls	4
'Draw me,' the cypress said	6
Dry were the words	76
Early last Sunday morning	119
Early morning boiler gives a bagpipe bellow	44
Eating crisp fried fish with plain bread	421
Entranced, he listens to salty tales	21
Every evening	311
Everyone is silent in the huge black car	350
Far too cold	231
Firing molten rock at the sky	110
First thing today before	302
Flap them in the air	277
Flash, crash, rock and roll	47
Friendship	319
From my window I see	114
Give yourself a hug	301
God said WORLD	246
Golden coin in blue	408
Graph	192
Great-grandad	347
Half a league, half a league	87
Harvey doesn't laugh about how I stay short while everybody grows	322
Have you heard Mouse laugh?	225
Have you seen the new girl?	325
He's been again	29
Henry the Seventh	78

Here lies the body	209
Hey. I'm cool	10
Hickory digital dock	168
Hill-tops: when getting there's been tough	429
History	63
Hold fast to dreams	432
Homework – to design and produce a flip-book	149
Horse rider	80
How do you keep your teeth so green	406
Hush, little alien, don't you cry	388
I always sat on his knee	305
I am a poet	20
I am a soft boomerang	411
I am a sundial, and I make a botch	158
I am a techno traveller	165
I am a teeming city	134
I am an astronaut	270
I am ten and you are two	194
I am the newest devil	84
I am waiting in the corridor	438
I am	249
I asked the little boy who cannot see	11
I breathe in	220
I did not promise	307
I don't like news	272
I don't much like this bedroom	313
I fear it's very wrong of me	321
I go out hunting rabbits	82
I have a friendly little mouse	171
I have a spelling chequer	167
I like electric guitars	46
I live in the city, yes I do	118
I love Geography	109
I love my teacher	189
I measure fun in grandads	200
I sat all morning in the college sick bay	353
I thank you Lord, for knowing me	237
I went to an art gallery with Dad	12
I'm a BIG BASS drum	55
I'm sitting	45
I'm so glad it's finally over	295

I'm the bongo kid	49
I'm the king of the keyboard, star of the screen	166
I'm tired this morning	73
I've always had a liking for the Viking	70
If all the numbers in the world were	183
If I could travel	126
If I had only one wish	274
If I should die, think only this of me	97
If I were a shape	201
If I were the conductor	52
Imagine that the earth was shaped	208
In 1943	99
In cowboy games we tumbled and cried in deaths so good	349
In marble walls as white as milk	407
In the bleak mid-winter	40
In the forest's shadows	225
In the sun's oven	140
It hurts when someone makes remarks	332
It takes so long for a tree to grow	291
It was 1953	160
It's a wonderful world, but they made a few mistakes	261
It's cold in here	22
It's easy – modern art is	8
It's tough bringing up a single parent	309
January cold desolate	413
January, sleep tight	412
Jim's dad has a motor mower	159
Ladies and Gentlemen	218
Leonardo, painter, taking	18
Lie in bed late lounging and lolling about	419
Life is a tree – rooted in the earth	241
Light the first of eight tonight	256
Light the lamp now	248
Light travels, said Miss	210
Liquorice plaits	98
Listen to the reading	255
Listen	282
Look	16
Matchstick girls and matchstick boys	13
'Maths gets everywhere,'	198
Miss says wilderness	365

Index of First Lines

Missing: our	377
Mist	27
Monday: Fell in Mother's pudding bowl! Kicked and	397
More black than white, Gran's photo	129
Moses supposes his toeses are roses	420
Mountains are today, yesterday, and for ever	124
Mr Khan's shop is dark and beautiful	423
Mr Mizen fell in the street	333
Mum said the dreaded words this morning	312
Music . . . is everywhere	35
My dad was a kung fu fighter in a video game called Death Cult Army	169
My dad's *amazing* for he can	418
My first is in two but not in a pair	409
My mother saw a dancing bear	94
My mum says I'm her sugarplum	303
My name is 'Couldn't care less'	374
My new paintbox's shining black lacquer lid	3
My sledge and hammer lie reclined	157
My teacher taught me how to see	6
My team	323
O praise God in his holiness: praise him	243
Of the three Wise Men	284
On the damp seashore	25
One pink sari for a pretty girl	179
Only part of me is metal	173
Our school's word processor	172
Our teacher likes us to	152
Our teacher told us one day he would leave	136
Out of the furnace	164
Out	304
Peace is a bird	264
Played softly	43
Poppies? Oh, miss	100
Prince was my dog	355
Quinquireme of Nineveh from distant Ophir	89
Rainbow	404
Rapunzel, let down your golden hair	416
Remember me when I am gone away	361
Rhythm in your breathing, rhythm in your heartbeat	36
Ring home, ring home	315
Roger's daddy's clever	337

Said Chuku, Creator of the world 267
Seashells on the beach 128
Seven fat fishermen 186
Shake your brown feet, honey 50
She licked the film of dust 132
She sells seashells on the sea shore 436
Silent nightingale 402
Sky so bright 252
Sky, grey. Late frost 427
Smells of bonfires 426
Smoke 131
Snow 417
So disembark! The storm has found its ending 242
Some Tudor folk 81
Sometimes I think the hills 123
Sometimes 331
Spring morning sun bathes 30
Steady explorer 226
Stream in the hillside 121
Swallows 415
Take a candle, take a feather 253
Ten tired teachers slumped in the staffroom at playtime 195
Thank You 263
The beauty of the trees 286
The blades of grass growing 184
The bushmen of the Kalahari desert 142
The Chinese write poems 24
The Cook and the Caretaker stirred their tea 395
The fish goes . . . Hip 53
The forest stretches for miles 368
The great lizards are gone 65
The Lord is my shepherd; I shall not want 244
The moon that once was full, ripe and golden 254
The night before a great moon full of honey 230
The noble King Canute, they said 71
The number 37 has a special magic to it 187
The Owl and the Pussy-cat went to sea 393
The reason i like chocolate 266
The rhythm of the tom-tom does not beat in my blood 56
The sky at night is like a big city 285
The soldiers came 342

The sun rises	227
The train goes running along the line	125
The wind of the north	401
The world is a beautiful place	337
The world with its countries	262
There is no needle without piercing point	360
There was a young lady of Riga	399
There wasn't much to do today	57
There's a girl at school	326
There's a lobster on the phone!	14
There's a plant in the garden with white flowers	338
They called me frog-face with ears like a bat	300
They used to fly	376
They're building a skyscraper	116
Think of a number from one to ten	193
This is our school	281
This is the moment I dread	85
This is the road down which I go	112
Thumb held tight on one	155
Tiger! Tiger! Turning white	370
Time's a bird, which leaves its footprints	185
Time-detective	64
To count myself	202
To every thing there is a season	299
To	190
Today, in strong colours	7
Tonight I saw the	403
'Twas brillig, and slithy toves	389
Twas Thursday and the bottom set	391
Twice one are two	180
Van Gogh thought to be a preacher	17
We are darters and divers	367
We can play reggae music, funk and skiffle too	39
We had to invent a toy	147
We yanked the wheels	156
We've done 'Water' and 'Metals' and 'Plastic'	216
Welcome to Cardboard City	335
Well, son, I'll tell you	269
Well, to start with	250
What do you collect?	425
What is Poetry? Who Knows?	387

When Amelia looks on the silver moon   359
When first I went to school   316
When I had   182
When I was down beside the sea   127
When it was time   128
When the jet sprang into the sky   111
When we buried   357
When you are very small   340
Where are your trainers and where is your coat   292
Where would you live if you were me?   115
Who's that knocking on the window   239
Why don't rainbows   233
Wild howler   405
With proud thanksgiving, a mother for her children 95
With snort and pant the engine dragged   154
World Wildlife Industries sadly announces   373
Worm shortage   396
You looked so sad when you came to us   342

Index of Poets

Agard, John 341
Andrew, Moira 264
Anon. 11, 118, 128, 180, 186, 187, 252, 399, 414, 420, 436
Baynton, Les 342
Belloc, Hilaire 158
Berry, James 37, 421
Bevan, Clare 49, 78, 90, 134, 147, 282, 395
Binyon, Laurence 95
Blance, Tracey 326
Bloom, Valerie 166, 185
Bonner, Ann 35, 248, 368
Bright, Paul 71, 121, 151, 207
Brooke, Rupert 97
Calder, Dave 65, 214, 339
Carroll, Lewis 389
Carter, James 45, 46
Causley, Charles 18, 94, 239
Clarke, Jane 366
Coldwell, John 349, 406
Collett, Andrew 55
Cook, Stanley 110, 112, 254
Cookson, Paul 193, 437
Cope, Wendy 20
Corbett, Pie 14, 22, 227, 233, 371, 408, 411
Cotton, John 262
Cowling, Sue 7, 115, 388, 396, 397, 416, 417
Dakos, Kali 182
Dean, Jan 200, 241, 247
Dixon, Peter 8, 152, 292, 336
Douglas, Lord Alfred 221
Douthwaite, Gina 44, 306
Dunmore, Helen 4
Dunn, Gwen 232
Dymoke, Sue 155

Eastwick, Ivy O. 263
Edwards, Richard 52
Farjeon, Eleanor 38, 387
Ferlinghetti, Laurence 337
Field, Rachel 123
Finney, Eric 276, 289, 415, 429
Fisher, Aileen 256
Florian, Douglas 153
Foster, John 159, 210, 332
Gallagher, Katherine 426
George, Chief Dan 286
Ghose, Zulfikar 111
Giovanni, Nikki 266
Gittins, Chrissie 17, 85
Green, Mary 42, 131, 149, 190, 191, 226
Gross, Philip 315
Harmer, David 82, 272, 291, 331, 335
Harvey, Trevor 98, 172, 220, 231
Hayley, William 157
Heaney, Seamus 353
Henri, Adrian 27
Hopkins, Lee Bennett 304
Houston, Libby 99
Hughes, Langston 50, 92, 269, 284, 431, 432
Hull, Robert 198
Jacinto, António 56
Jennings, Elizabeth 24, 321
Johnson, Mike 192, 216, 369, 377
Johnson, Mina 129
Jubb, Mike 36, 402, 435
Kay, Jackie 307
Kent, Penny 76, 229, 343
Kenward, Jean 255
King James Bible 243, 244, 245, 299

449

Index of Poets

Kirkup, James 3, 25
Kitching, Daphne 265, 405
Kitching, John 7, 13, 30, 63, 64, 81, 109, 189, 209
Kuba 360
Kuskin, Karla 59, 202
Lear, Edward 393
Leavy, Una 156
Leighton, Patricia 67, 84, 225, 226, 327, 355
Linden, Ann Marie 179
Livingston, Myra Cohn 128
MacRae, Lindsay 350
Magee, Wes 161, 184, 425
Masefield, John 89
McGough, Roger 21, 438
Millum, Trevor 391
Mitchell, Adrian 169
Mitton, Tony 253
Moon, Pat 208
Morgan, Michaela 370
Moses, Brian 57, 75, 195, 201, 305, 374
Moss, Jeff 295
Munro, Madeline 224
Muslim prayer 237
Nagle, Frances 218, 312, 323, 359
Nicholls, Judith 43, 100, 160, 249, 367, 401, 427
Nichols, Grace 301
Nourallah, Riad 287
Owen, Gareth 164, 250, 313, 316
Patten, Brian 39, 136, 197, 309, 357
Peake, Mervyn 242
Playdell, Sue 409
Poulson, Joan 12, 347, 365, 376
Priestley, Janis 274
Rago, Henry 6

Rice, John 173, 212, 223, 311, 333, 400, 412, 428
Rieu, E. V. 5
Rossetti, Christina 40, 238, 361, 410, 413
Rumble, Coral 80, 165, 330
Sackett, Anita Marie 132
Sansom, Clive 125
Sedgwick, Fred 16, 302, 403, 404, 419, 423
Sensier, Danielle 217, 325
Serraillier, Ian 124
Shakespeare, William 433
Souter, Ian 47, 114, 119, 183, 418
Steven, Kenneth C. 230
Stevens, Roger 9, 10, 73, 216, 267, 270
Stevenson, Robert Louis 127
Tadjo, Véronique 319
Tagore, Rabindranath 122
Tennyson, Alfred Lord 87
Thomson, Charles 188, 300
Tippett, James S. 116
Traditional 53, 281, 285, 407
Turner, Steve 168, 246, 277
Tweedie, Jennifer 126
Vandal, Norman 167
Viorst, Judith 138, 261, 303, 322
Waddell, Philip 194, 338, 373
Wade, Barrie 140
Warren, Celia 70
Whitehead, David 171
Williams, Brenda 29
Worsley-Benison, H. 154
Wright, Kit 279
Zephaniah, Benjamin 142

Acknowledgements

The compilers and publishers wish to thank the following for permission to use copyright material:

John Agard, 'The Soldiers Came' from *Laughter is an Egg* by John Agard, Viking (1990), by permission of Caroline Shelden Literary Agency on behalf of the author; **Moira Andrew**, 'All in the Mind', first published in *Dove on the Roof*, ed. Jennifer Curry, Mammoth (1992), by permission of the author; **Les Baynton**, 'Stranger', by permission of the author; **Hilaire Belloc**, 'Progress' from *Complete Verse* by Hilaire Belloc, Random House, by permission of PFD on behalf of the Estate of the author; **James Berry**, 'Everyday Music' from *A Nest Full of Stars*, Macmillan Children's Books, and 'Childhood Tracks', by permission of PFD on behalf of the author; **Clare Bevan**, 'The Tudors', first published in *Hysterical Historicals – The Tudors*, ed. Brian Moses, Macmillan Children's Books (2000), 'Coral Reef', first published in *A Sea Creature Ate My Teacher*, ed. Brian Moses, Macmillan Children's Books (2000), and 'The Music Lesson Rap', first published in *The Rhyme Riot*, ed. Gaby Morgan, Macmillan Children's Books (2002), 'The Housemaid's Letter', 'Listen', 'The Cook and the Caretaker' and 'Technology Lesson', by permission of the author; **Laurence Binyon**, 'For the Fallen (September 1914)', by permission of The Society of Authors on behalf of the author's Estate; **Tracey Blance**, 'Shame'. Copyright © Tracey Blance 1999, by permission of the author; **Valerie Bloom**, 'Time' and 'Mega Star Rap', by permission of the author; **Ann Bonner**, 'Dipa', first published in *Let's Celebrate*, ed. John Foster, Oxford University Press (1989), 'Forest', first published in *Earthwise, Earthways*, ed. Judith Nicholls, Oxford University Press (1993), and 'Music', by permission of the author; **Paul Bright**, 'Up in Smoke', first published in *Shorts*, ed. Paul Cookson, Macmillan Children's Books (2000), 'The Oojhamaflip', 'Stream Story' and 'King Canute', by permission of the author; **Dave Calder**, 'Citizen of the World', 'Information for Travellers' and 'The Great Lizards', by permission of the author; **James Carter**, 'Electric Guitars' from *Cars, Stars and Electric Guitars* by James Carter. Copyright © 2002 James Carter, by permission of Walker Books Ltd; **Charles Causley**, 'My Mother Saw a Dancing Bear', 'Innocent's Song' and 'Leonardo' from *Collected Poems* by Charles Causley, Macmillan, by permission of David Higham Associates on behalf of the author; **Jane Clarke**, 'Web of Life', by permission of the author; **John Coldwell**, 'Two Witches Discuss Good Grooming', first published in *Read Me* 2, ed. Gaby Morgan, Macmillan Children's Books (1999), and 'Cowboy Games and the Good Death', by permission of the author; **Andrew Collett**, 'Making Music', by permission of the author; **Frank Collymore**,

Acknowledgements

'Phinniphin', by permission of Ellice Collymore; **Paul Cookson**, 'Barry and Beryl and the Bubble Gum Blowers' from *Tongue Twisters and Tonsil Twizzlers* by Paul Cookson, Solway Publishing (1998), and 'Mathematically Telepathically Magical', first published in *Sing That Joke*, ed. Paul Cookson, Macmillan Children's Books (1998), by permission of the author; **Wendy Cope**, 'The Uncertainty of the Poet' from *Serious Concerns* by Wendy Cope, Faber, by permission of PFD on behalf of the author; **Pie Corbett**, 'Who's That on the Phone?', first published in *Junior Education*, Scholastic. Copyright © Pie Corbett 2000, 'The Day's Eye', first published in *Writer's World*, Heinemann (2001), 'The Wobbling Rainbow', first published in *Junior Education*, Scholastic (2001), 'The Artist's Model Daydreams', 'The Last Wolf Speaks from the Zoo', 'One Line Riddles' and 'What am I?', by permission of the author; **John Cotton**, 'The World with its Countries', by permission of the author; **Sue Cowling**, 'Alien Lullaby' from *Space Poems*, Oxford University Press (2002), 'Houses' from *What Is A Kumquat*, Faber and Faber (1991), 'Song Thrush Poster', 'The Witch, the Prince and the Girl in the Tower', 'Litter Lout', 'Today in Strong Colours' and 'Tom Thumb's Diary', by permission of the author; **Kali Dakos**, 'Why Must it Be Minus 3?' from *Don't Read This Book, Whatever You Do!* by Kali Dakos, by permission of the Simon & Schuster Books for Young Readers, an imprint of Simon & Schuster Children's Publishing Division; **Jan Dean**, 'Dedicating a Baby', 'Prayer for When I'm Cross' and 'The Unit of Sleep', by permission of the author; **Peter Dixon**, 'Problem Solving', 'My Daddy Dances Tapstep', 'Modern Art' and 'Grown-Ups', by permission of the author; **Lord Alfred Douglas**, 'The Shark', by permission of John Rubinstein and John Stratford, Joint Literary Executors of the Estate of the author; **Gina Douthwaite**, 'Divorce' and 'A Crack Band', by permission of the author; **Helen Dunmore**, 'What Shall I Draw?' from *Secrets* by Helen Dunmore, by permission of A P Watt Ltd on behalf of the author; **Gwen Dunn**, 'Dandelions', by permission of the author; **Sun Dymoke**, 'Scissors', by permission of the author; **Ivy O. Eastwick**, 'Thanksgiving' from *Cherry Stones! Garden Swings* by Ivy Eastwick, by permission of Abingdon Press; **Richard Edwards**, 'If I Were the Conductor' from *I Wish I Were a Teabag* by Richard Edwards, Viking (1990), by permission of the author; **Eleanor Farjeon**, 'Poetry' from *Blackbird Has Spoken* by Eleanor Farjeon, Macmillan, and 'J is for Jazz-Man' from *Silver Sand and Snow*, Michael Joseph, by permission of David Higham Associates on behalf of the Estate of the author; **Laurence Ferlinghetti**, 'The World is a Beautiful Place' from *A Coney Island of the Mind* by Laurence Ferlinghetti. Copyright © 1955 by Laurence Ferlinghetti, by permission of New Directions Publishing Corporation; **Rachel Field**, 'The Hills' from *Branches Green* by Rachel Field. Copyright © 1934 Macmillan Publishing Company, renewed copyright © 1962 Arthur Pederson, by permission of the Simon & Schuster Books for Young Readers, an imprint of Simon Schuster Children's Publishing Division; **Eric Finney**, 'Simple Seasons', 'Best Places', 'Thank You Letter' and 'Finding Magic', by permission of the author; **Aileen Fisher**, 'Light

Acknowledgements

the Fesitve Candles' from *Skip Around the Year* by Aileen Fisher. Copyright © 1967, 1995 Aileen Fisher, by permission of Marian Reiner on behalf of the author; **John Foster**, 'Mowers', first published in *Four O'Clock Friday,* Oxford University Press. Copyright © 1991 John Foster, 'Summer Storm' from *Standing on the Sidelines*, Oxford University Press. Copyright © 1995 John Foster, 'It Hurts' from *Making Waves*, Oxford University Press. Copyright © 1997 John Foster, by permission of the author; **Katherine Gallagher**, 'Bonfire Night', by permission of the author; **Zulfikar Ghose**, 'Geography Lesson', by permission of Sheil Land Associates Ltd on behalf of the author; **Chrissie Gittens**, 'The Powder Monkey', 'The British Museum Print Room' from *Pilot*, Dagger Press (2001), by permission of the author; **Mary Green**, 'Teacher's Torture', 'Pyramid Pie', 'Excuses', 'Volcano', 'Seaside Sonata' and 'Mouse Laughing', by permission of the author; **Philip Gross**, 'This is a Recorded Message' from *Scratch City* by Philip Gross, by permission of Faber and Faber Ltd; **David Harmer**, 'Our Tree', 'On The Streets', 'The News', 'Dobbo's First Swimming Lesson' and 'Cutpurse Kit', by permission of the author; **Trevor Harvey**, 'Printout, Wipe Out', first published in *Techno Talk*, compiled by Trevor Harvey , Bodley Head (1994), 'Growing Up in the 1930's', first published in 'How We Used to Live', *Projects Magazine*, Scholastic (2001), 'The Hedgehog' and 'Breath', by permission of the author, **Seamus Heaney**, 'Mid-Term Break' from *Death of a Naturalist* by Seamus Heaney, by permission of Faber and Faber Ltd; **Adrian Henri**, 'Notes for an Autumn Painting' from *Adrian Henri – Collected Poems*, Allison and Busby (1986). Copyright © Adrian Henri 1986, by permission of Rogers, Coleridge & White on behalf of the author; **Lee Bennett Hopkins**, 'Staring' from *Been to Yesterdays* by Lee Bennett Hopkins. Copyright © 1995 Lee Bennett Hopkins, by permission from Boyds Mills Press; **Libby Houston**, 'Post-War' from *Cover of Darkness, Selected Poems 1961-1998* by Libby Houston, Slow Dancer Press. Copyright © Libby Houston (1967) 1999, by permission of the author; **Langston Hughes**, 'Mother to Son', 'Carol of the Brown King', 'Aunt Sue's Stories', 'Dreams, 'The Dream Keeper' and 'Song for a Banjo Dance' from *Selected Poems* by Langston Hughes, by permission of David Higham Associates on behalf of the author; **Ted Hughes**, 'Robin Song' from *Crow* by Ted Hughes, by permission of Faber and Faber Ltd; **Robert Hull**, 'Maths Person' from *Stargazer* by Robert Hull, Hodder, by permission of PFD on behalf of the author; **Elizabeth Jennings**, 'Friends' and 'A Sort of Chinese Poem' from *Collected Poems* by Elizabeth Jennings, Carcanet, by permission of David Higham Associates on behalf of the author; **Mike Johnson**, 'Tall Story', first published in *The Upside-Down Frown*, ed. Andrew Peters Fusek, Wayland (1999), 'Science Lesson', first published in *Ridiculous Rhymes*, ed. John Foster, Collins (2001), 'Missing' and 'Natural Numbers', by permission of the author; **Mina Johnson**, 'Points of View', by permission of the author; **Mike Jubb**, 'We got Rhyme', first published in *A Poetry Teacher's Toolkit, Vol. 2, Rhymes, Rhythms and Rattles* by Collette Drifte and Mike Jubb Fulton (2002), 'The Emperor and the Nightingale', first published in *A Poetry*

Acknowledgements

Teachers' Toolkit, Vol. 3, Style, Shape and Structure by Collette Drifte and Mike Jubb Fulton (2002), and 'Camilla Caterpillar', by permission of the author; **Jackie Kay**, 'Divorce', by permission of the author; Penny Kent, 'Arturi's Story', 'Winter Seeds' and 'A Sense of History', by permission of the author; **Penny Kent**, 'Arturi's Story', 'Winter Seeds' and 'A Sense of History', by permission of the author; **Jean Kenward**, 'Mela', by permission of the author; **James Kirkup**, 'The Sand Artist' and 'First Art Lesson', by permission of the author; **Daphne Kitching**, 'Job Description' and 'Kennings' from *As long as there are trees* by Daphne Kitching, Kingston Press (2001), by permission of the author; **John Kitching**, 'My Teacher Taught Me How to See', first published in *Schools Out*, compiled by John Foster, Oxford University Press (1988), 'Short Livers', first published in *Hysterical Historical Poems*, compiled by Brian Moses (2000), 'History', 'Science Graveyard', 'A Bit of a Problem', 'Historian', 'Art Year Haikus', 'Geography' and 'Matchstick King', by permission of the author; **Karla Kuskin**, 'Lewis Has a Trumpet' from *In the Middle of the Trees* by Karla Kuskin. Copyright © 1959, renewed 1986 by Karla Kuskin; and 'Counting' from *The Rose on My Cake* by Karla Kuskin, copyright © 1964, renewed 1992 by Karla Kuskin, by permission of Scott Treimel NY on behalf of the author; **Una Leavy**, 'Go-cart', by permission of the author; **Pat Leighton**, 'Bullied', 'Wonder Birds', 'Voice from the Pharaoh's Tomb', 'My First Dog', 'Snail' and 'Printer's Devil', by permission of the author; **Myra Cohn Livingston**, 'Shell' from *Worlds I Know and Other Poems* by Myra Cohn Livingston, McElderry Books/Artheneum. Copyright © 1986 Myra Cohn Livingston, by permission of Marian Reiner on behalf of the author; **Roger McGough**, 'Having my Ears Boxed' and 'The Boyhood of Raleigh', by permission of PFD on behalf of the author; **Lindsay MacRae**, 'The Funeral' from *How to Avoid Kissing Your Parents in Public* by Lindsay MacRae, Puffin (2000). Copyright © Lindsay MacRae, 2000, by permission of the author; **Wes Magee**, 'What do you collect?' 'What is a million?' and 'The Electronic House', by permission of the author; **John Masefield**, 'Cargoes', by permission of The Society of Authors as the Literary Representative of the Estate of the author; **Trevor Milum**, 'Jabbermockery', by permission of the author; **Adrian Mitchell**, 'Techno Child' from *Balloon Lagoon and the Magic Islands of Poetry* by Adrian Mitchell, by permission of PFD on behalf of the author; **Tony Mitton**, 'Hunting the Leaven Passover', included in *Festivals*, ed. Andrew Fusek Peters, by permission of David Higham Associates on behalf of the author; **Pat Moon**, 'Earth's Clock' from *Earthlines* by Pat Moon, Pimlico (1993), by permission of the author; **Michaela Morgan**, 'Blake's Tyger – revisisted', by permission of the author; **Brian Moses**, 'The Group', first published in *Turn that Racket Down*, ed. Paul Cookson, Red Fox (2001). Copyright © Brian Moses, 'Entering a Castle' from *Don't Look at Me in that Tone of Voice*, poems by Brian Moses, Macmillan (1998). Copyright © Brian Moses, 'Behind the Staffroom Door' from *The Secret Life of Teachers*, ed. Brian Moses, Macmillan (1996). Copyright © Brian Moses, 'Names' from *Knock Down Ginger and Other Poems* by Brian Moses,

Acknowledgements

Cambridge University Press (1994). Copyright © Brian Moses, 'If I Were a Shape' and 'It's Not the Same Without Dad', by permission of the author; **Jeff Moss**, 'The Last Day of School' from *The Other Side of the Door* by Jeff Moss, Bantam Books, by permission of ICM, Inc on behalf of the author; **Frances Nagle**, 'My Gang' and 'Dream Team', first published in *My Gang*, ed. Brian Moses, Macmillan (1999), 'Silver Moon' and 'Star Turn', by permission of the author; **Judith Nicholls**, 'Remembrance Day', 'Haiku of the Four Winds', 'Notes towards a Poem', 'Dolphin Dance', 'First Television', 'Drum' and 'Plague Frogs'. Copyright © Judith Nicholls 2002, by permission of the author; **Grace Nichols**, 'Give Yourself a Hug' from *Give Yourself a Hug*. Copyright © 1994 by Grace Nichols, by permission of Curtis Brown Ltd, London, on behalf of the author; **Gareth Owen**, 'The New House', 'Friends', 'Space Shot' and 'Jonah and the Whale' from *Collected Poems for Children* by Gareth Owen, Macmillan Children's Books (2000). Copyright © Gareth Owen 2000, by permission of Rogers, Coleridge & White on behalf of the author; **Brian Patten**, 'Burying the Dog in the Garden' and 'Embryonic Mega-Stars' from *Gargling with Jelly* by Brian Patten, Viking (1985). Copyright © Brian Patten, 1985, by permission The Penguin Group (UK) Ltd; and 'Bringing up a Single Parent', 'Three Frazzles in a Frimple' and 'Geography Lesson' from *Juggling With Gerbils* by Brian Patten, Puffin Books (2000). Copyright © Brian Patten 2000, by permission of Rogers, Coleridge & White on behalf of the author; **Mervyn Peake**, 'Disembarkation Chorus' from *Peake's Progress*, ed. M. Gilmore, Penguin, by permission of David Higham Associates on behalf of the author; **Joan Poulson**, 'Jacob and the Angel', 'Dragonflies', 'Wilderness' and 'All That Space', by permission of the author; **Janis Priestley**, 'Just One Wish', by permission of the author; **John Rice**, 'A Minute to Midnight', first published in *The Great Escape – A World Book Day Poetry Book*, Macmillan Children's Books (2000), 'Low Owl' and 'Cousins', first published in *Bears Don't Like Bananas*, Hodder Wayland (1991), 'Mr Mizen', 'Constant, Constant Little Light', 'The Tree Spell', 'The Machine of the Three Big Ears' and 'Gannet Diving', by permission of the author; **E V Rieu**, 'The Paint Box', by permission of the Authors Licensing & Collecting Society Ltd on behalf of the estate of the author; **Coral Rumble**, 'Guess Who?', first published in *The Works*, ed. Peter Cookson, Macmillan Children's Books (2000), 'Sometimes' and 'New Frontiers', by permission of the author; **Anita Marie Sackett**, 'Rain', *Seam Poetry Magazine*, 14 (2001), by permission of the author; **Clive Sansom**, 'The Train', by permission of David Higham Associates on behalf of the author; **Fred Sedgwick**, 'First Thing Today', 'Mr Khan's Shop', 'December Cinquain', 'Red Leaves', 'Things to Do on the First Day of the Summer Holidays' and 'After Giacometti', by permission of the author; **Danielle Sensier**, 'New Girl' and 'experiment', by permission of the author; **Ian Serraillier**, 'Mountains', by permission of Anne Serraillier; **Ian Souter**, 'From My Window', 'Heavy Metal, Stormy Weather', 'My Dad's Amazing', 'Early Last Sunday' and 'Numberless', by permission of the author; **Kenneth C. Steven**, 'Mushrooms',

Acknowledgements

by permission of the author; **Roger Stevens**, 'Julius Caesar's Last Breakfast' from *I Did Not Eat the Goldfish* by Roger Stevens, Macmillan Children's Books (2002), 'The Most Important Rap', first published in *Performance Poems*, ed. Brian Moses, Southgate Publishers Ltd (1996), 'The Dawdling Dog', 'Chalk', 'The Museum Says' and 'The Art Gallery Says', by permission of the author; **Véronique Tadjo**, 'Friendship' from *Talking Drums*, ed. Véronique Tadjo, by permission of A & C Black (Publishers) Ltd; **Rabindranath Tagore**, 'Day by Day I Float My Paper Boats' from *Collected Poems and Plays of Rabindranath Tagore*, by permission of Visva-Bharati University, Calcutta; **Charles Thomson**, 'Name-calling' and 'Counting Horrors', by permission of the author; **James Tippett**, 'Building a Skyscraper' from *Crickety Cricket! The Best Loved Poems of James S Tippett* by James Tippett. Copyright © 1933, renewed 1973 by Martha K. Tippett, by permission of HarperCollins Publishers, Inc; **Steve Turner**, 'In the Beginning' from *The Day I Fell Down the Toilet*, Lion Publishing (1996), 'With My Hands' and 'Hickory Digital Clock' from *Dad, You're Not Funny*, Lion Publishing (1999), by permission of the author; **Jennifer Tweedie**, 'Ocean Travel', first published in *Another Very First Poetry Book*, Oxford University Press (1992), by permission of the author; **Judith Viorst**, 'Some Things Don't Make Sense at All' and 'It's a Wonderful Life' from *If I Were in Charge of the World and Other Worries* (1981). Copyright © Judith Viorst 1981, 'Harvey' and 'Someday Someone Will Bet That You Can't Name All Fifty States' from *Sad Underwear* by Judith Vorist, by permission of A M Heath & Co Ltd on behalf of the author; **Philip Waddell**, 'Important Notice', 'Puzzler' and 'In the Garden', by permission of the author; **Barrie Wade**, 'Haiku Calendar: Southern Version', by permission of the author; **Celia Warren**, 'A Liking for the Viking' and 'Roman Invasions', by permission of the author; **David Whitehead**, 'My Pet Mouse', first published in *Pet Poems*, ed. Jennifer Curry, Scholastic (2001), by permission of the author; **Brenda Williams**, 'Jack Frost', by permission of the author; **Kit Wright**, 'All of Us' from *Great Snakes* by Kit Wright, Penguin (1994), by permission of the author; **Benjamin Zephaniah**, 'Fearless Bushmen' from *Wicked World* by Benjamin Zephaniah, Puffin (2000). Copyright © Benjamin Zephaniah, 2000, by permission of The Penguin Group (UK) Ltd.

Also by Fiona Rule...

LONDON'S DOCKLANDS
The Lost Quarter

A lively volume exploring an area of London which for many years has remained steeped in mystery.

Uncovers a wealth of evidence left behind by the people who lived and worked in the docks to provide a glimpse into the world they once populated.

Perfect for all those with an interest in London's rich culture and history.

Published September 2009

SAUCY JACK
The Elusive Ripper

Gavin Baddeley and Paul Woods

behind the legend of Jack the Ripper,

Challenges established thinking on who
the Ripper was, and puts forward a

Launches the 'Devil's Histories' series
- a range of sensational history books
which focus on 'the dark side' of our

Published November 2009

GOD'S ASSASSINS
The Medieval Roots of Terrorism

Gavin Baddeley and Paul Woods

A fascinating exploration of the
founding fathers of terrorism and their
belief in Islamic martyrdom and the
parallel with today's suicide bombers.

Unusual format combining interviews
with a unique range of modern
commentary, pop culture references
and vivid illustrations.

A title in the 'Devil's Histories' series
which will captivate readers with its

Published November 2009

CAPITAL PUNISHMENT IN BRITAIN

Richard Clark
Foreword by Rt Hon Anne Widdecombe, MP

A thought-provoking analysis of the
history, ethics, and gruesome methods
of capital punishment throughout
British history.

Foreword by the Rt Hon Anne
Widdecombe, whose views on
the death penalty are well known
and respected.

A perfect read for social historians
and those interested in the darker side
of justice.

Published November 2009

BEDLAM
London's Hospital for the Mad

Paul Chambers

A compelling history of one of the oldest and most notorious of Britain's mental health care institutions.

Written in a highly readable narrative format, this book raises crucial questions about our own attitudes towards mental health.

A gripping read for all interested in an institution with a colourful and lurid past.

Published September 2009

Ian Allan
PUBLISHING